Berkeley!

Heyday Books

Berkeley, California

Berkeley!

a literary tribute

edited by DANIELLE LA FRANCE

introduction by MALCOLM MARGOLIN

Publisher's Cataloging-in-Publication Data:
(Provided by Quality Books, Inc.)

Berkeley! : a literary tribute / edited by Danielle La France ;
    foreword by Malcolm Margolin.—1st ed.
      p. cm.
    ISBN: 0-930588-94-0
    1. Berkeley (Calif.)—Literary collections. I. La France, Danielle.
    PS509.B57 1997   810.8'03279467
                             QBI97–40517

Cover Design: Jack Myers, DesignSite, Berkeley
Interior Design and Typesetting: Laura Harger
Printing and Binding: Patterson Printing
Cover Illustration: *Berkeley #4*, Richard Diebenkorn. Courtesy of the
University of California, Berkeley Art Museum; gift of Joseph M. Bransten
in memory of Ellen Hart Bransten.

Please address orders, inquiries, and correspondence to:
Heyday Books
Box 9145
Berkeley, CA 94709
Phone: (510) 549-3564
Fax: (510) 549-1889

Printed in the United States of America
10 9 8 7 6 5 4 3 2 1

Contents

Acknowledgments

IN MANY WAYS, BERKELEY IS A SMALL TOWN, AND THIS ANTHOLOGY IS THE PRODUCT OF dozens of chance meetings, conversations, and suggestions—too many for adequate thanks.

We would, though, like to acknowledge the following people for their significant contributions: Carol Christensen for her willingness to share her encyclopedic knowledge; Laura Harger for her meticulous proofing and clean, supple text design; Mark Leonard for his assistance with the text; Melissa Sankary, Elizabeth Wlordarzak, and John Barrios for their tireless assistance in collecting the pieces included in this anthology; Sayre Van Young and the entire staff at the Berkeley Public Library for suggestions and involvement; Josh Paddison for his good-humored checking of frequently astonishing facts; Wendy Low and Dolores Jalbert for organizing the text; and Linda Jordan at the Bancroft Library for her continued assistance and considerable sense of humor.

Introduction

BERKELEY, CALIFORNIA, WAS NOT NAMED AFTER A SAINT, AS WERE NEARBY SAN FRANcisco and San Jose. Nor was it named after an early settler, as were other Bay Area cities—Hayward, Livermore, and Daly City, for example. Nor after a geographical feature (Oakland, El Cerrito, Redwood City), an East Coast city (Richmond and Albany), or a real estate promoter's fantasy (Sunnyvale and Pleasanton). Rather, and one might say prophetically, Berkeley was named for a poet and philosopher, and a somewhat radical one at that. While Bishop George Berkeley is best known in popular culture for his exasperating question about whether a tree falling in a forest outside of human earshot can properly be said to have made a noise, it was for one of his now all but forgotten poems that the city commemorates his name. A century before the University of California's founding in the mid-1860s, he envisaged the decay of Europe with its "pedantry of courts and schools" and foretold a westward land "where nature guides and virtue rules." Here would blossom a renaissance of learning "such as [Europe] bred when fresh and young."

The allusion in Bishop Berkeley's poem to ancient Greece predicted a major concern, even an obsession, of those who established the University of California and guided its growth during its early years. The general area upon which the campus was built had been sparsely settled since about 1850. It was a rural, work-a-day community of farms, houses, and a few factories clustered around the eastern shoreline of San Francisco Bay, exactly opposite the Golden Gate. The founding of the University here was a visionary act, recognizably utopian and heroic even when the mythology that has sprung up around it is pruned back. Its founders sought nothing less than an ideal university in an ideal community, and in its early years Berkeley (both the university and town) was commonly referred to as "the Athens of the Pacific." Today this phrase might be uttered only with a roll of the eyes and a shrug of the shoulders, but originally the phrase and the vision behind it had a surprising and touching fervor. Surveying a landscape of California live oaks, California bay-laurel trees, and California poppies, the university founders saw Athens. Like Athens, Berkeley was bounded by hills to the east and to the west by a plain sloping toward a seaport. It had a Mediterranean climate, groves of trees, and a clear stream running through it. "I do believe the second Greece, a greater Greece, will come to the world here," intoned Henry Durant, one of the University's founding fathers. This noble vision carried Berkeley through its early years, and although it might be embarrassing to admit to it, I believe that at least a touch of that fervor and idealism still pervades the Berkeley air.

Today, of course, when people mention Berkeley and the Sixties in the same sentence, they are not referring to the university's founding in the 1860s but to events that took place a century later. During the early 1960s university communities throughout the country were animated by demands for racial freedom and civil rights. As the decade progressed, demands for other free-doms followed: the freedom to experiment with drugs, sexual freedom, free-dom from the draft, and freedom from the threat of destruction by mass warfare or environmental degradation. Berkeley was in the forefront of the agitation—synonymous with it in some circles. But the freedom that first galvanized this university was, interestingly enough, freedom of speech. The Free Speech Movement insisted upon the right of students and others to say what they wanted without censorship, a right essential to any community that values words and the flow of ideas.

Reverence for words and respect for ideas have been a constant part of Berkeley's heritage from its founding to the present. Berkeley has always nourished an astonishingly strong literary community, never more so than today. There are many reasons for this—size, for one. Berkeley, with a popu-lation of slightly more than one hundred thousand people, is a small city—small enough that the creative, literary people (except for the deliberately re-clusive) tend to know one other. It is virtually impossible to walk in the downtown or campus areas for ten minutes without passing a bookshop or two or without meeting an author, publisher, bookseller, reviewer, editor, teacher, or someone deeply engaged in the literary life. Yet while offering the comfort and social density of a small college town, Berkeley adjoins blue-collar Oakland and is twenty minutes from cosmopolitan San Francisco, and thus shares enough of a big-city atmosphere to keep it from becoming too inbred, precious, or provincial.

The beguiling climate and natural beauty of the area surely deserve some credit as well, not only for attracting writers who luxuriate in its mild winters and moderate summers, but for giving much of Berkeley writing a decidedly environmental focus. Here one can hike the Berkeley Hills in shirt-sleeves most Thanksgiving mornings, and early February finds the magnolias and flowering plum trees blossoming with springtime abandon. Such beauty! Yet Berkeley is no Shangri-la. It has its poorer neighborhoods too, the troubling heritage of generations of racial and economic injustices, which keep Berkeley writers rooted in the contradictions and challenges of a diverse, struggling American culture.

Berkeley also seems to have developed the infrastructure necessary to support a vigorous literary community: strong coffee served in a multitude of settings where writers can sit for half a day with a pad of paper or a laptop computer; an amazing number of inexpensive restaurants and movie theaters that interrupt the isolation of long writing stints; a wonderful public library; and, of course, a world-class university which attracts prestigious speakers and visiting scholars, maintains an extraordinary faculty, supports one of the world's great libraries, and each year draws thousands of young, eager students to repopulate poetry readings and inspire even the most jaded author with a sense of renewed hope and belief.

There is more to a literary community than writers. Berkeley and its surrounding areas support, for example, close to one hundred book publishers. These range in size from the huge University of California Press to tiny houses that put out an occasional book of poetry. Berkeley is also home to dozens of periodical publishers, including the vital bimonthly *Poetry Flash*, which announces poetry events, profiles poets, and reviews poetry. The local give-away entertainment weekly, the *Express*, features a high-quality monthly book review supplement. And three major national book distributors—BookPeople, Publishers Group West, and Small Press Distribution—are located in Berkeley or a stone's throw away. All this publishing and wholesaling activity makes Berkeley home to hundreds of editors, typographers, designers, sales representatives, publicists, agents, book packagers, and others who are a vital part of Berkeley's literary community.

The glue that holds all these elements together is surely the bookstores. Berkeley is blessed with more than fifty bookstores. These include a number of strong independent general bookstores, a chain "superstore," and stores that specialize in such subjects as western Americana, used first editions, Judaica, textbooks, travel, small press, new age, comics, science fiction, fine art, university press books, etc. It has been said that Berkeley has the highest number of bookstores per capita of any place in America.

It is not just the number of Berkeley bookstores that astounds and delights, but their size and the variety of their offerings. Moe's Books, with its four floors of well-chosen used and new books, is widely acknowledged to be one of the three or four great used bookstores in the nation. Elegant Black Oak Books, founded by some of Moe's ex-employees, provides a cultural nexus for Berkeley's north side. And Cody's Books, which sells only new books, is an international phenomenon. With about 140,000 scholarly, literary, and popular titles to choose among, its selection is staggering. To quote a recently published guide, here you can find "twelve shelves devoted to architecture, twenty to the history of science, thirty to philosophy, forty to poetry, and so on…. Are you looking for a German-English dictionary? Cody's has over twenty different ones."

Berkeley's bookstores provide more than books. They are intellectual centers, social centers, even clubs, each with its characteristic "membership." This is especially apparent at the readings many bookstores sponsor, often featuring world-famous authors, but also at other times of day and night as writers and publishers, editors and agents stroll into their favorite bookshop with studied casualness to check whether their books are still stocked and well displayed, to see what their associates have been up to, and (perhaps most importantly) to mingle with other browsers in an environment where literature is alive. It is impossible to visit the bookstores of Berkeley without being simultaneously humbled and exhilarated by the fecundity and breadth of publishing, without feeling that one is taking part in a passionate, vigorous, noble enterprise.

Berkeley provides a uniquely nourishing environment for writers, and over the last century it has had more than its share. Nationally renowned literary figures who have lived in Berkeley, studied or taught at the University, or who at some stage of their careers have been associated with Berkeley include Frank Norris, Lincoln Steffens, Jack London, Robert Duncan, Josephine Miles, Jack Kerouac, Allen Ginsberg, Gary Snyder, Louis Simpson, Joan Didion, Philip K. Dick, David Brower, Eldridge Cleaver, Timothy Leary, Susan Griffin, Ishmael Reed, Theodore Roszak, Alice Walker, Bharati Mukherjee, Fritjof Capra, Pauline Kael, Barry Gifford, Maxine Hong Kingston, Czeslaw Milosz, and Ursula Le Guin, to name only a fraction. As I write this introduction in the spring of 1997, Robert Hass, Berkeley resident and professor at the University, is stepping down as Poet Laureate of the United States, to be replaced by Robert Pinsky, who for many years was associated with Berkeley as well.

With so many writers, it was inevitable that Berkeley would become the setting for dozens of novels and short stories, the subject of much excellent poetry, the background to hundreds of thoughtful essays. If Berkeley has nourished its writers, the relationship is certainly reciprocal: many of Berkeley's best authors, whether by praising Berkeley's virtues or laying bare its follies, have provided a dense, rich portrait of this most vigorous, contradictory, and literary of American cities.

A couple of years ago I set out to assemble some of this wealth of material into an anthology. I was at first assisted by Melissa Sankary, a student at the University, later by John Barrios and Elizabeth Wlordarzak, and finally by Danielle La France, who with great skill, intelligence, and dedication finished collecting the material and helped put it into its final shape. It was a labor of love for everyone, most of all for me. From the time some twenty-five years ago when Fred Cody looked at my first published book, threw his long arm over my shoulder, took two dozen copies and laid them conspicuously next to the cash register of Cody's Books—thus making me feel like the most important person in the entire world—I have felt myself warmly welcomed by the literary community of Berkeley. I hope this anthology serves to express something of my enjoyment, bemusement, and most of all my gratitude.

MALCOLM MARGOLIN
Publisher, Heyday Books
Berkeley, April 1997

Berkeley!

From The Works of George Berkeley, Vol. II, Misc. Works 1707-50. Published by Clarendon Press (1901). First published in the ? vollume (1725).

Bishop George Berkeley

Verses on the Prospect of Planting Arts and Learning in America

The Muse, disgusted at an age and clime
   Barren of every glorious theme,
In distant lands now waits a better time,
   Producing subjects worthy fame:

In happy climes, where from the genial sun
   And virgin earth such scenes ensue,
The force of art by nature seems outdone,
   And fancied beauties by the true:

In happy climes, the seat of innocence,
   Where nature guides and virtue rules,
Where men shall not impose for truth and sense
   The pedantry of courts and schools:

There shall be sung another golden age,
   The rise of empire and of arts,
The good and great inspiring epic rage,
   The wisest heads and noblest hearts.

Not such as Europe breeds in her decay;
   Such as she bred when fresh and young,

From *The Works of George Berkeley, Vol. IV, Misc. Works 1707–50*. Published by Clarendon Press (1901). First published in the *Miscellany* (1752).

When heavenly flame did animate her clay,
  By future poets shall be sung.

Westward the course of empire takes its way;
  The four first Acts already past,
A fifth shall close the Drama with the day;
  Time's noblest offspring is the last.

Lincoln Steffens

🌾 I Become a Student

IT IS POSSIBLE TO GET AN EDUCATION AT A UNIVERSITY. IT HAS BEEN DONE; NOT OFTEN, but the fact that a proportion, however small, of college students do get a start in interested, methodical study, proves my thesis, and the two personal experiences I have to offer illustrate it and show how to circumvent the faculty, the other students, and the whole college system of mind-fixing. My method might lose a boy his degree, but a degree is not worth so much as the capacity and the drive to learn, and the undergraduate desire for an empty baccalaureate is one of the holds the educational system has on students. Wise students some day will refuse to take degrees, as the best men (in England, for instance) give, but do not themselves accept, titles.

My method was hit on by accident and some instinct. I specialized. With several courses prescribed, I concentrated on the one or two that interested me most, and letting the others go, I worked intensively on my favorites. In my first two years, for example, I worked at English and political economy and read philosophy. At the beginning of my junior year I had several cinches in history. Now I liked history; I had neglected it partly because I rebelled at the way it was taught, as positive knowledge unrelated to politics, art, life, or anything else. The professors gave us chapters out of a few books to read, con, and be quizzed on. Blessed as I was with a "bad memory," I could not commit to it anything that I did not understand and intellectually need. The bare record of the story of man, with names, dates, and irrelative events, bored me.

But I had discovered in my readings of literature, philosophy, and political economy that history had light to throw upon unhistorical questions. So I proposed in my junior and senior years to specialize in history, taking all the courses required and those also that I had flunked in. With this in mind I listened attentively to the first introductory talk of Professor William Cary Jones on American constitutional history. He was a dull lecturer, but I noticed that, after telling us what pages of what books we must be prepared in, he mumbled off some other references "for those that may care to dig deeper."

When the rest of the class rushed out into the sunshine, I went up to the professor and, to his surprise, asked for this memorandum. He gave it me. Up in the library I ran through the required chapters in the two different books, and they differed on several points. Turning to the other authorities, I saw that they disagreed on the same facts and also on others. The librarian, appealed to, helped me search the book-shelves till the library closed, and then I called on Professor Jones for more references. He was astonished, invited me in, and began to approve my industry, which astonished me. I was not trying to be a good boy; I was better than that: I was a curious boy. He lent me a couple of his books, and I went off to my club to read them. They only deepened the mystery, clearing up the historical question, but leaving the answer to be dug for and written.

The historians did not know! History was not a science, but a field for research, a field for me, for any young man, to explore, to make discoveries in and write a scientific report about. I was fascinated. As I went on from chapter to chapter, day after day, finding frequently essential differences of opinion and of fact, I saw more and more work to do. In this course, American constitutional history, I hunted far enough to suspect that the Fathers of the Republic who wrote our sacred Constitution of the United States not only did not, but did not want to, establish a democratic government, and I dreamed for a while—as I used as a child to play I was Napoleon or a trapper—I promised myself to write a true history of the making of the American Constitution. I did not do it; that chapter has been done or well begun since by two men: Smith of the University of Washington and Beard (then) of Columbia (afterward forced out, perhaps for this very work). I found other events, men, and epochs waiting for students. In all my other courses, in ancient, in European, and in modern history, the disagreeing authorities carried me back to the need of a fresh search for (or of) the original documents or other clinching testimony. Of course I did well in my classes. The history professors soon knew me as a student and seldom put a question to me except when the class had flunked it. Then Professor Jones would say, "Well, Steffens, tell them about it."

Fine. But vanity wasn't my ruling passion then. What I had was a quickening sense that I was learning a method of studying history and that every chapter of it, from the beginning of the world to the end, is crying out to be rewritten. There was something for Youth to do; these superior old men had not done anything, finally.

Years afterward I came out of the graft prosecution office in San Francisco with Rudolph Spreckels, the banker and backer of the investigation. We were to go somewhere, quick, in his car, and we couldn't. The chauffeur was trying to repair something wrong. Mr. Spreckels smiled; he looked closely at the defective part, and to my silent, wondering inquiry he answered: "Always, when I see something badly done or not done at all, I see an opportunity to make a fortune. I never kick at bad work by my class: there's lots of it and we suffer from it. But our failures and neglects are chances for the young fellows coming along and looking for work."

Nothing is done. Everything in the world remains to be done or done over. "The greatest picture is not yet painted, the greatest play isn't written (not even by Shakespeare), the greatest poem is unsung. There isn't in all the world a perfect railroad, nor a good government, nor a sound law." Physics, mathematics, and especially the most advanced and exact of the sciences, are being fundamentally revised. Chemistry is just becoming a science; psychology, economics, and sociology are awaiting a Darwin, whose work in turn is awaiting an Einstein. If the rah-rah boys in our colleges could be told this, they might not all be such specialists in football, petting parties, and unearned degrees. They are not told it, however; they are told to learn what is known. This is nothing, philosophically speaking.

Somehow or other in my later years at Berkeley, two professors, Moses and Howison, representing opposite schools of thought, got into a controversy, probably about their classes. They brought together in the house of one of them a few of their picked students, with the evident intention of letting us show in conversation how much or how little we had understood of their respective teachings. I don't remember just what the subject was that they threw into the ring, but we wrestled with it till the professors could stand it no longer. Then they broke in, and while we sat silent and highly entertained, they went at each other hard and fast and long. It was after midnight when, the debate over, we went home. I asked the other fellows what they had got out of it, and their answers showed that they had seen nothing but a fine, fair fight. When I laughed, they asked me what I, the D.S., had seen that was so much more profound.

I said that I had seen two highly-trained, well-educated Masters of Arts and Doctors of Philosophy disagreeing upon every essential point of thought and knowledge. They had all there was of the sciences; and yet they could not find any knowledge upon which they could base an acceptable conclusion. They had no test of knowledge; they didn't know what is and what is not. And they have no test of right and wrong; they have no basis for even an ethics.

Well, and what of it? They asked me that, and that I did not answer. I was stunned by the discovery that it was philosophically true, in a most literal sense, that nothing is known; that it is precisely the foundation that is lacking for science; that all we call knowledge rested upon assumptions which the scientists did not all accept; and that, likewise, there is no scientific reason for saying, for example, that stealing is wrong. In brief: there was no scientific basis for an ethics. No wonder men said one thing and did another; no wonder they could settle nothing either in life or in the academies.

I could hardly believe this. Maybe these professors, whom I greatly respected, did not know it all. I read the books over again with a fresh eye, with a real interest, and I could see that, as in history, so in other branches of knowledge, everything was in the air. And I was glad of it. Rebel though I was, I had got the religion of scholarship and science; I was in awe of the authorities in the academic world. It was a release to feel my worship cool and pass. But I could not be sure. I must go elsewhere, see and hear other professors, men these California professors quoted and looked up to as their high priests. I decided to go as a student to Europe when I was through Berkeley, and I would start with the German universities.

My father listened to my plan, and he was disappointed. He had hoped I would succeed him in his business; it was for that that he was staying in it. When I said that, whatever I might do, I would never go into business, he said, rather sadly, that he would sell out his interest and retire. And he did soon after our talk. But he wanted me to stay home and, to keep me, offered to buy an interest in a certain San Francisco daily paper. He had evidently had this in mind for some time. I had always done some writing, verse at the poetical age of puberty, then a novel which my mother alone treasured. Journalism was the business for a boy who liked to write, he thought, and he said I had often spoken of a newspaper as my ambition. No doubt I had in the intervals between my campaigns as Napoleon. But no more. I was now going to be a scientist, a philosopher. He sighed; he thought it over, and with the approval of my mother, who was for every sort of education, he gave his consent.

Frank Norris

The "English Courses" of the University of California

IN THE "ANNOUNCEMENT OF COURSES" PUBLISHED ANNUALLY BY THE FACULTY OF THE University of California the reader cannot fail to be impressed with the number and scope of the hours devoted by the students to recitations and lectures upon the subject of "literature." At the head of this department is Professor Gayley (the same gentleman who is to edit the volumes of Shakespeare for Macmillan at the expense of the State of California). Be pleased for a moment to consider these "literary" courses. They comprise "themes" written by the student, the subject chosen by the instructor and the matter found in text books and encyclopedias. They further include lectures, delivered by associate professors, who, in their turn have taken their information from text books and "manuals" written by other professors in other colleges. The student is taught to "classify." "Classification" is the one thing desirable in the eyes of the professors of "literature" of the University of California. The young Sophomore, with his new, fresh mind, his active brain and vivid imagination, with ideas of his own, crude, perhaps, but first hand, not cribbed from text books. This type of young fellow, I say, is taught to "classify," is set to work counting the "metaphors" in a given passage. This is actually true—tabulating them, separating them from the "similes," comparing the results. He is told to study sentence structure. He classifies certain types of sentences in De Quincey and compares them with certain other types of sentences in

Excerpted from *Frank Norris: Novels and Essays*, edited by Donald Pizer. Published by Literary Classics of the U.S., Inc. (1986). First published in *The Wave* (November 28, 1896).

Carlyle. He makes the wonderful discovery—on suggestion from the instructor—that De Quincey excelled in those metaphors and similes relating to rapidity of movement. Sensation!

In his Junior and Senior years he takes up the study of Milton, of Browning, of the drama of the seventeenth and eighteenth centuries, English comedy, of advanced rhetoric, and of aesthetics. "Aesthetics," think of that! Here, the "classification" goes on as before. He learns to read Chaucer as it was read in the fourteenth century, sounding the final e; he paraphrases Milton's sonnets, he makes out "skeletons" and "schemes" of certain prose passages. His enthusiasm is about dead now; he is ashamed of his original thoughts and of those ideas of his own that he entertained as a Freshman and Sophomore. He has learned to write "themes" and "papers" in the true academic style, which is to read some dozen text books and encyclopedia articles on the subject, and to make over the results in his own language. He has reduced the writing of "themes" to a system. He knows what the instructor wants, he writes accordingly, and is rewarded by first and second sections. The "co-eds" take to the "classification" method even better than the young men. They thrive and fatten intellectually on the regime. They consider themselves literary. They write articles on the "Philosophy of Dante" for the college weekly, and after graduation they "read papers" to literary "circles" composed of post-graduate "co-eds," the professors' wives and daughters and a very few pale young men in spectacles and black cutaway coats. After the reading of the "paper" follows the "discussion," aided and abetted by cake and lemonade. This is literature! Isn't it admirable!

The young man, the whilom Sophomore, affected with original ideas, does rather different. As said, by the time he is a Junior or Senior, he has lost all interest in the "literary" courses. The "themes" must be written, however, and the best way is the easiest. This is how he oft-times goes about it: He knows just where he can lay his hands upon some fifty to a hundred "themes" written by the members of past classes, that have been carefully collected and preserved by enterprising students. It will go hard if he cannot in the pile find one upon the subject in hand. He does not necessarily copy it. He rewrites it in his own language. Do you blame him very much? Is his method so very different from that in which he is encouraged by his professor; viz., the cribbing—for it is cribbing—from text books? The "theme" which he rewrites has been cribbed in the first place.

The method of English instruction of the University of California often develops capital ingenuity in the student upon whom it is practiced. We know of one young man—a Senior—who found himself called upon to write four "themes," yet managed to make one—re-written four times—do for the four. This was the manner of it. The four "themes" called for were in the English, chemical, German and military courses respectively. The young fellow found a German treatise on the manufacture of gunpowder, translated it, made four copies, and by a little ingenuity passed it off in the four above named departments. Of course the thing is deplorable, yet how much of the blame is to be laid at the door of the English faculty?

The conclusion of the whole matter is that the literary courses at the University of California do not develop literary instincts among the students who attend them. The best way to study literature is to try to produce literature. It is original work that counts, not the everlasting compiling of facts, not the tabulating of metaphors, nor the rehashing of text books and encyclopedia articles.

They order this matter better at Harvard. The literary student at Cambridge has but little to do with lectures, almost nothing at all with text books. He is sent away from the lecture room and told to look about him and think a little. Each day he writes a theme, a page if necessary, a single line of a dozen words if he likes; anything, so it is original, something he has seen or thought, not read of, not picked up at second hand. He may choose any subject under the blue heavens from a pun to a philosophical reflection, only let it be his own. Once every two weeks he writes a longer theme, and during the last six weeks of the year, a still longer one, in six weekly installments. Not a single suggestion is offered as to subject. The result of this system is a keenness of interest that draws three hundred men to the course and that fills the benches at every session of the class. The class room work consists merely in the reading by the instructor of the best work done, together with his few critical comments upon it by the instructor in charge. The character of the themes produced under this system is of such high order that it is not rare to come across one of them in the pages of the first-class magazines of the day. There is no sufficient reason to suppose that the California collegians are intellectually inferior to those of the Eastern States. It is only a question of the means adopted to develop the material.

Benjamin Ide Wheeler

It Is Good to Be Here

This address, the first given by University of California Presi-
dent Benjamin Ide Wheeler, was delivered to the student body on
October 3, 1899.

STUDENTS OF THE UNIVERSITY OF CALIFORNIA, I REJOICE THAT MY FIRST INTRODUC-
tion to the University takes the form of an introduction to you. Heretofore this
University has been to me more or less a thing of the imagination: I have
known of it in the form of statutes and reports, names and titles, forms and
observances; I have seen its admirably edited register; I have seen its hon-
orable governing board in session; I have seen its buildings, its equipment, its
mechanism, its gardens and its trees; but now, standing here in the golden
sunlight, by its help under this real blue canopy, I look into the faces of the
real blue and gold that constitutes the real living University of California.
From this hour I know that I am a member in a real living association, because
I am joined in association with men. The only thing that is of interest to me in
a university is men and women. As long as I live, I trust I may never be
interested in a university of mechanisms, reports, and papers; but only in a
university of human beings.

It has been a solicitude on my part, lest in entering a presidential office,
I might be so absorbed in administrative things, that my own loved work of
teaching might be taken from me, and it will be a disappointment to me if in

Excerpted from *The Abundant Life* by Benjamin Ide Wheeler, edited by Monroe
Deutsch. Published by the University of California Press (1926).

any wise my work here shall separate me from active interest in student affairs. Almost the only consolation I have this morning in entering upon my work is the belief that I am going to know you and to have to do with you intimately; for all this work of the presidential office is burden and care. It is only done in order that the real thing may be reached, the real object, the bringing forward of a university made of students. I want you to find in me— to believe from the beginning and throughout, that you have in me a personal friend. I shall regard my mission here a failure if that is not the case. I want you to come to see me, and come to me as persons. Tell me your names—I beg of you, tell me your names whenever you see me; for whenever I see a man that I have seen before, I am apt to remember his face and to remember a good deal about him—almost everything except his name. So please come up to me and say "My name is —," and if it happens to be Smith, give the initial. Please do not be afraid to come about petty matters, little matters. What interests you will interest me. And I hope I am going to have time enough to know about your petty affairs.

Now there are a great many things that I am moved to say on this occasion. This is a stimulating sight. The golden sunshine coming down in genial, lazy haze, smiling upon the ripened brown of these magnificent hills, reminds me of my beloved Greece. It is more than Hellas that we have here. Greece looked out toward the old oriental world, Berkeley looks out through the Golden Gate to the oriental world that has meaning for today.

I should like to talk to you about the glorious future that I discern for this University. I should like to talk to you about the work we have in hand, but in the few moments that I have in this supreme opportunity, I want to speak to you about the one thing that in my idea is fundamental in the life of a university—and that is university loyalty.

A university is not a place where you come as empty buckets to the well to be filled. People are going to pump things into you, to be sure, but you are going to pour most of it out again. I believe from my own experience, that after all, we must take to ourselves the consolation that that educative material does us the most good which we forget most entirely. Those things which hover on the superfices of the mind are oftener a stumbling block than a help. It is what goes over into spinal marrow, what goes over into real life that makes us; and what we are likely to gain from our university life is not bits of knowledge, is not maxims and rules for getting this or that; but after all it is this one thing that we talk so much about and understand so imperfectly—it is character. The men you tie to are men of character. As I grow older I come less and less to respect men of brilliancy and to tie to men for their characters. And what men are going to get out of their university life is not what is pumped into the pail, but what goes over into life. And it comes not only from the lecture room, but from association with the best minds they find in the faculty, alumni, and student body—association with the whole life and character of the University. This University is a living thing. The real university is alive. Blood pulses through its veins. The spiritual life of the men who have gone before is in it. It is not a thing of buildings, of statutes, of courses—it is a thing of life. What you will get out of this University that is worth your while, that will stand by you, is what you will get out of association with it as a living thing.

Therefore I say we are not a mechanism to furnish people with equipments; we are alive; we have a heart. And to that family life I charge you, students of the University of California, be loyal. It is worth your while. It is your duty. Be loyal to the University; be loyal to all its parts.

Those who take the misunderstandings and quarrels of the inside to ventilate them in the outside world are traitors to us. We are a family. You cannot make a university out of minds and brains. In a university, as elsewhere in the world, heart is more than head, love is more than reason.

Hold fast to that love for the University. Stand strong, shoulder to shoulder, when you do its work. Let every man according to his ability do what the University asks of him, and let every man do in support of the other man's work what he can. Let the quarter-back pass the ball, let the line stand solid, let the men guard the half-back when he comes racing round the end. Let us stand together. Let us have at the University of California what we call in football "good interference."

This University shall be a family's glorious old mother, by whose hearth you shall love to sit down. Love her. It does a man good to love noble things, to attach his life to noble allegiances. It is a good thing to love the church, it is a good thing to love the state, it is a good thing to love one's home, it is a good thing to be loyal to one's father and mother, and after the same sort it is good to be loyal to the University, which stands in life for the purest things and the cleanest, loftiest ideals. Cheer for her; it will do your lungs good.

It has done me good to hear your cheer ringing over the campus. My little boy (five or six years old), who is already a loyal Californian, asked me, when I started to come out here, if I would please instruct him in the California yell; and I to my regret was unable to give it to him in the original. He looked at me and shook his head, entertaining some serious doubts whether I had any right to be the President of the University of California; and I shared his doubts. But we had not been in San Francisco many hours when the yell was learned.

And so I say cheer for her; it will do your lungs good. Love her; it will do your heart and life good.

Mr. F. G. Dorety, President of the Associated Students, spoke briefly on their behalf. After hearty cheers for the President, he rose again and said:

It has been good to be here. I thank you, I thank you, I thank you a thousand times for your cordiality and welcome. May we meet together in the future often, to consult, and arouse our enthusiasm together. Now it has been good to be here and we will go unto our homes in peace.

John F. Boyd

⚡ The Berkeley Heroine

"YOU WILL HAVE TO TAKE YOUR LUNCH TO SCHOOL TO-MORROW, ALICE," SAID MRS. Foster to her daughter, a bright young miss of sweet sixteen, who her teacher said was the brightest scholar in the Kellogg school; "You will take your lunch as your father is going to take your grandma and me over to see the landing and reception of the California volunteers who have just returned from Manila. It will be a grand sight, and your father has secured seats for us on Market street which a friend of his has kindly placed at his disposal. We have seats at a second-story window. You know your cousin Edward is a lieutenant now in the regiment in which he enlisted as a private, and which promotion he gained by strict attention to his duties and to his soldierly conduct. Ah! 'twill be a proud day for his mother, whom he parted with in tears about a year ago, to see him return wearing an officer's uniform and sword—in fact, returning a hero." And Mrs. Foster thought of her own darling boy who, had he lived, might have followed "Old Glory" to the far-away Philippines and returned a hero. "Yes," replied Alice, "boys can become heroes, and get all the praise and have all the glory, while we poor girls can never achieve greatness or do any heroic deed. Oh dear, some times I wish I was a boy. No, I don't either," said she, blushing, "but—but—"

"Nonsense," said Mrs. Foster, "you are entirely wrong Alice. Think how many women have made a name for themselves throughout the civilized world by their womanly conduct or heroic actions. Remember the mother of Washington; remember Grace Darling; think of brave Florence Nightingale

---

From *Under the Berkeley Oaks: Stories by Students of the University of California.* Published by A. M. Robertson (1901).

and scores of other noble women who have made heroines of themselves by their noble deeds. Think of that noble woman, Mrs. Hearst, who has come to reside in Berkeley. Pause and reflect on the immense amount of good she is doing to our grand University, and see the helping hand which she holds outstretched to the students of both sexes.

"Remember, Alice, that when the names of the present generation shall be forgotten the names I have mentioned will be revered by thousands. Think you that the name of Phoebe Hearst will not be remembered with gratitude by thousands yet unborn? Think by what a noble, yet simple deed, the name of Barbara Frietchie has been told in song and story." "Yes," said Alice, "but there is no hopes of my ever gaining a great name or becoming a heroine. In the first place, I haven't got the wealth to follow the noble actions of the lady you last named. Then, let me see, Grace Darling saved some men from drowning, didn't she? Well, the first time anybody falls into Strawberry Creek I am going to rush out and save them; providing there is not over two inches of water in the bed of the creek; and then, hurrah! I'll get my name in the Berkeley and San Francisco papers, and perhaps some city reporter will come over and say, 'Mrs. Foster, would you be kind enough to lend us a photo of your daughter who so heroically saved those persons from drowning the other day? We want it to use in the Sunday edition of the San Francisco *Howler*'"; and gay-hearted Alice gave the house cat, who was sleeping on the lounge, a sly pinch on one of her ears, and then petted poor kitty and inquired what troubled her.

The household was astir at sunrise and an early breakfast was prepared and eaten, as Mrs. Foster was determined to get a start to avoid the rush, which in all probability would take place on both ferry-boat and street-car on that day. Breakfast over, a light lunch was put up for Alice to enjoy at the noon hour, and as soon as grandma (who took a long time to dress) was ready, Mr. and Mrs. Foster, accompanied by grandma and Alice, took their seats in the carriage, which on account of grandma's infirmities had been engaged to convey them to Berkeley station, where Alice was to leave them and proceed to school.

After kissing ma and grandma good-bye, and receiving instructions as to where the kitchen door key had been hidden, and told to go in and help herself to the eatables in the pantry if she felt hungry, and receiving a "good-bye" kiss from her father, the latter said, "Alice, I wish to warn you not to go near or handle my shot-gun which I loaded a few days ago to shoot those cats that have been troubling our chickens. It stands in the closet off the washroom and is loaded with coarse birdshot; and although it may not kill, it would severely wound any one who stood in front of it, or at least make them think that a whole hive of bees had stung them. So be careful darling and don't trouble it. We shall be home on the five o'clock train if possible; not later than 5:30 at the latest. So good-bye, and as they used to say when I was a youngster:

> Go to school, go to school,
> And tell the teacher you're a fool.

"But no," said Mr. Foster, gazing affectionately at his pet, "papa is wrong to call you such names. You are the bonniest lass, as the Scotch say, in Berkeley." "Yes," said Mrs. Foster, smiling, "and she wants to be a heroine; to make a name for herself in the world," and she gave a ludicrous account of Alice's remark on the preceding evening and added:

"Why, what do you suppose papa? Alice actually wished she were a boy and could go and fight the Philippinos." "Oh no," said Alice, blushing furiously, "I only said I wished to make a name in the world; to gain name and fame by some heroic action." "Well," said Mr. Foster, "one more sweet kiss from my darling, then go to school and imagine that you have captured Aguinaldo single-handed, and received the thanks of the U.S. government and also the plaudits of the whole Yankee nation for your heroic action. But, good-bye dear, here comes our train." And waving adieu to Alice, the party boarded the Berkeley train.

Mr. Foster was a merchant doing business in the city, but making his home in beautiful Berkeley. He had built himself a home near the State University where he resided with his wife and daughter Alice who, as the only child, was the pet of the family. The only other occupant of the house besides the Chinese servant was Grandma Farquhar, who was proud of her descent from the Farquhar family of Georgia, whose broad plantation and countless slaves, situated in the upper part of the State, had been her childhood's home; and she often entertained and amused Alice and her schoolmates with tales of "slavery days" and incidents of the war of the Rebellion and the sights she had witnessed during that eventful period.

The day at school passed off without any unusual event, although Alice made some blunder in her Latin which caused a look of surprise on Professor James' face, as usually she was letter-perfect in her studies. But to-day her thoughts were with her parents across San Francisco bay, and Alice felt relieved when school closed.

School was dismissed and Alice walked along toward home accompanied by some of her schoolmates whose homes lay in the same direction. Slowly they sauntered along, gayly discussing the events of the day and the merits and demerits of Professor Waterman, Mr. James, Miss Edmonds and Miss McClean.

When she parted from her companions Alice took a short cut through the University grounds as the nearest way home. As she slowly walked along thinking over the events of the day she was surprised to see two rough-looking, ill-clad men smoking short clay pipes and reclining at the foot of an old oak tree. Alice was somewhat startled and was about to retrace her steps when her attention was arrested by hearing one of the men say, "I tell you it's a safe job, the hull of the family is gone to the city to see the big parade and there's a host of silverware in the china closet. I peeked through the winder this mornin' when they was eatin' breckfus and seed it all glistenin'. I tell yer we can 'crack the crib' as easy as I can light this pipe. I'll bet there's two or three hundred dollars' worth of silverware and it'll make us rich. Dunno but what I'll take a trip to Yurop when I get it in old Jerry's meltin' pot, and bid farewell to the Barbary Coast and wipe my weepin' eyes, as the Salvation Army sings. Come let's make a break, or old man Foster will be comin' home with the woman and kid, and then there'll be no chance to handle all the purty silver jimcracks. Come, shake a leg and let's travel."

Alice stood petrified. All the ruffians' talk indicated their intention to rob her father's home. What could she do to prevent it? There was no near neighbors to call on for assistance, and to run down to Shattuck avenue and obtain help would be useless; besides, she was afraid to stir lest the ruffians should overhear her. The group of bushes behind which she stood effectually concealed her from the sight of the tramps, and fear kept her quiet.

"I say, Mose," said the elder of the two villains, "you jest run over to the house and ring the front door bell and make sure there is nobody at home. If anybody comes to the door give them a song and dance about wood to saw, or garden to spade. If nobody comes to the door, hoof it round to the winder and take a peep in. I'll stay here and if I see anybody coming I'll whistle." "All hunky," said the one called Mose, "I'll be back in a jiffy;" and away the younger robber started, while his companion in crime lazily reclined on the bank smoking, the fumes of which was anything but pleasant to the nostrils of poor Alice who stood motionless, not daring to move.

In a few moments the younger ruffian returned and with an oath declared that the coast was clear and "all quiet on the Potomac."

His partner then inquired regarding the window fastenings, and on receiving an answer said, "Well, come ahead then, I want to handle some of that purty silverware I seed this mornin'."

The mention of the silverware caused poor Alice a sad pang. Every piece, consisting of a massive tray, sugar bowl, cream pitcher, tea pot and one dozen large, and the same number of small teaspoons, butter bowl and knife, had been in grandma's family for generations back, and were valued heirlooms. Grandma Farquhar had inherited them from her ancestors in her old Georgia home. The silverware had been buried time after time during the civil war of '61–'65, and it had been Alice's delight to listen to grandma's stories of the events of that stirring period. How when Sherman's army made its celebrated march through Georgia the Farquhar plantation lay directly in its road, and horrible rumors were circulated regarding the thievish propensities of the Yankee army. How all the valuable jewelry and silverware had been hastily buried by one of the negroes, an old slave named Hector, who was born on the plantation and was regarded and trusted as one of the family. Grandma who was a young girl at that time, used to relate how old Hector came in quite pleased, and assured "Old Missus" that "dat dem Yankees done walked right ober de spot whar dem tings war buried and neber saw dem."

The Union officers were, however, very polite to the ladies of the Farquhar family, even applauding when Miss Belle (as grandma was then called,) in a spirit of defiance sang the "Bonnie Blue Flag," and they lost nothing but some chickens and sweet potatoes which the Yankee soldiers gobbled up.

After the Yankees left, a detachment of the Confederate cavalry encamped near the plantation and remained about ten days. Again was the silverware and other valuables buried by old Hector, and although the soldiers helped themselves to the hay and grain for their horses, nothing else was missed, and the family was not disturbed or molested. After both armies left the vicinity a gang of ruffians and outlaws, known as "Red Burns'

Guerrillas," made their appearance in the neighborhood, and although claiming to belong to the Confederate army, robbed both friend and foe alike. Again was the treasure buried, and although the guerrillas questioned every slave on the plantation, they received no information, for the simple reason that none but old Hector and the whites of the family knew where it was.

Grandma used to describe to Alice the terrible scenes which took place when Red Burns and his gang arrived on the plantation. How they invaded the home, ripped up the carpets, plunged swords into the feather beds and searched high and low for the valuables they were certain were concealed somewhere, and to add insult to injury, threatened to burn the house and slave quarters unless the valuables were handed over to them. However, they succeeded in sending news of the situation to the male members of the family who were serving in the Confederate army.

Hon. Col. DeCourcey, an uncle of grandma's, arrived with a company of cavalry, with orders from Gen. Sinclair of the Confederate forces to draft every one of the cowardly guerrillas into the Confederate army or wipe them off the earth, and the general said he did not give a hang which.

That very morning some of the guerrillas having learned from a slave who was jealous of the popularity of old Hector with the whites, and likewise having been threatened by some of the gang, confided to them that probably old Hector was aware of any hiding place which held the family belongings as he was acquainted with a great many family secrets, and had even been allowed to carry the key of the smoke-house.

The ruffians had already placed a rope around Hector's neck, and with a refinement of cruelty had forced all the females of the family, (the males were all away in the army) to come out and see the nigger hang, no doubt, hoping that sympathy for the poor fellow would induce some of the females to betray the hiding place of any valuables they might have concealed.

In fact, the mistress of the plantation, grandma's mama had just started forward with an offer to surrender all the valuables on condition that the ruffians should spare old Hector, but at this juncture a cheer was heard down the lane, a few shots were fired and the guerrillas ordered to surrender.

The new arrivals were Col. DeCourcey and a company of Confederate cavalry. Old Hector was at once released, while the band of outlaws were placed under arrest and sent to the nearest Confederate camp.

Alice never grew weary of hearing her grandma relate the stirring events of the Rebellion. She knew that grandma valued the silverware far above its intrinsic worth as a souvenir of her girlhood days; and now to think that these ruffians were planning to steal and carry it off. But what could she do—no one was in sight. Oh! if pa, or even the Chinese boy was at home, but he too, had been granted a holiday and had gone to see his cousin over in San Francisco. Oh! if she were only in the house she might scream from an up-stairs window and frighten the ruffians away. But no,—there she was in that clump of bushes, not daring to stir, scarcely to breathe lest she should be overheard.

In a few minutes the younger ruffian returned and with a great many slang expressions, explained that he "rang the bell and made a circuit of the house and there was no one at home."

After a short talk the two desperadoes agreed to break one of the dining-room windows and effect an entrance that way. As they moved off, tears came in Alice's eyes as she thought how bad her grandma would feel at the loss of her silverware. Oh! what could she do to save it! She thought of the events of the night before. How she wished she were a boy. Then of her wish to be a hero-ine. Suddenly the thought struck her if she could save grandma's precious silverware from the hands of the robbers, would it not be a heroic action? Would not her dear mama and papa praise her? And the gratitude of grand-ma! Oh! yes, she must save that silverware at any cost.

But how? No help was near. She must do it alone. Suddenly she thought of her father's words about the shotgun, "it might not kill, but you would think a hive of bees had stung you." It was in the washroom and the key of the kitchen door was hidden in the woodshed under an old coat which hung there.

She would softly unlock the kitchen door, gain access to the washroom, seize the gun, throw open the dining-room door and order the villains to sur-render. She glanced toward the house; the tramps were under the dining-room window, and one was standing on the other's shoulders. She heard the sound of breaking glass. She saw one of the villains raise the window, crawl through and assist his companion in crime up. Now was her time.

Quickly hurrying around the other side of the house she gained the woodshed, and in a moment had possession of the key. As she turned, the sight of a large American flag, which her father hoisted on the flagpole in front of the house on all holidays, caught her eye. She remembered that one time when the janitor of the Kellogg school had hoisted the school flag upside down by mistake, how that bold, bad expressman, John Boyd, had criticised his doing so in the Berkeley *Advocate*. How he said that a flag was never hoisted "Union down" unless in case of distress; and surely this was a case of deep distress. Besides, her father would see the flag while up the road and would hasten to see what was the matter.

Alice quickly seized the flag, and running around the opposite side of the house bent it on, Union down, and was glad when the breeze streamed it out.

Now for the shotgun. One moment! How should she accost the thieves? Why, put on a bold face, rush in, point the gun at the burglars and force them to remain quiet until her father came. She at first thought of repeating to the villains her favorite lines in her best loved poem "Barbara Frietchie":

> "Who touches one hair of yon gray head
> Dies like a dog. March on," he said.

But as the intruders were not touching any gray head, that would not be appropriate; but she would trust to circumstances and proceed to action. Carefully grasping the gun Alice crept cautiously to the dining-room door and threw it open, and what a sight met her eyes! Seated on the floor were the two ruffians, one holding a grain sack while the other placed the different articles of silverware in it. Other articles usually kept in the closet were scattered on the floor, showing that the closet had been thoroughly overhauled and all the contents thrown out. The sight of Alice caused the ruffians to rise to their feet. But as the young lady pointed the gun and cried out "Surrender or die," they sank back in dismay.

After a moment's pause the elder ruffian said: "Say, Miss, jest pint that gun the other way and me and my pard will jump out of the winder and say *au revoir* and vamoos the ranch."

"Please sit still," replied Alice, "or you die like a dog."

Now the truth must be told; Alice had never handled a gun before and did not know enough to raise the hammer and cock the gun. But this the tramps did not perceive, and like cowards as they were, sat trembling and did not dare to move. One of the ruffians did propose to "jump up and choke the kid." But when Alice (with her heart in her mouth) answered boldly "come on and try it," the ruffians sat still. Again when one of the scoundrels drew an old sooty clay pipe from his pocket and prepared to smoke, Alice simply said: "My ma does not allow any smoking in the house. Put that pipe away," and the command was obeyed so promptly that it gave Alice courage, though she constantly held the gun in readiness to bring it to her shoulder. All of a sudden Alice heard the sound of approaching wheels, and one of the tramps exclaimed with an oath: "There's a kerreige comin' down the road."

Alice was overjoyed and made a step toward the window; upon seeing which one of the robbers started to arise from the floor. Quick as a flash Alice turned and leveled the weapon, at the same time exclaiming: "Please sit down;" a polite request which the man, with one glance at the shotgun in the hands of the young girl was good enough to obey.

The sound of wheels grew nearer, and as Alice caught sight of her father seated on the front with the driver, Alice screamed with all her might: "Fire! robbers! help! murder! fire! thieves! help!" Mr. Foster heard and recognized the voice of his daughter, and his first thought was of fire. Jumping from the carriage he seized an empty water pail which stood out on the flower beds; he sprang through the rear of the house into the dining-room and one glance told the story. The leveled gun held by his daughter, the silverware and other articles scattered over the floor, the crouching robbers. Seizing the gun from his daughter's hands he cocked both barrels and shouted, "Surrender, you villains, or I will fill you full of lead."

"Yes," shouted Alice (remembering her last lesson in history relating to the capture of Crown Point by Ethan Allen during the war of the Revolution). "Surrender in the name of the Great Jehovah and the Continental Congress!" and turning to her mama, who had just hurried in, Alice fell into her arms exclaiming: "They—were—going—to—rob—grandma—of—her—silverware," and fainted. Laying Alice on the lounge Mrs. Foster called in Joe Frick, the driver of the carriage, and bade him drive down to Shattuck avenue and request Marshal Lloyd, or one of his deputies, to return with him to arrest the captured outlaws.

Frick soon returned with the Marshal and also a reporter of the *Advocate*, who had heard the news and had visions of a "scoop" before his eyes, and to Alice's confusion skillfully drew from her a full account of the day's happenings. Alice very modestly told her story, after which Marshal Lloyd handcuffed the two villains and started for the county jail. Alice received the congratulations of her friends and neighbors, who crowded in to hear of her strange adventure, and to her surprise the Berkeley *Advocate* came out with a two-column account of her daring act headed in large letters: "A Heroic Berkeley Girl. She Captures Two Burglars and Saves the Family Jewels. A Young Lady of Whom Berkeley Should Be Proud." And it made Alice feel proud to read the kind commendations, which the big-hearted editor of the *Advocate* showered on her.

But what a welcome she received the next morning when she entered Kellogg school yard. How her schoolmates petted and admired her. How Prof. Waterman shook hands and congratulated her on her pluck and courage, and said he was proud of her as a pupil. It was a disagreeable feature of the case when Alice had to go down to the Superior Court as witness in the case for the People vs. Moses Riley and Peter McCann. Alice dreaded the ordeal; but when in simple language she told how she had followed the burglars, how she had covered them with the shotgun and forced them to surrender, the court rang with applause. How the judge in his charge to the jury called her a "brave American girl"; how the jury, after finding the prisoners guilty, begged the privilege of shaking hands with her. But it must be confessed that Alice felt sorry when she heard the prisoners sentenced to ten years in San Quentin.

A few days after, grandma sent for lawyer Graber and added a codicil to her will, which read:

"And in addition to the bequest heretofore made to my beloved granddaughter Alice Foster, I hereby bequeath to her all my silverware known as the 'Farquhar silverware,' which I wish her to keep in memory of the giver."

James Hopper

The Proud Dig and the Lazy Student

ONCE UPON A TIME, LONG, LONG AGO, BEFORE THE UNIVERSITY HAD ITS NEW BUILD-
ings, before Stanford had invented football, when Professor Putzker spoke
only nineteen languages, and co-eds were yet a minority, there lived in
California a Lazy Student.

O but he was lazy—a masterpiece of perfected laziness! On sunny days
he spent his time on the steps of North Hall (then a temporary building),
puffing at a charred piece of corncob with just enough nicely calculated force
to keep a light. His long legs stretched over half-a-dozen steps; his hazy blue
eyes wandered over the landscape. Passers-by stumbled regularly over the
legs; they looked into the hazy blue eyes, and their wrath was quelled.

Once in a while, as the North Hall bell toned musically, he seemed to
remember something. His face contracted in agony; his dreamy blue eyes took
tints of nameless terror; he half-rose, stiff with resolve. But his muscles would
relax; he fell back limply on his steps, took a puff of relief, and a wave of
beatitude smoothed the face to its customary placidity. These paroxysms
came about fifteen times a week, and observers noticed that, on a small piece
of cardboard lined in little squares, the Lazy Student had marked with crosses
the time of occurrence of these dreadful attacks.

Sometimes, on warm spring days, the Lazy Student forsook North Hall.
Early in the morning he sauntered up Eglantine Canyon (this was before the
supremacy of co-eds). In short, laborious relays, cut by long periods of de-
licious rest, he puffed and sighed his way to a little knoll, where he threw

From *Under the Berkeley Oaks: Stories by Students of the University of California.*
Published by A. M. Robertson (1901).

himself down in the supreme ecstasy of toil done. There, lying on his back in the high grass, he passed the day. Golden beams stealing through the grass-blades played merrily about his nose. The air vibrated with mysterious sounds of throbbing life; the quail called from afar; the lark tinkled; and, nearer, there were nameless little chirps and squeaks and little cries—rustlings, scamperings, whisperings. For the little beasts of the hill liked this lazy man, and he was so nice, so quiet, so beautifully lazy that they took all sorts of liberties with him. Often a scurrying squirrel ran plumb over him, and spiders were wont to weave their webs all about him. Once, one of these tire-less little spinners, a tiny golden-hued thing, had built a bridge from the tip of his shoe to the tip of his nose. He watched her with one eye as on this foundation she elaborated a fragile net. Then a happy, buzzing flylet had be-come entangled, and the Lazy Student underwent a terrible moral crisis. Should he save the fly and disappoint the spider, or should he please the spi-der and see the fly devoured? The spider was certainly his first friend, and saving the fly would be a deliberate breach of trust. He decided for the spider. But just as she was pouncing on the struggling, helpless little fly, his innate sympathy for the weak suddenly got the better of him. He moved his foot, straightened his nose, and piff! the web broke, and buzz! the fly was off. The little golden spider jumped on his knee, hurried up and down to view the catastrophe, then resolutely began weaving again. Suddenly the Lazy Student had a vision of her sensation. He imagined the affrighted and questioning dismay at the sudden destructive act of the great unknown, brutal force, the passionate "why?" of the little spider. And a big tear dropped languidly a-down his nose. Ah, the life of a lazy man is not always a happy one!

Above, lazy, fluffy clouds floated across the blue—eternal invitation to airy, floating life. He loved the clouds, did this Lazy Student.

One day, as he lay in this interesting position, he suddenly felt an impulse to yell.

Where he got that idea I will not attempt to tell. The act necessitated a considerable amount of physical exertion. He had to draw in a big breath of air, then expel it; the vocal clouds must be set vibrating. Could he have for-gotten to calculate this? I fear it. Communion with nature is intoxicating. I know of a dignified professor who, when in the mountains, rolls down every hill of slope gentle enough to impart some slight degree of decorum to such indecorous action. Our hero did not roll down the hill, but he yelled, and,

worse, he yelled in German, something that he had heard in his childhood—
in the happy days when there was a nurse to take care of him and tell him
stories—and which suddenly rhythmed back into his head:—

O, was soll es bedeuten
Das ich so traurig bin.

(He might have said *faulig*.)

Soft, far, dreamily indistinct, the echo came floating back. He started!
Again he yelled. Again the echo returned. He took a big gasping breath; then,
leaning back, he closed his eyes, overcome by the sudden realization of what
might be.

The remainder of that term the North Hall station was abandoned. The
Lazy Student passed his time on the hill.

At the beginning of the next semester there went through college vague
rumors that the Lazy Student had reformed.

It was true. He was attending recitations. One morning, registration
week, he had sauntered into the recorder's office.

He had been at college three years and a half. He found that he had five
hours' credit. He calmly put down one hundred and twenty hours on his
registration-card. This, happening a long, long time ago, before red tape had
been invented, was quite possible.

But what was singular was his choice of studies. His card read something like this: German I, do. 2, do. 3, and so on to German 58; French I, do.
2, do. 3, and so on to French 51. Spanish, Italian, Hebrew, Chinese, Sanskrit, Icelandic appeared in the same proportion. One hundred and twenty
hours in languages! Putzker paled before this.

One day, during German 46 b., the Dig, glancing over his spectacles
toward a corner of the room, was startled at the sight of the Lazy Student,
sprawled comfortably in a corner chair, with half-shut eyes permeating himself with the atmosphere of lore. An hour later, at French 53 c., the Dig,
making for a seat, stepped on some one's feet. Turning to apologize, he met
the mournful, reproachful look of two hazy blue eyes. At Spanish 37, everywhere he went that day, he met our lazy friend.

It puzzled him and it irritated him. What right had this long, lazy,
unkempt personage to profane the learned haunts with his languid presence?
It was positively insulting.

But he had to stand it. The ex-bum attended recitations religiously. Half-asleep most of the time, when called upon to recite he was transformed. His body stiffened with a snap, his eyes opened and flashed genius, and he translated, translated, translated, tearing his way along like a torrent, rushing over all obstacles. He tossed his head like a fiery nag, snorted and charged on till the moderating, imploring "Kritisch! kritisch!" of the professor became mild open-mouthed astonishment. When finally stopped, he dropped to his seat and, after a final tremor, regained his usual indescribable ease of posture, while the professor muttered, "Ya, gut; you haf—you haf de geeft of languish." And a stinging envy penetrated the heart of the Dig.

Every day at four o'clock the Lazy Student could be seen making his way by easy stages toward Eglantine Canyon. Under his arm he had a pile of books—a Tower of Babel of Greek, Sanskrit, Latin, German, Hebrew, etc. In the evening he returned, flushed and happy with the sense of duty done. He certainly had a remarkable gift for languages. And the Dig who toiled and toiled over a paltry twenty hours a week was taken with a formidable hate for that lazy, worthless, shiftless Rip Van Winkle who bummed along one hundred and twenty hours of the same subjects.

One day after Hebrew 27, during which the Lazy Student had starred the Dig into the shades of mediocrity, the latter made a mighty resolution. He would follow his rival; he would cling to him like a leech and spy his method, wrest the secret of his success!

The Lazy Student started for the hill, and the Dig followed. It was not difficult to keep up. The Lazy Student sighed along one hundred feet, then rolled limply on the ground. There he recuperated a few minutes, his legs stretched like some gigantic compass. With a heart-rending groan he started up again, to repeat the same performance with gradual diminuendo of walking stages and crescendo of resting periods. The Dig followed these maneuvers, wondering. Creeping through the grass, jumping from tree to tree, he followed our unconscious hero. Two or three times he almost stumbled upon him during one of his numerous rests. At last an ecstatic sprawl in the grass, a formidable sigh of relief, and a total immobility lasting many minutes told that the destination had been reached.

Silence reigned. The Dig heard his heart pitapatting. The Lazy Student did not budge. A butterfly perched on his nose, a squirrel peeped at him through the grass; but he did not move. A minute passed. Another. The Dig began to feel ridiculous. The laborious puffing of a train toiling up a grade seemed to reproach him for his momentary idleness. He was wasting his time up here, with Sanskrit 36 to prepare. He metaphorically kicked himself. It was ridiculous. He was just on the point of sneaking away when a great crackling sent the butterfly off in winged flurry and the little squirrel scampering in laughable terror. The Lazy Student was stretching himself. A majestic and resounding yawn followed. Then a rustling of paper. He had picked up a book. He began reading aloud:—

"Wenn ich ein Pferd hatte, so wurde ich nach San
Francisco reiten."

Far, musical, prolonged, came back a voice:—

"If I had a horse I would go to San Francisco."

The echo was translating!

A great wrath nearly choked the Dig. So that was the way! While he digged and toiled laboriously, painfully, ceaselessly, that lazy, worthless, shiftless bum merely— A great indignation throbbed in his head. But he kept quiet. Ah, two could play the same game!

For two hours the Lazy Student read—read in French, in German, in Spanish, in Hebrew, in Greek, in Latin, in Syriac, in Sanskrit, in other languages. And the echo translated—translated in its measured, melodious, golden voice.

Many of the lessons were also the Dig's, and the echo was doing double duty. When the Lazy Student had finished the sun had set. A gray, melancholy, foggy night was falling. The Dig remained. The Lazy Student took not Old English. The Dig did. And he wanted a translation.

That night was a bad one for the inhabitants of the little town of Berkeley. Up in the hills the elements seemed to groan in terrible nightmare. Thunder rolled menacingly; lightning seared the sky. Sudden gusts of wind howled past dismally. In the morning only did the struggle cease, and a bright sun dispelled all gloom.

A rancher came down from the hills. He told a queer story. Passing along a ridge at night, he had witnessed a strange spectacle. On a knoll, erect, defiant, a young man with long black hair and shining spectacles, holding a book at arm's-length read aloud in some weird tongue. It sounded something like this: "Gewat him tha on uhtan mid aerdage ofer sandhleothu to saes farude," and other kindred buzzing, rasping, whirring cries. At each word thunder answered from the hill as if the elements revolted at such sounds. The wind hooted dismally; nameless shrieks and groans came from the canyons. With a sort of frenzy, the weird reader shouted louder and louder,—seemed to taunt and defy the elements. A yellow moon glancing at intervals through dirty, sulphurous clouds glamoured the scene in sickly light. The rancher had fled in terror.

That afternoon the Lazy Student, on the point of spreading himself in his accustomed pastoral study, found it occupied. A man was stretched in his customary place. The Lazy Student approached. The man did not move. When nearer, the Lazy Student remarked that the body was stark and stiff. The face was black.

One glance was sufficient. With a howl of terror the Lazy Student scampered down the hill. He got down without one stop. He gave the alarm and the body was brought down.

It was the Dig. He was not quite dead. In a few days he regained consciousness, but only to fall into the hallucinations of a terrible fever. In his delirium, he imagined himself engaged in a terrible struggle with the echo of the hills. The Dig had got it into his head to make the echo translate Old English. The latter had vigorously protested, and an epic struggle had taken place. To scraps of Old English the tortured echo had hurled back nameless imprecations—thunder, lightning, earthquake. The proud student had persisted, and an extra-vigorous retort had felled him to the earth.

For weeks he struggled in the throes of his hallucinations. Finally, little by little, his mind cleared of its fearful fantasies and he became convalescent. But he had forgotten all his languages, and had acquired an overpowering repugnance to language-study. A word of Old English whispered in his ear would cause an epileptic fit. Poor fellow! He turned to mathematics.

The Lazy Student graduated. He was the class medalist. He now translates great works of foreign tongues. Although famous, he has always clung with touching fidelity to the home of his childhood.

Jack London

🌿 *from* Martin Eden

As Martin Eden went down the steps, his hand dropped into his coat pocket. It came out with a brown rice paper and a pinch of Mexican tobacco, which were deftly rolled together into a cigarette. He drew the first whiff of smoke deep into his lungs and expelled it in a long and lingering exhalation. "By God!" he said aloud, in a voice of awe and wonder. "By God!" he repeated. And yet again he murmured, "By God!" Then his hand went to his collar, which he ripped out of the shirt and stuffed into his pocket. A cold drizzle was falling, but he bared his head to it and unbuttoned his vest, swinging along in splendid unconcern. He was only dimly aware that it was raining. He was in an ecstasy, dreaming dreams and reconstructing the scenes just past.

He had met the woman at last—the woman that he had thought little about, not being given to thinking about women, but whom he had expected, in a remote way, he would sometime meet. He had sat next to her at table. He had felt her hand in his, he had looked into her eyes and caught a vision of a beautiful spirit;—but no more beautiful than the eyes through which it shone, nor than the flesh that gave it expression and form. He did not think of her flesh as flesh,—which was new to him; for of the women he had known that was the only way he thought. Her flesh was somehow different. He did not conceive of her body as a body, subject to the ills and frailties of bodies. Her body was more than the garb of her spirit. It was an emanation of her spirit, a pure and gracious crystallization of her divine essence. This feeling of the divine

---

Excerpted from *Martin Eden* by Jack London. Published by Macmillan (1909). First published serially by the *Pacific Monthly* (1908–1909).

startled him. It shocked him from his dreams to sober thought. No word, no clue, no hint, of the divine had ever reached him before. He had never believed in the divine. He had always been irreligious, scoffing good-naturedly at the sky-pilots and their immortality of the soul. There was no life beyond, he had contended; it was here and now, then darkness everlasting. But what he had seen in her eyes was soul—immortal soul that could never die. No man he had known, nor any woman, had given him the message of immortality. But she had. She had whispered it to him the first moment she looked at him. Her face shimmered before his eyes as he walked along,—pale and serious, sweet and sensitive, smiling with pity and tenderness as only a spirit could smile, and pure as he had never dreamed purity could be. Her purity smote him like a blow. It startled him. He had known good and bad, but purity, as an attribute of existence, had never entered his mind. And now, in her, he conceived purity to be the superlative of goodness and of cleanness, the sum of which constituted eternal life.

And promptly urged his ambition to grasp at eternal life. He was not fit to carry water for her—he knew that; it was a miracle of luck and a fantastic stroke that had enabled him to see her and be with her and talk with her that night. It was accidental. There was no merit in it. He did not deserve such fortune. His mood was essentially religious. He was humble and meek, filled with self-disparagement and abasement. In such frame of mind sinners come to the penitent form. He was convicted of sin. But as the meek and lowly at the penitent form catch splendid glimpses of their future lordly existence, so did he catch similar glimpses of the state he would gain to by possessing her. But this possession of her was dim and nebulous and totally different from possession as he had known it. Ambition soared on mad wings, and he saw himself climbing the heights with her, sharing thoughts with her, pleasuring in beautiful and noble things with her. It was a soul-possession he dreamed, refined beyond any grossness, a free comradeship of spirit that he could not put into definite thought. He did not think it. For that matter, he did not think at all. Sensation usurped reason, and he was quivering and palpitant with emotions he had never known, drifting deliciously on a sea of sensibility where feeling itself was exalted and spiritualized and carried beyond the summits of life.

He staggered along like a drunken man, murmuring fervently aloud: "By God! By God!"

A policeman on a street corner eyed him suspiciously, then noted his sailor roll.

"Where did you get it?" the policeman demanded.

Martin Eden came back to earth. His was a fluid organism, swiftly adjustable, capable of flowing into and filling all sorts of nooks and crannies. With the policeman's hail he was immediately his ordinary self, grasping the situation clearly.

"It's a beaut, ain't it?" he laughed back. "I didn't know I was talkin' out loud."

"You'll be singing next," was the policeman's diagnosis.

"No, I won't. Gimme a match an' I'll catch the next car home."

He lighted his cigarette, said good night, and went on. "Now wouldn't that rattle you?" he ejaculated under his breath. "That copper thought I was drunk." He smiled to himself and meditated. "I guess I was," he added; "but I didn't think a woman's face'd do it."

He caught a Telegraph Avenue car that was going to Berkeley. It was crowded with youths and young men who were singing songs and ever and again barking out college yells. He studied them curiously. They were university boys. They went to the same university that she did, were in her class socially, could know her, could see her every day if they wanted to. He wondered that they did not want to, that they had been out having a good time instead of being with her that evening, talking with her, sitting around her in a worshipful and adoring circle. His thoughts wandered on. He noticed one with narrow-slitted eyes and a loose-lipped mouth. That fellow was vicious, he decided. On shipboard he would be a sneak, a whiner, a tattler. He, Martin Eden, was a better man than that fellow. The thought cheered him. It seemed to draw him nearer to Her. He began comparing himself with the students. He grew conscious of the muscled mechanism of his body and felt confident that he was physically their master. But their heads were filled with knowledge that enabled them to talk her talk,—the thought depressed him. But what was a brain for? he demanded passionately. What they had done, he could do. They had been studying about life from the books while he had been busy living life. His brain was just as full of knowledge as theirs, though it was a different kind of knowledge. How many of them could tie a lanyard knot, or take a wheel or a lookout? His life spread out before him in a series of pictures of danger and daring, hardship and toil. He remembered his failures and scrapes in the process of learning. He was that much to the good, anyway. Later on they would have to begin living life and going through the mill as he had gone. Very well. While they were busy with that, he could be learning the other side of life from the books.

Cornelius Beach Bradley

⁜ Walks about Berkeley

THE CASUAL OBSERVER MIGHT FIND VERY LITTLE OF PROMISE IN THE BERKELEY HILLS
to lure him on to their exploration. Their brown slopes, wrinkled and thread-
bare as the sleeve of a hunter's jacket, seem to reveal to the very first glance
all that they hold in store. No surprise, surely, can be waiting for one on those
bare, open hillsides. The imagination pictures no secret nooks, no wooded
ravines, no crag or waterfall behind the straggling screen of fern and scrub
that fringes its waterways. Yet, after all, the charm of surprise is a veritable
feature of the walks about Berkeley—surprise not keen and startling, to be
sure, but genuine and of the quality that does not pall by frequent repetition.
Thus it is that the number and variety of these rambles is a source of unend-
ing pleasure to those who have come to know them. There is a large gradation
too in their extent and in the effort they require:—the quiet saunter up
Strawberry Cañon in the gloaming, the long afternoon ramble over the hills
to Orindo Park, the all-day tramp by the Fish Ranch to Redwood Cañon and
Maraga Peak, or more strenuous still, the cross-country trip to Diablo. You
may follow the quiet country lanes with pastures, orchards, and grainfields
dotted about here and there among the enveloping wildness. You may even
find abandoned roadways leading nowhither, constructed at large expense by
some one who surely was a lover of his kind, and now bequeathed to your sole
use and behoof. You may thread some cool, mossy ravine where the stream
runs deep in its rocky channel, under a close roof of alders and redwoods. Or

From *A Berkeley Year: A Sheaf of Nature Essays*. Published by the Women's Aux-
iliary of the First Unitarian Church of Berkeley (1909).

you may breast the steep slope, each step opening up a wider and wider prospect, until from the east you catch the exultant flash of Sierra snows, and on
the west, far beyond Golden Gate and Farallones, you gaze with awe on the
immensity of the Pacific.

I do not mean to weary the reader with an itinerary of these various
routes, or a tabulation of their peculiar charms. Such things are best learned
when they come with the zest of discovery. To one quaint nook only would I
offer to conduct my reader, and with the more reason, perhaps, because while
it is easy enough of access, it seems to be very little known. The place is called
Boswell's, though why so called I have never been able to guess. The name
suggests human habitation at least, if not also vulgar resort and entertainment; but both suggestions are wide of the mark. Our visit shall be on some
bright morning in April. We take the train to Berryman station, and zig-
zagging thence northwestward, we soon are clear of the thin fringe of dwelling-
houses, and out among the fields. Our course so far has been as if for Peralta
Park; but instead of turning sharply down to the west at the margin of a little
creek, we cross the bridge, and follow the country lane northward. When the
lane also turns abruptly westward, some half-mile further on, we abandon it
altogether, continuing our former direction over fields and fences, and across
two little waterways. Beyond the second rivulet we reach a broad slope thickly
strewn with rocks and boulders, and dotted about with low trees and shrubs.
This is Boswell's.

The air all along has been full of the sounds and scents of spring:—the
gurgling notes of the meadowlark, the rich smell of newly-ploughed fields, the
warm breath of mustard in bloom. But this untamable rock-strewn area, like
the Buddhist monasteries of the Far East, has become a veritable sanctuary
for plants and living creatures that could not maintain themselves in the open
in their unequal struggle with that fell destroyer, man. Here the wood-rat has
piled undisturbed his huge shelter of sticks. The warbler and the thrush are
singing from every covert. The woodpecker and the squirrel shadow you from
behind tree-trunk or rock to discover your intent in trespassing thus upon
their private domain; while the flycatcher flashes his defiance in your very
face, if you venture too near his mate on her nest. Nor is it otherwise with the
plants. Delicate species that are fast disappearing before cultivation—the
blue nemophila, the shy calochortus, the bright pansy-violet—bloom here

undisturbed in all their pathetic beauty. "If God so clothe the grass of the field, which to-day is, and tomorrow is cast into the oven, shall he not much more clothe you, O ye of little faith?"

But we linger here too long upon the threshold. The tract is a considerable one, and midway there is thrust up into it from the west a sombre wedge of eucalyptus forest, contrasting strangely with the rest of the scene. For here we seem to be in a region three thousand miles away,—in a veritable bit of New England hill-pasture with its labyrinthine paths, its ever-changing short vistas, its endless series of little secluded alcoves walled about with shrubbery and carpeted with grass and flowers. The rocks too are of striking size and form, and culminate near the lower end of the tract in a bold, fantastic crag, in itself well worth the effort to visit it. But the most unlooked-for feature of the place is its air of remoteness and seclusion. Here it lies, spread out on the open hillside, in full view from bay and from town. Yet as we thread its quiet alleys, or lie dreaming in the sunshine under the lee of its rocks, we seem to have journeyed leagues from the work-a-day world we left behind us but an hour ago.

It is good to be here! And good it is also to return to the world. The joy of the scene and the season, the clearer brain and quickened pulses we shall bring back with us as we take up again the effort and struggle. And more than this we may sometimes bring from such a sanctuary,—some heavenly vision,—some far-seen glimpse of a transfigured life that may be ours—in the strength of which we shall go many days, even unto the mount of God.

Henry F. May

A House in Berkeley

IF A WELL-INFORMED SOCIAL HISTORIAN SUDDENLY FOUND HIMSELF IN OUR LIVING ROOM in 1925, he would, I think, expect to walk out into a Boston suburb. Instead, all around lay Berkeley and California. Berkeley in those days was a quiet, rather staid university town of about twenty-five thousand, attractive to well-to-do commuters. I hardly ever saw the flat part of town, where there were small factories and a population of Italians, Finns, and a small number of highly respectable blacks, some of them railway porters or cooks. The three parts that I knew as a child were Claremont, the campus, and North Berkeley.

Claremont was full of houses much like ours—some much bigger and handsomer. I knew the names of everybody within ten or fifteen houses on each side and was known in the local stores. One reached the campus by walking about two miles, crossing on the way the grounds of the California School for the Blind and Deaf, where there was an exciting life-size statue of two Indians fighting a grizzly bear who had bitten halfway through the arms of one of them. Nearer the campus one passed fraternities, where tall young men in sweaters and cords lounged on the porches, watching for girls to go by. The campus itself was huge, mostly made up of white stone buildings and green lawns, surmounted by the tall campanile that bonged the hours. To the west were the broad dusty fields where the ROTC marched. From most of the campus one could see either San Francisco Bay or the swelling oak-dotted hills.

Excerpted from *Coming to Terms: A Study in Memory and History*, copyright 1987 by Henry F. May. Reprinted by permission of the author.

I knew that North Berkeley and the few blocks south of the campus were supposed to be more interesting than Claremont, mainly because they were close to the University. A few of the family's university friends suggested even to a child some very special quality. The Misses Hilgard, for instance, were daughters of a famous agricultural scientist and lived on Bancroft Way. Miss Louise was tall, musical, a little scatterbrained perhaps, and devoted to my mother and my aunt, whom she called the Pink (of Perfection). Miss Alice was handsome, slightly severe looking with her brushed-back iron-gray hair and her pince-nez, erudite and dryly humorous. The Hilgards' pleasant frame house was surrounded by an impeccably tended garden. One story has it that Professor Gayley of the English department came up to the front door carrying, in mock horror, one leaf that he had found in the sandy path. The Hilgards, like many others, employed college boys to take care of the garden, probably paying them very little but supervising their manners. (One of the boys, Miss Alice reported once in a horrified whisper, had to be told not to *expectorate.*) When each boy graduated, he received a gold watch. Next door to the Hilgards was a particularly rowdy fraternity with which the Hilgards were in a state of intermittent war. Shrill female screams, carefully faked, sometimes rang out from the upper floors in the middle of the night, freezing the blood of the ladies next door. Yet at the appropriate times the fraternity house asked the Hilgards in for tea with parents, and the tone in which the ladies told about the scandalous goings-on was as much amused as really horrified. Much later, when I had learned about such things, I found out that the Hilgards, unlike most family friends, were political liberals, members of the ACLU and friends of Oswald Garrison Villard, the editor of *The Nation.*

On the campus Sanskrit and Greek plays were presented in the Greek Theater, and each spring I was taken to the Parthenia, a dance drama in which young women in beautiful gauzy costumes ran trippingly across the grass under the auspices of the physical education department. In fall, when a new class appeared, the streets near the campus blossomed with horrible posters, threatening death and worse to freshmen who wore jeans or cords or didn't wear dinks on their heads. When the Memorial Stadium was being built (in 1922), I was often taken to watch the steam shovels scooping out the mighty crater. Of course I was for Cal as soon as I heard about intercollegiate football.

41

Behind the town lay the Berkeley hills, to me as a child and later as an adolescent the most beautiful and inviting wilderness in the world. One could walk up the dirt road behind the Claremont Hotel and branch off onto trails. Eventually one would get to lonely hillsides, brown in summer, green in winter, flowery in spring, as I thought all the world should be. Finally one came to dense and fragrant pine woods—to me part of immemorial nature, though they had actually been planted twenty years before by the water company. In openings one could see the campus, the town, and beyond them the Bay and the white towers of the City.

One could see the City also from our front window. The Bay spread below us and on the other side, after the sun went down into the Bay, lighthouses winked from the two sides of the Golden Gate and Alcatraz in the middle, and San Francisco glittered in more and more splendor. To get to San Francisco one took the Key train for half an hour and then waited on the pier for the ferry, looking at the barnacles and starfish on the pilings. When the boat warped carefully in, people streamed aboard. Some met their regular bridge group for the half-hour's trip, others went to the galley for excellent corned beef hash and apple pie à la mode. For a child, the best of all was to stand on the stern with a bag of bread fragments, tossing them to the gulls who circled in endless formation, usually catching the crust in effortless flight, a few feet from the water. For the last few minutes people crowded onto the bow, watching the Ferry Building come closer and closer until the boat ground alongside and people rushed out into the noise of shouting paperboys and streetcar conductors: " 'Xaminer, Chronicle, Call. Get your San Francisco papeh! All the way up Market, City of Paris Shopping District!"

In the city people walked faster, looked brisker, and were far more various. In Chinatown one very occasionally saw a queue, in North Beach the signs were in Italian and there were wonderful pastry smells. In Union Square everybody was always dressed up—men wore suits and hats and women black dresses and hats. Naturally! This was the City!

As a child the rest of my California included Mount Tamalpais with its funicular winding endlessly up through the bay and madrone, and Carmel, still a village smelling everywhere of pines, dusty roads, and the ocean. When we had a car we went for long drives through Contra Costa County, often between rows of walnut or fruit trees. Several times we drove for two interminable days all the way to La Jolla, next door to Mexico, where my father's sister lived in a small pink auto-court surrounded by bee-buzzing lantana. One summer after my brother learned to drive, we made it all the way to Tahoe, first putting the car on a riverboat to Sacramento and then struggling up the steep and winding Strawberry Grade, lined with cars waiting with their hoods up for the engines to cool down. There we stayed for a wonderful month in a cottage at Glenbrook, on the Nevada side. My father and brother fished, while I played with friendly kids who didn't know my dubious place in the home-playground pecking order. When someone caught a lake trout it was served for dinner with ceremony. Every Saturday night a three-piece band ground out "Moonlight and Roses" while the slightly older kids solemnly circled.

The East existed only in school geography books or very occasional and baffling group reminiscence. Snow was an exciting legend except once when a freak sprinkling of white caused the schools to close. Winter meant greenness. In summer, of course, the hills smelled of dry grass in the afternoon sun before the white fog rolled in through the Golden Gate. An old house was one built in 1900. That my parents' furniture, books, and loyalties went back even farther than this and were associated with other parts of the country was something I sensed dimly and only later came gradually to understand.

John Kenneth Galbraith

Berkeley in the Thirties

ONE DAY IN THE AUTUMN OF 1930 I WAS GAZING AT THE NOTICE BOARD IN THE POST office of the main men's residence at the Ontario Agricultural College at Guelph in Canada, where I was then a senior. It was usually an unrewarding vision but on this day it advertised a number of research assistantships at the Giannini Foundation of Agricultural Economics at the University of California. The annual stipend was $720 for unmarried scholars. I copied down the details and applied. Sometime later I received a letter from George Peterson, Associate Professor of Agricultural Economics, saying that I had been selected. I was surprised and so were my professors, who detested me and thought the people at Berkeley were crazy. I quickly accepted; in that second year of the Great Depression the monthly salary of sixty dollars, if not princely, was by far the best offer of any kind I had. In fact it was the only offer of any kind I had. From that day on the University of California has engaged my affection as no other institution—educational, public or pecuniary—with which I have ever been associated.

One Sunday afternoon in the summer of 1968, with my wife and oldest son (who followed me to be an assistant at the University of California Law School) I strolled across the California campus—over Strawberry Creek, by the Campanile, down by the Library, out Sather Gate. I was taught, as were most of my generation, that no one should allow himself the weak luxury of sentiment or even emotion. To this day when I write "Love" at the end of a letter I always remind myself that it is only modern affectation, in all respects a matter of form. I was suddenly overwhelmed by the thought that I loved this place—the paths, trees, flowers, buildings, even the new ones. I was deeply embarrassed.

In the thirties, for some reason related either to the eccentricities of the California crop year or climate, the university opened in August. Accordingly in July of 1931 I borrowed $500 from an aunt, one of the few members of our rural family still to command such capital, and, almost literally, set sail for California. I boarded the steamer which plied between Port Stanley on the north shore of Lake Erie and Cleveland, where, by prearrangement with our local jeweler and oculist, I met his nephew who had a graduate fellowship at California in astronomy. At five o'clock the following morning we set out in the 1926 Oakland automobile my companion had acquired for this trip. The car was in terrible condition and almost immediately got worse. To save money he had bought a five-gallon gasoline tin and a one-gallon container for oil so that we could stock up on these products whenever, as happened in those days, our path led us through a region being ravaged by a price war. Such at least was the theory. About thirty miles out of Cleveland my friend stopped to check the gas (the gauge was broken) and look at the oil. The car absorbed the whole five gallons of gasoline and the whole gallon of oil. For the rest of the trip we averaged around a quarter gallon of gas and a half pint of oil to the mile. To this day I shudder at the cost.

The journey took ten days not counting twenty-four hours at Casey, Iowa, where we were laid up with a broken connecting rod. That, too, had a lasting effect. It was raining hard, and as we waited for the repairs, we listened to the local farmers, who used the garage as a club, discuss Hoover. I became a life-long Democrat. It was about six o'clock on a bright summer evening when we got to Berkeley and drove up Bancroft Way to the International House. The hills behind were very bleached and sere but the low sun glistened on the live oaks and the green lawns and the masses of pink geraniums, which elsewhere are only geraniums but in Berkeley are the glory of the whole city. The sun also lit up the vast yellow-buff facade of the International House with the large Spanish arches of the portico below. We passed into the great hall, then gleaming new, and combining the best mission style with the finest in

Moorish revival. I thought it a place of unimaginable splendor.

Eventually the International House was to prove a bit too expensive even for one who earned sixty dollars a month and was, as a result, one of the more affluent members of the community. My capital had been depleted by that terrible car. But for the first few months at Berkeley this nice Rockefeller benefaction—it had counterparts in New York, Chicago, Paris and Tokyo—housing several hundred students of both sexes from the United States and many foreign lands, was to be my window on the Berkeley world. Never before had I been so happy.

The world on which I looked down could not be recognized in important respects by Mario Savio or his successors. I must stress that I had just emerged from the Ontario Agricultural College and this could have distorted my vision. Once I was asked by *Time* magazine about this academy; I replied, thoughtlessly, that in my day it was certainly the cheapest and possibly the worst in the English-speaking world. This was tactless and wrong and caused dissatisfaction even after many years. (No one questioned my statement that the college was inexpensive.) At OAC students were expected to keep and also to know and cherish their place. Leadership in the student body was solidly in the hands of those who combined an outgoing anti-intellectualism with a sound interest in livestock. This the faculty thought right. Anyone who questioned the established agricultural truths, many of which were wildly wrong, was sharply rebuked, and if he offended too often he was marked down as a troublemaker. A fair number of faculty members had effectively substituted the affable and well-clipped manner and moustache of the professional countryman for the admitted tedium of science. But unquestionably the place did build health.

At Berkeley I suddenly encountered professors who knew their subject and, paradoxically, invited debate on what they knew. They also had time to talk at length with graduate students and even to come up to International House to continue the conversation. I first discovered at Berkeley from Henry Erdman, who had until recently been the head of the Agricultural Economics Department, and Howard Tolley, who had just succeeded him as the Director of the Giannini Foundation, that a professor might like to be informed on some subject by a graduate student—might not just be polite but pleased. So profound was that impression that I never stopped informing people thereafter. The pleasure I have thus given has been very great. (Howard Tolley, after a year or two, went on to Washington to become head of the Agricultural Adjustment Administration under FDR. I shall mention him again in a moment. In 1968, after the elapse of a third of a century, I was back in Berkeley one Sunday to urge the case and, more important, since everyone was persuaded, to raise money for Eugene McCarthy. I was not at all surprised to see Henry Erdman in the front row. He believed strongly in keeping informed.)

Although we had stipends, we agricultural economists were second-class citizens. Our concern was with the prices of cling peaches, which were then appalling; the financial condition of the Merced irrigation district, which was equally bad; the prune industry, which was chronically indigent; and other such useful subjects. I earned my research stipend by tramping the streets of Los Angeles and also Oakland and San Jose to ascertain the differing preferences as to package and flavor—sage, orange blossom, clover—of Mexican, Jewish, Negro and (as we then thought of them) ordinary white Americans, for honey. No differences emerged. This kind of work was not well regarded by the nonagricultural, or pure, economists. Thorstein Veblen was still being read with attention in Berkeley in the thirties. He distinguishes between esoteric and exoteric knowledge, the first having the commanding advantage of being without "economic or industrial effect." It is this advantage, he argues, which distinguishes the higher learning from the lower. Ours, obviously, was the lower.

We suffered from another handicap. Agriculturalists, in an indistinct way, were considered to be subject to the influence of the California Farm Bureau Federation and, much worse, of the opulent and perpetually choleric baronage which comprised the Associated Farmers of California. Actually our subordination was not all that indistinct. Both organizations told the Dean of the College of Agriculture and the Director of Extension what they needed in the way of research and also conclusions. They were heard with attention, even respect. No one was ever told to shape his scholarly work accordingly; men were available who did it as a matter of course.

The nonagricultural economists, whatever their differences in other matters of doctrine, were united in regarding the farmers, even more than the bankers or oilmen, as an all-purpose class enemy. In time I acquired a certain reputation in economic theory and other branches of impractical knowledge

47

and also as a rather circumspect critic of the agricultural establishment. So I was accorded an honorary status as a scholar, my agricultural handicaps notwithstanding. I was then even more happy.

The Department of Economics at Berkeley has never been considered quite as eminent as that at Harvard. The reason is that the best Californians have always come to Harvard. As this is written of the twenty-three full professors of economics at Harvard no fewer than seven, nearly one-third, were recruited at one stage or another in their careers from the University of California at Berkeley. And economics at Berkeley has long had a marked personality. In the early thirties, years before the Keynesian revolution, Leo Rogin was discussing Keynes with a sense of urgency that made his seminars seem to graduate students the most important things then happening in the world. I learned Alfred Marshall from Ewald Grether, who taught with a drill-master's precision for which I have ever since been grateful. Marshall is the quintessence of classical economics and much of what he says is wrong. But no one can know what is wrong if he does not understand it first. My memory also goes back to M. M. Knight's seminar in economic history, a gifted exercise in irrelevancy. Once Robert Gordon Sproul, then the president of the university, said in one of his booming speeches that, after all, a university was run for the students. Knight, a brother of the even more noted Frank H. Knight of the University of Chicago, attacked this doctrine for two full sessions. A university, he argued with indignation, was run for the faculty and, to affirm the point, he announced his intention of introducing a resolution at some early faculty meeting to exclude the students from the library. They got in the way.

We graduate students were also fond of Paul Taylor, who spoke out unfailingly for the small farmer in California; Charles Gulick, who spoke out for the farm workers, who then as now aroused great animosity and a measure of righteous anger for wanting a union and a living wage; and Robert Brady, who was the friend of the consumer and other lost causes. Brady taught courses in the business cycle and set great store by exhaustive bibliographic research. One of my friends met this requirement by going to the card catalogue in the library and copying into the appendix of his thesis everything that appeared there under the headings Cycle, Business, and Cycle, Trade. Brady sent over for some of the latter items which were new to him and they turned out to be works on bicycles, tricycles, and motorcycles published by the Cycle Trades of America. We always heard there was quite a scene.

A few years after I left Berkeley I became deputy head of the Office of Price Administration in charge of the World War II price controls. This was a post with unlimited patronage—eventually, as I recall, I had some seventeen thousand assistants. In addition to Mr. and Mrs. Richard Nixon and many other promising people, numerous of my former professors, including Howard Tolley, Harry Wellman (later the acting president of the university) and Robert Brady turned up on our staff. Brady had scarcely arrived before he was assaulted hip and thigh by the Dies Committee—later better known as HUAC and now as HSC—for saying in a book on German fascism that American capitalism was only technically better. To complicate matters further, Dies had got hold of the edition published by the Left Book Club in England. It had something on the cover about not being for public sale. I handled the defense on the Hill with the handicap of knowing that everything I said in favor of Bob would immediately be used against me. Brady later attributed his troubles to the oil companies and said I was their tool. He had proposed that people conserve oil by not draining the crankcase for the duration of the war or ten thousand miles, whichever was less. I did not endorse the idea. This was mostly because with everything else it never got to my attention. But if it had, I might have remembered that Oakland car and the way it changed itself and wondered if it would have made much difference.

The graduate students with whom I associated in the thirties were uniformly radical and the most distinguished were Communists. I listened to them eagerly and would liked to have joined both the conversation and the Party but here my agricultural background was a real handicap. It meant that, as a matter of formal Marxian doctrine, I was politically immature. Among the merits of capitalism to Marx was the fact that it rescued men from the idiocy of rural life. I had only very recently been retrieved. I sensed this bar and I knew also that my pride would be deeply hurt by rejection. So I kept outside. There was possibly one other factor. Although I recognized that the system could not and should not survive, I was enjoying it so much that, secretly, I was a little sorry.

In the ensuing twenty years many of those I most envied were accorded an auto-da-fé by HUAC, James Eastland or the late Joseph M. McCarthy.

49

Their lives were ruined. Phrases about the unpredictable graces of God kept constantly crossing my mind.

One man who did not get called by Joe McCarthy was Robert Merriman, a vital and popular graduate student and teaching assistant who came down to Berkeley from Nevada in the early thirties. As an undergraduate he had been wholesome and satisfactory and even took an interest in ROTC. But Berkeley had its effect and so (as he told friends) did the great waterfront strike of 1934, where he saw soldiers deployed against the strikers. Hugh Thomas' brilliant book, *The Spanish Civil War*, tells the rest of his story. Interrupting a traveling fellowship in Europe in 1936, Merriman went to Spain, where (one assumes as an uncalculated consequence of ROTC) he commanded the Abraham Lincoln Battalion on the Jarama and then went on through many battles to be chief of staff of the XV International Brigade. A major and by now long a veteran, he was killed (possibly executed after capture by the Nationalists) on the Aragon front in 1938. He must have been the bravest of our contemporaries; he so impressed Ernest Hemingway that he became in part the model for Robert Jordan (the professor from Montana in *For Whom the Bell Tolls*). The California campus has ornaments for lesser heroes who died nearer home for more fashionable beliefs. There are some naïve, haunting lines written by John Depper, a British volunteer, of the Battle of Jarama that might serve:

> *Death stalked in the olive trees*
> *Picking his men*
> *His leaden finger beckoned*
> *Again and again.*

A year ago in Chicago I was on a television discussion program with Robert Merriam, a White House aide to President Eisenhower and once Republican candidate for mayor of Chicago against Richard Daley. He said that for many years he had been investigated assiduously by the FBI because of his name. Merriman was not wholly forgotten.

I would not wish it thought that our life in the thirties was limited to politics and great matters of the mind. One roamed through San Francisco, climbed Mt. Diablo, went up to the Sierras, where someone was always imagining that the Depression might make panning gold profitable again, and consumed (I most diffidently) alcohol stolen from the chemistry laboratories and mixed with grapefruit juice and, after repeal, a blended whiskey of negligible cost called, to the best of my memory, Crab Orchard. I have difficulty in believing that the latter-day intoxicants and suffocants do worse. In any case, we were all greatly impressed one night when a girl who had been overstimulated by these products ceremoniously removed her clothes in the patio of the International House and spent the late hours of the evening doing orgiastic obeisance to the heavens above and, more than incidentally, to the windows of the men's rooms around.

In these days people came to Berkeley from all over the world and, naturally enough, no one ever left. The reasons were social and economic as well as cultural. As a student, teaching fellow, or even a nonstudent, one could be a respected member of the *community* and it counted against a person not at all to have no income. But the moment one left Berkeley he became a member of the great army of the unemployed. As such, he was an object of sympathy and lost his self-respect. In general, graduate students avoided taking their final degrees lest they be under temptation, however slight, to depart. When, in 1933 and 1934, jobs suddenly and unexpectedly became available in Washington—NRA, PWA, AAA—almost everyone got busy and finished up his thesis. Even my Communist friends reacted favorably to the exorbitant salaries which economists commanded in the New Deal.

Among the people who appeared in Berkeley, my mind returns to a slim, boyish-looking girl who, improbably in light of her build, claimed to have been in Texas Guinan's chorus before turning to higher learning. More recently she had been in Tahiti and then in Bora Bora, where she had gone native and had as proof a comprehensive suntan. Now she was doing graduate work in anthropology on the basis of credentials, partly forged and partly imaginary, from a nonexistent undergraduate institution in the city of New York. I fell deeply in love with her; on our second or third date, as we were walking up Strawberry Canyon back of the stadium, she asked me if I thought it right, as an economist, to be wasting both her time and mine. Nothing in my Canadian and Calvinist background had prepared me for such a personal concept of efficiency. A little later, after an all-night party in San Francisco, she insisted on being taken to the Santa Fe Station. She had just remembered that, on the day following, she was scheduled to marry a banker in New

Mexico. Much later I met her in New York. She was just back from Haiti (not Tahiti) and was preparing to marry a Pan Am pilot. She told me she was working on her memoirs and was being encouraged to the task by Westbrook Pegler. I was by then a promising young member of the Harvard faculty. I first worried that she would publish her recollections and then, after a time, that she would not.

Though we graduate students expected the revolution very soon and planned to encourage it, we did not expect any help from the Berkeley undergraduates. Not that they would oppose—they would simply, as usual, be unaware that anything was happening. A singular accomplishment of American higher education, as one reflects on it, was the creation of a vast network of universities, public and private, which for a century, until the sixties, caused no one any political embarrassment of any kind. In other countries they created trouble from time to time, but not here. A control system which subtly suggested that whatever the students most wanted to do—i.e., devote themselves to football, basketball, fraternities, college tradition, rallies, hell-raising, a sentimental concern for the old alma mater and imaginative inebriation—was what they should do, was basic to this peace. The alumni rightly applauded this control system and so, to an alarming extent, did the faculty. An occasional non-political riot was condoned and even admired; some deeper adult instinct suggested that it was a surrogate for something worse. At Berkeley in the thirties this system was still working perfectly. Coming up Bancroft Way to the International House of an evening one saw the fraternity men policing up the lawns of their houses or sitting contentedly in front. Walking along Piedmont at night one heard the shouts of laughter from within, or occasional bits of song or what Evelyn Waugh correctly described as the most evocative and nostalgic of all the sounds of an aristocracy at play, the crash of breaking glass. Here were men with a secure position in society and who knew it and who were content. On a Friday night they would do their duty at the pep rally shaming the apathetic; on Saturday they would be at the stadium and on Saturday night, win or lose, they joined with the kindred souls of earlier generations, men they did not hesitate to call brother, to whoop it up as a college man was meant to do. The *Daily Californian* was the approving chronicle of this world—of the Big Game, the Axe, the cards turned in unison in the cheering section to depict an Indian or a bear, the campaign to send the band to Oregon to support the team. In 1932 Norman Thomas came to the campus and spoke to a small assembly in a classroom. Neither Hoover nor Roosevelt dreamed of favoring us. Hoover did speak to a vast audience of indigent citizens from the local Hooverville down on the Oakland flats and was cheered uproariously when he told them that, at long last, the Depression was over. They had not heard. Only once was there a suggestion of student involvement. The financial condition of the state of California in those days was appalling. State workers were being paid with tax-anticipation certificates. Even the governor, James (Sunny Jim) Rolph, sensed that something was wrong. In 1932 and 1933 there were threats to cut the university budget. When it seemed that these were serious, the students were encouraged to assemble and ask their relatives and friends to petition their legislators to relent. Perhaps that was the camel's nose, the seed of the Frankenstein. As to persuading the legislature, however, it was considered less important than a promise by the university to retrench voluntarily and to begin with the Agricultural Extension (Farm Adviser) Service. No one said so but we agriculturalists certainly felt that our pragmatic approach to scholarship had paid off for everybody.

In the 1960s Dean Rusk, Lyndon Johnson, General Westmoreland, Lewis Hershey and Ronald Reagan accomplished what not even the most talented of our teachers had ever hoped to achieve. The undergraduates became politically concerned. When the time comes to award honors to those who made our universities the center of our political life, it will be a great injustice if the men of affirmative, as distinct from the negative, influence are featured. Now, I would suppose, Berkeley is the most intense intellectual and political community in the world; perhaps, indeed, it is the nearest thing to a total university community in modern times. As such it would be silly to suppose that it could be altogether tranquil. Often in these past years, following some exceptionally imaginative outbreak on Telegraph Avenue, I've heard a colleague say: "You know that sort of thing could never happen here." I've always been too polite to say why I agreed. And the statement could be wrong. As other university communities succumb to the concerns so long a commonplace at Berkeley, they, too, cease to be tranquil.

Not everyone is as restrained as I am about Berkeley. A few weeks ago I shared a seat on an airplane with a young colleague newly recruited, like so many before him, from the University of California. I asked him if he missed it. He replied, "Christ, yes! At Berkeley you worked all morning in the library and then at noon you went out into the sun and there was always a demonstration going on or something. Man, that was living!"

The days passed. During my second year my stipend was raised to seventy dollars a month, allowing me to save a little money and also to have a larger social life. Then in my third year I was sent to Davis, which, for the benefit of non-Californians, is in the Sacramento Valley not far from Sacramento. It is now a full-fledged university but in those days it was the center of agricultural research and instruction too closely associated with orchards, insects and the soil to be carried on at Berkeley. It cultivated, in other words, the lowest of the lower learning. At Davis I was the head of the Departments of Economics, of Agricultural Economics, of Accounting and of Farm Management. I also gave instruction in all of these subjects and, with the exception of one elderly dean who gave lectures to nondegree students, I was also the total teaching staff in these disciplines. During the year I also had time to write my Ph.D. thesis and I do not recall that I was especially rushed. Certainly such was my love for Berkeley that I went there every weekend. At Davis my pay was $1,800 and I was able (by way of repayment of my own college debts to my family) to send my younger sister to college.

The Davis students were also highly stable. My course in beginning economics was required for some majors. The scholars so compelled shuffled in at the beginning of the hour, squeezed their yellow corduroy-clad bottoms into the classroom chairs, listened with indifference for an hour and then, by now conveying an impression of manfully suppressed indignation, shuffled out. Only once in the entire year did I arouse their interest. I gave some support to the textbook case for lower tariffs. Coming as they did from the sugar beet fields, olive orchards, cattle ranches and other monuments to the protective tariff, they knew that was wrong and told me so. My best remembered student that year was a boy who had an old Ford runabout who spent his weekends putting up signs on the highways which warned motorists to repent and prepare at a fairly early date to meet their God. In response on an examination to a question about the nature of money, he stuck resolutely to the proposition that it (not the love of money but money itself) was the root of all evil. I tried to reason with him, but in vain. So I flunked him, for his contention seemed to me palpably untrue. That was my only personal encounter in those years with any form of student dissent.

One day in the spring of 1934 I was in Berkeley putting the finishing touches on my thesis. A Western Union boy came into the room with a telegram offering me an instructorship at Harvard for the following year at $2,400. I had not the slightest idea of accepting, for I was totally happy at California. But my rapid advance in economic well-being, plus no doubt the defense of my faith against that student, had made me avaricious and I had heard that one won advances in academic life by flashing offers from other universities. I let it be known over the weekend that "Harvard was after me," and, on the following Monday, went by appointment to see the Dean of the College of Agriculture to bargain. I carried the telegram in my hand. The dean, a large, handsome and highly self-confident man named Claude B. Hutchison, who later became the Mayor of Berkeley, was excellently informed on all matters in the college and his intelligence system had not failed him on this occasion. He congratulated me warmly on my offer, gave me the impression that he thought Harvard was being reckless with its money and said that, of course, I should go. In a moment I realized to my horror I had no choice. I couldn't now plead to stay at two-thirds the price. The great love of my life was over. I remember wondering, as I went out, if I had been right to flunk that nut.

Yoshiko Uchida

🦙 *from* A Jar of Dreams

I NEVER THOUGHT ONE SMALL LADY FROM JAPAN COULD MAKE SUCH A BIG DIFFERENCE in my life, but she did. I'm talking about my Aunt Waka who came to visit us the summer a lot of things changed in our house, including me.

That summer turned special from the day Mama got the letter that caused her strange behavior. It was on a Tuesday, one of the days Mama went to work for Mrs. Phillips to clean her house and scrub her floors. The minute I got home from school and walked into the kitchen, I knew something was wrong. Well, not wrong exactly, but strange. I felt the way I do when I've got one sweater button in the wrong hole or when I put my left slipper on my right foot.

In the first place, water was dripping from the kitchen faucet and splashing on dishes Mama had left in the sink. Ordinarily Mama never leaves the house without checking the faucets to see that they're turned off good and tight. And she never leaves dirty dishes sitting in the sink when she goes to work.

But that wasn't all. She'd left so many things scattered over the kitchen table, I couldn't even see the yellow oilcloth cover. The Japanese newspaper was spread out on the table with a square hole in it where Mama had cut out the recipe for the day. And she hadn't even bothered to put away the scissors she'd used. There were two or three bills Mama hadn't opened and a five-page letter from Japan that hadn't been put back in its envelope. The table was a mess, and if I had left it that way, or my little brother, Joji, we sure would have heard about it from Mama.

I looked at the Japanese writing in the letter, squiggling up and down the soft rice paper like a lot of skinny black spiders, and wished I could read it. But of course I couldn't, because I don't study very hard at Japanese Language School, and besides I'm not far enough advanced to read that kind of writing. All I could read were the numbers that said, first day of the fifth month, 1935. I had a hunch, though, that whatever was in the letter was the reason Mama had gone off acting like Joji instead of her own neat self. And I couldn't bear to wait until she got home to tell me what was in the letter.

I stuffed the letter in the envelope, grabbed an apple from the bin in the sunporch, and headed for Papa's barbershop. It was a hot day, but I ran all the way to Shattuck Avenue and forgot to wait until I'd gotten to Channing Way before crossing Shattuck. That meant I'd have to walk by the Starr Laundry, which I usually avoid like a nest of cobras because of Mr. Wilbur J. Starr, the owner.

The reason I hate and despise Wilbur J. Starr is because he is so mean and nasty. Once when I was in the fourth grade, Joji and I walked by his laundry on the way home from Papa's shop. Old Wilbur J. Starr was standing in the doorway of his laundry, and when Joji and I walked by minding our own business, he yelled, "Get outta here you damn Jap kids!"

Joji dropped my hand and began to run. "Come on, Rinko," he yelled. "He's gonna git us." And he went steaming on ahead of me, pounding hard on his fat little legs.

I wanted to run with him, but when I heard Wilbur Starr laughing behind us, I just held up my head and said to Joji, "Pretend you never heard him." But my knees were shaking so hard, I could barely walk home.

Ever since that day, I try never to walk by the Starr Laundry if I can help it, because I hated the way I felt when Wilbur Starr called me a Jap. It made me really mad, but it also made me feel as though I was no good. I felt ashamed of who I was and wished I could shrink right down and disappear into the sidewalk.

There are a few white girls in my class at school who make me feel that way too. They never call me "Ching Chong Chinaman" or "Jap" the way some of the boys do, but they have other ways of being mean. They talk to each other, but they talk over and around and right through me like I was a pane of glass. And that makes me feel like a big nothing. Some days I feel so left out, I hate my black hair and my Japanese face. I hate having a name like Rinko Tsujimura that nobody can pronounce or remember. And more than anything, I wish I could just be like everybody else.

Gale Wilhelm

from Torchlight to Valhalla

LATE IN THE AFTERNOON FRITZ TAPPED ON HER DOOR AND OPENED IT. THE LIGHT'S getting bad, he said. I'm going to lie down now. You'd better stop too and go out for a walk.

All right, she said.

He was lying on his bed when she went past the open door, and she said softly, I won't stay out long, but he was already asleep. She went out and went swiftly down the steps and around the shoulder of the hill and then up past Mark's, past the little vacant house and on, breathing deeply and not letting herself slow her steps, until she was in the canyon. She rested then, looking down into the canyon, listening to the small sounds of birds moving unseen, a smaller sound of water and to the sound and movement of her breathing.

When she started back she left the trees and the soft young twilight of the canyon and went up a narrow trail onto the bare hill. She stopped again and stood watching the fog moving in the wind and then suddenly a voice close beside her said, It's marvelous, isn't it?

She turned quickly but the wind whipped her hair across her face. She pushed back her hair with both hands and saw a tall man standing beside her, smiling at her hands and her hair trying to escape them. He stepped up in front of her. There, he said. Now the wind's with your hair. You can put your hands back in your pockets.

She put her hands in her pockets and looked at him.

When he saw her eyes he stopped smiling and something in him seemed to hesitate, but he said, I'm lost. The fog's shut everything out. If I could find the campanile I'd be all right.

Why, there, Morgen said, nodding to it.

He glanced over his shoulder and laughed. As close as that! It looks like a little tent pitched in snow, doesn't it? I'd like to walk down the hill with you anyway.

Morgen looked at the campanile and then looked at him. All right. It isn't far.

He smiled and said, Thank you, as though he were clicking his heels. He wore a bright blue tie and when he turned it snapped out and lay shivering along the wind. He went beside her silently, looking out at the fog, looking often at her, looking at their feet walking in step. Finally he said, You know all the trails, don't you?

With my eyes closed.

That would mean you live close by.

About ten minutes from here, she said.

The trail narrowed and she walked ahead for a few moments and then it widened and he came up alongside her and said, If you live ten minutes from here we're in an awful hurry.

Well, Morgen said, when you walk this way it's twenty.

Let's walk this way then. He looked at her walking beside him with her hands in the deep pockets of her coat and her fair hair smoothed back away from her face by the wind. You know, he said, when I first saw you standing so still on the hill I thought you were a statue. What do you think about to keep as still as that? Wait, he said suddenly, and put out his hand and stopped her. He looked at her so intently she smiled, but he said, Have you ever been modeled? I mean, have you ever had a portrait painted?

Oh, she said, many times.

Well, good Lord, he said, catching step with her. What do you know about that? Why, it's marvelous! I never heard of anything so marvelous! He walked looking at her. She was just the same, the long throat and the hair like fine white wine held to the light. Her face had the still listening look and her eyes were that clear deep blue over darkness. He pushed his hands down into the pockets of his jacket and stumbled over a stone. He wanted to stop her again and look at her eyes but he didn't. She was walking as though she were walking alone and he didn't dare change that.

At the foot of the steps she stopped and said, I live here. If you'll follow this road down around the hill to the first street, you'll—

Later, he said, shifting his weight onto one foot. Right now I'm going to ask myself to tea. What do you say?

She looked at him. I'm sorry, we never drink tea and my father's resting.

I promise not to disturb your father.

She felt all along the insides of her pockets for a moment. All right, she said.

He followed her up the steps, looking at her thin ankles in calyxes of dark green wool socks worn over stockings, thinking what a marvelous thing it was. She went up the veranda steps quietly. At the door he said, My name's Royal St. Gabriel and yours is—

She said, Morgen Teutenberg, and opened the door.

He followed her inside, trying to make his footsteps sound as light as hers and she smiled at this and went to Fritz's door and looked in and then closed the door softly. She slipped off her coat and said, Won't you sit down? and put her coat over the back of the divan and pulled down the cuffs of her sweater.

Royal said, Thanks, but didn't sit down.

Would you like beer or coffee?

He would have liked beer but he said, Coffee, because it would take longer to prepare.

She left him then and he stood perfectly still, looking out of his enchantment at the room. It was a long low room, ceiled in redwood, unfinished and beautifully seasoned and the rafters were decorated with red and blue and yellow sawtooth designs. He saw an easel standing under the skylight in a sort of alcove, lifted a couple of steps above the floor level. There was some very simple unfinished furniture. The divan was long and low and there was a narrow runner in front of it, woven in a sort of geometry lesson of many colors. The drapes at the windows were made of some heavy blue stuff and the divan was covered with it and the cushions were beginning to break along the edges. He went slowly to the fireplace and put his foot up on the hearth. He heard Morgen in the kitchen and he smiled at the fire, at his foot on the hearthstone. He couldn't believe it.

She came in carrying a tray and he started toward her, but she said, Will you move the table up to the hearth, please? and he turned back and moved the coffee table up. He pushed aside a tobacco jar and a pair of woolen socks and she put the tray down.

There, she said, sitting on the hearth. I'm not going to insist but I know you'd be more comfortable if you'd sit down.

He smiled and sat on the end of the divan nearest her. He ran his hands back over his short hair. I hate that jack-in-the-box business of jumping up every time a woman comes near me, he said. I always wait till the preliminaries're over. I'll have cream, thanks, no sugar. He took the cup and sat back, crossing his knees. She offered him a plate of little dark brown cakes and he took one and said, Thanks. A moment later he said, These are marvelous. Did you make them?

Oh, no.

He finished the cake and set his cup on the edge of the table and got his cigarettes out of his jacket pocket and drew two from the pack and gave one to her. I wish you had a piano, he said. I love to play for people I like and I think I like you. She was looking into her cup and she didn't look up and he leaned forward and poured himself more coffee and she poured in the cream. He lit their cigarettes. The room was filling up with shadows and he sat back and looked at her and said, Morgen, aren't you a little surprised we get along so nicely?

Her eyes came up out of their own shadow and she said, Why, no.

He smoothed his hand back over his hair. Well, some other time I'll ask if you're glad. He got his cup and drank some coffee and got another cake off the plate. Your father's the painter? She nodded and he finished the cake. These remind me of cakes I used to eat at tea-time when I was little.

She smiled and said, More coffee?

He shook his head, smiling, and rose. No, thanks. I'm going now.

She went with him to the door and looked out over his shoulder, feeling the air cold and moist on her face.

I'm awfully glad you let me come up, he said. He held out his hand. And I didn't thank you for rescuing me, did I? She looked at him and he looked down at her hand and smiled at it. Anyway, he said, I feel rescued. He hesitated over what he wanted to say and then decided to let everything stay exactly as it was. He unclasped his fingers and she put her hand into the pocket of her sweater. Good-bye, Morgen.

She took a step backward. Good-bye, she said.

When he went in Barton was sitting in his chair at the window and Gildo was pouring whisky into a tall glass. He bowed to them. Gentlemen, he said.

Hello.

Have a drink? Gildo said.

He took off his jacket and lit a cigarette and said, No, thanks. He sat down at the piano and when his fingers touched the keys he felt a shock go through him to the soles of his feet. He sat frozen for a moment and then his body relaxed and he began to play.

Gildo said, Listen, Barton.

Royal lifted his hands abruptly and swung around. Say, Barton, he said, do you know anything about a fellow named Teutenberg, a painter?

Barton's eyebrows went up. The tall bearded Jesus of Berkeley?

That's the one, Royal said.

Barton rose and went over to the piano. Do I know anything about Teutenberg! He laughed.

Seriously I mean, Royal said.

Very seriously then, Barton said, looking at the ice in his glass, Fritz Teutenberg is probably one of the most important painters in the world today. As a man, nobody knows much about him but I gather he's rather a disagreeable old boy, very snooty. Lubansky gave half his fortune recently for one of his blonde young ladies. He has a penchant for blonde ladies, Teutenberg I mean, but no—

You're a dumb ox, Royal said, but thanks. He turned back to the keyboard and his hands settled. This, he said, glancing up at Barton, is for one of Teutenberg's blonde young ladies.

Thomas Parkinson

Berkeley 1947

Your Eisenhower jacket showed your bone-thin wrists
Contemptus mundi with a cat's grin
You jigged in cast-off army shoes
And maddened by the lack of care you chewed
Your spleen to prove your hate was right
And seared your liver, stomach, lungs,
And burned your clothes caked with dribbled food
And found your crackling line in book-piled rooms.

In Wheeler Hall you smelled the sham around you.
Half-poets, half-intellects, and all
Preferred. Hell is the state that grew
From San Diego up to Klamath Falls
Hot pavements, smogged skies, ranch houses
Hitch-hiking on a treadmill packed
With Cadillacs. A few simple hearts
Protected you, your slant intelligence.
Chants rose from Kantorowicz.
Tolman proved that some rats jump the wall
And leave the labyrinth to pointless drones.
The prize is cheese and not the Minotaur.
You brooded underneath the bevatron
And checked some words and graphed some idiolects.
The candor of poetry you kept inviolate.

George R. Stewart

🕊 *from* The Year of the Oath

THIS ACCOUNT OF THE OATH CONTROVERSY, THEY TELL ME, NEEDS A LITTLE LIGHTEN-
ing. Well, here goes! Hear all about the slapstick shenanigans of Professor
Elmer Bopp and Regent Ben Calef. Get ready to laugh. Only don't bother to
unbutton your vest. It's not going to be that funny!

You understand that my name is not Elmer Bopp, and I say thank the
Lord for that too! Also, I am not an ornithologist, and there is no such organization as the California Society of Bird and Lizard Watchers, and there
is no such bird (so far as I know) as the white-footed titmouse. There is,
however, such a bird as Ben Calef, though that is not his name either. The only
real name is that of Bob Sproul, but since he comes off very well in this whole
affair, I see no reason for changing that one.

It all began when the department secretary left a note for me: "Professor Bopp: Please call the President's Office. They are trying to get in touch
with you." All this happened, I should say, several years ago, and so in these
reported conversations I am not necessarily supplying the exact words, but I
am sure that the essential outline of facts is correct.

Well, I called the President's Office immediately, as a professor always
does when he receives such a message. They connected me with Mrs. Groueber, although that is not her name either.

"Oh yes," she said, "I've been trying to get you, Professor Bopp. Regent Calef has just written to President Sproul. He wants you to come and talk
to the Society of Bird and Lizard Watchers on the nesting habits of the white-

footed titmouse at their October meeting. Regent Calef is president of the society."

Perhaps she did not say "wants you to." Perhaps it was a stronger statement. I am sure, however, that it was not one of the usual polite expressions, "would be happy if you would," ... "would like you to."

I thought fast, and by long habit a professor is likely to be extremely respectful and obliging when he is dealing with the president and particularly when a regent stands in the background, if you could even call this "background." Then I sparred for time.

"I'm very busy," I said. "That means a five-hundred-mile trip. I hardly think that I can take the time this fall."

There was a pause at the other end of the line, and I took it as indicating a certain dramatization of shock.

"But," she said, "Regent Calef has written a letter!"

At that moment I had an image of Bob Sproul as the keeper of a livery stable and of all the professors as livery horses and of Regent Calef ordering out a horse for his own purposes.

"Well, I'm sorry," I said, "but as I think things over, I find that I really am too busy to take most of two days for that purpose. Will you please tell President Sproul that I'm sorry and ask him to express my appreciation to Regent Calef that he thought I would make a good speech?"

I supposed that the matter had ended there. I get a fair number of invitations to speak. Since I really am busy, I turn down nearly all of them, particularly when they make no mention of honorarium or even of traveling expenses. I didn't for a moment consider that Bob Sproul would hold the matter against me, and as for Regent Calef, I figured that he was so far away, academically speaking, that any resentment he might feel would have no very good route by which to express itself.

Within two hours I had another call from the President's Office. This time it was the president himself. "HELLO, ELMER," he said.

"Hello, Bob," I said in reply.

"About this speech to the Bird and Lizard Watchers," he said, "Calef would really like to have you do that. He thinks that you're the best possible man for the topic."

"Well, that's very complimentary of him. Possibly I am. Of course it's a long time since I did that monograph on the titmouse, and I really haven't much interest in the topic any more."

"Yes, I'd say that you'd gone on to higher and bigger things. But still, you could make the talk."

"Naturally I can't say that I couldn't make it. But, as I told Mrs. Groueber, I'm very busy just now, and I've turned down various invitations to speak."

"I know," he said, "I realize that. Still, this would be a service. This would be a personal favor to me."

Bob Sproul has been a good friend to me and he has a lot of charm too. When he spoke of a personal favor, I felt myself weakening fast. Then the image of the livery stable came into my mind.

"All right, Bob," I said, "I might as well tell you. Of course I could squeeze out the time somewhere, but what I really object to is being ordered out like a livery-stable horse by means of a letter that a regent writes to the president."

There was a pause on the line again.

"All right," he said then, "I think I understand. I'll take care of it. It won't be easy, but I'll take care of it."

He hung up, and I hung up. I thought again that the matter was finished.

Next day I had a third call from the President's Office. It was the president himself again.

"I've talked with Calef on the telephone," he said. "He really is very much worked up about having you come to speak."

I'm afraid that I can be just as stubborn as the next one. Anyway, I'd gone too far, I felt, to back down.

"I'm sorry, and I mean it, Bob. I'd like to help you out here. But I took my position really as a moral issue, and I don't see how I can back down."

"Well, I wish you could! With things as they are, this would be a University service. It would make my job easier."

I was really beginning to feel like a heel now, letting the University down, and Bob too. Still, it would be worse to yield now than it would have been in the first place. I thought fast for still another time and checked the sudden emotional impulse to be a good fellow.

"Look here, Bob. How about this? Why doesn't Mr. Calef write me a letter on their stationery as president of the society, not as a regent? In that case I'll consider it."

This didn't seem to please him. I gathered that Calef wasn't likely to back down any more than I was and that such a situation left Bob Sproul badly caught in between.

"I'm sorry!" I said once more. "This probably leaves you in a bad fix."

"Oh, don't worry about me! I'm used to that!" He seemed a little pathetic.

"Well," I said, perhaps nervously defensive, "I'd think you'd like having a good, vigorous, independent-minded faculty that doesn't like to take orders."

"Yes," he said, "I do." But he didn't seem very enthusiastic, and I can't say that at the moment I blamed him. And again I thought the matter was all over.

Two or three days later, at my home, I received a letter, and the envelope bore the return address of the California Society of Bird and Lizard Watchers. It contained a polite letter requesting that I speak, etc., etc. It was signed Ben Calef, and underneath the signature was typewritten, "President of the Society."

There I was, caught in my own trap! I really didn't want to make that trip and to talk to that society—let alone on that subject. But I had to write to Mr. Ben Calef, President of the Society, and accept. His letter had made no statement as to compensation. I think, however, that it is indecent for a man to pay his own expenses to make a speech. I therefore inserted the sentence that I would expect my expenses....

So I went and I made my speech. Mr. Calef, incidentally, was not there. They told me that he was out of town. People came up and complimented me after I had finished. I don't think, however, that it was a very good speech. The way I had got into making it did not arouse much enthusiasm in me.

When I was about to leave, the secretary spoke to me and said that President Calef—or she may have said Regent Calef—would take care of my expenses if I would submit a bill. I thanked her.

I spent that night with a friend and ate breakfast at his house. When I got back home I sent in a bill for expenses, which consisted exactly of my round-trip airplane fare—$42.50.

I waited a month. Then I got another call from the President's Office, and it was Bob Sproul again.

"Say, Elmer," he said, "Calef has sent me the bill for those expenses on your trip to speak to his society. It's only for $42.50. That's not very much. Was that all the expense you had?"

I was flabbergasted at just how the bill had got to him, but I answered his question first:

"That's all the bill I sent in. I stayed with a friend. I just sent the bill for my airplane ticket."

"Well, if that's all you think is right—"

"No, I don't want to charge anything more. As you remember, my heart wasn't in that affair. I'm afraid I didn't make a very good speech."

"Well—" he said doubtfully. "If you only made them the $42.50 speech, I suppose that's all right not to get any more money than that."

"But how's it happen," I said, sensing my chance to get a word in, "how's it happen that Mr. Calef sent the bill to you?"

"Don't worry," he said, "I won't have to pay it out of my own pocket. There's a fund for these things. Calef just sent me the bill and said the University could pay it."

"I don't like it," I said. "Even if the University has a public relations fund for sending professors around the state to spread culture, I think the Club should pay the expenses, for they originated the idea."

He replied to the general effect that I might as well take the money and consider the affair finished. I was sure that that would be the easiest way for him, and I agreed.

I promptly got a check for $42.50, signed by the president personally....

This is my own little affair, and I think that it has its comical sides, although before the end all the farce becomes pretty stale. And even in my little story there are some bits of seriousness. Perhaps they should be clear enough to anyone, but I am going to point them out anyway.

First—and this, I think, irritates me most of all—the president's time was taken up to a disproportionate and alarming degree because, apparently, a regent was involved. The president made three personal telephone calls to me. He called Calef at least once, perhaps oftener. He signed me a check personally. The president is very busy, chronically overworked. But just because a regent was involved, he had to expend all this time, not to mention what worry was involved!

Second—Regent Calef felt that he could incur expenses for the benefit of a society of which he was president and then make the University foot the bill.

Third—Regent Calef seemed to feel that a professor is a livery horse so far as a regent is concerned and can be ordered out by the process of writing a letter to the stablekeeper. The matter involved here is not merely that the professor's own sense of worth and dignity is impaired, but also that no option is left either to the President or to the professor as to whether the professor's time can be expended better in that particular way or in some other for the greater benefit of the people of the state.

Josephine Miles

To Make a Summer

Sandy says his high-school daughter
Keeps exclaiming joy, joy.
The burden of my joy lightens
With her exclamation.

It's a generality, it takes
From my heart the sting of the singular, it sets moving
In the easy early Berkeley air
What we incommunicably share.

From *Poems, 1930–1960*, copyright 1960 by Josephine Miles. Reprinted by permission of Indiana University Press.

Simone de Beauvoir

🌿 Berkeley

TODAY I HAD TO SPEAK AT THE UNIVERSITY OF CALIFORNIA IN BERKELEY. A YOUNG writer, who ran a bookshop there, called for me in his car. He edited an avant-garde review influenced by Surrealism and Henry Miller. There is an intellectual regionalism in America; Henry Miller has little importance in New York, but on the West Coast, where he lives, he is taken for a genius. Many of his books are banned, but copies are passed around from hand to hand; passages have even been recorded. The bookshop to which V. took me reminded me a bit of Adrienne Yonnier's; it was quite small, with a tiny picture gallery. Many of the names I read on the shelves were unknown to me; I wanted to inform myself about the new generation of writers, and I asked his opinion; the replies I received were not at all identical with those I got in New York. No one seemed to agree about the older writers either, with the exception of Faulkner and Melville. It is true that in France we also have our coteries, our prejudices, our likes and dislikes, but here indecision symbolizes a certain disorder; writers, with no inkling of their future, turned their backs on the past. Yet nearly everyone agrees that there is a great revival of poetry.

While we were talking, V., himself a poet, gave me books and reviews and a record, a fragment of *Tropic of Cancer*. Books and records also figured in the conversation at the Faculty Club—an austere dining room all in black, with a big family table in the center and, around it, serious old gentlemen. As

Excerpted from *America Day by Day*, copyright © 1953 by Simone de Beauvoir. Reprinted by permission of Grove Press.

in France, but even more so, most of the universities are cut off from literary and artistic avant-garde movements. They seem to be as sharply cut off from life. We may certainly not look to the universities for the spark which will stimulate doubt and a sense of responsibility in the young people in their charge. The universities only confirm these young people in their apathy and conformity. I looked at the athletic-looking young people, the smiling young girls in my audience, and I thought that certainly, like the students in Los Angeles, there were no more than one or two who were concerned about the news of the day. They sometimes say that America is the land of youth. I am not so sure. Real youth is that which exerts itself in forging ahead to an adult future, not that which lives confined with accommodating resignation in the limits assigned to it.

Raquel Scherr

⚘ La Japonesa

My mother, Juana Estela Salgado de Scherr, came home from her English class and said, in Spanish, "I had a very interesting conversation with a Japanese woman while I was waiting for the bus." Her eyes glistened with amusement and she cupped her mouth when she laughed. "The woman came up to me and started speaking Japanese. I told her in Spanish that I did not speak Japanese. She laughed too. She thought I was Japanese." I could understand why—my mother's black black eyes, their Indian slant, straight black hair, cinnamon-and-lemon colored skin, cheekbones tilted toward the sun. My father's Baltimore Jewish family, who had never seen a Mexican before, said my mother "looks like Madame Chiang-Kai-Shek."

In the 1950s, in Berkeley, foreign faces looked familial to me, rather like seeing an American in a Mexican town—an instantly familiar stranger. We lived in Albany's Codornices Village, on Sixth Street, a mostly Black neighborhood. My father, Max Scherr, often took me to the Piccolo, a popular coffee shop near the Berkeley campus where he'd meet his friends. They were mainly Jewish or Black. How different they seemed from college men with crewcuts slicked in vasoline, and college women in tight skirts, cashmere sweaters, and duck-tailed hair. I thought they all came from places like Modesto. My friend Judy Nikaido referred to them as "white people." She was born in a detention camp in California. After the war a young white couple helped ease the Nikaidos' financial pressures by taking the youngest of seven children until things got better. When things got better, they refused to give her back. Nothing could be done because she didn't want to come back. Mrs. Nikaido cried in the corner of her living room which smelled strongly of incense, while Judy and I played Monopoly. Neither of our mothers spoke English.

I asked my mother how she was able to have a conversation with the woman at the bus stop. "A little Spanish, a little Japanese, a little English, and a lot of hands. We understood each other very well." She would always say this about the people in her classes. "We understand each other very well." She told me about her good friend, "el Peruano" (the Peruvian), who was putting himself through college and supporting his aunt and invalid mother by working at Larry Blake's restaurant, or about "la joven Pakistani" (the young Pakistani woman) who wanted to go back home, but her husband wanted to stay. There were also the Delgados, a Cuban family who came to California before the revolution. Their kids went to school with my brothers and me. They were the only "latinos," besides the Randalls' kids who were mixed like us, and my Mexican friend Gloria who insisted she was Spanish. In later years, my mother told me about "la Vietnames" whose husband was killed while carrying medical equipment in Saigon. She brought her son to the U.S., but left her small daughter behind. "And your father writing about hippies," my mother said, meaning the *Berkeley Barb*, an underground newspaper my father started in 1965.

My mother kept going back to school to practice her English; not to learn it but to be with friends: "el Colombiano," "la Nicaraguense," "la Koreana," "el Panameño," "la Japonesa," "la China," "la Filipina."

She had been in her last year of medical school at the University of Mexico when she met my father, a young lawyer who rode the rails to California, then hitchhiked to Mexico. My mother had read the Classics. Octavio Paz had been her schoolmate. Her first few years in Berkeley she wore long handpainted Mexican skirts and thickly colored embroidered blouses. "The whole world comes to my English class," she'd say. "The whole world comes to California. We understand each other very well." I think of her talking to the woman at the bus stop, and it seems, thousands of years ago, my Mexican mother—part Aztec, French, and Spanish—was Japanese.

Shelley Singer

🖋 *from* Full House

I STILL HAD PLENTY OF THE DAY LEFT, SO I DECIDED THAT, BEFORE I DID ANY MORE work, I would take Carleton up on his invitation to visit the hat shop and look around. I found a parking place a block down from Telegraph on Dwight and strolled into the dim narrow shop for the second time in three days. I nodded to Carleton, who, busy with a customer, nodded back.

This time, I was looking at the merchandise. I ignored the rack of berets. After slouching around Berkeley-style for a few minutes, sneering at the over-crowded, ceiling-high shelves of headgear, I spotted a glass case, along one side, in which were perched about a dozen very beautiful fedoras. Soft felt in beige, brown, black, blue, and forest green.

I approached the counter. "What do I have to do to try on one of those fedoras?" I asked.

"Just go around the back of the case and slide the door open." He looked pleased with me for some reason.

I did as he said. I found a brown one in my size and tried it on in front of a mirror that needed resilvering. Gorgeous. I was Alan Ladd. No, too tall. George Raft? Scott Brady? Thirty-five dollars. Not much for a great image. I wore it up to the counter.

"Mm-hm!" Carleton said admiringly. I grinned crookedly, film noir style, and paid the man.

"I guess you remember when guys wore those things the first time around, right, Jake?" He smiled innocently.

"I guess I should warn you," I said, smiling back, "that Victor's a little pissed off that you sent me over there."

"Yeah?" He laughed. "What's he gonna do, smear me with grease? Anything new on the case?"

"Hard to tell," I said cryptically, and headed for the door.

"Maybe the hat will help," he called after me. I did not turn back or answer him.

My car and my hat suited each other. First of all, there was none of that nonsense about headrests. People were tough in the fifties and didn't worry about things like broken necks. You can wear a hat in a 1953 Chevy. Modern cars, on the other hand, were built for an era of hatlessness. You cannot comfortably wear a hat, except a beret, in a modern car with a headrest. First of all, the ceilings are low. If you're even moderately tall, you'll smash your hat against the ceiling. If you slump to avoid this, or if you're short, you collide with the headrest. The back of the hat gets squashed, or the hat gets pushed down on your nose or off your head altogether.

I wonder what will happen if hats continue to be popular once again. Will cars change? Will hat racks and hatcheck concessions return to public places? I've seen people sticking their hats under their chairs in restaurants, sometimes forgetting them. Or stepping on them. And it's not much fun to wear a hat to go someplace when you have to take it off to drive there and back. The point of a hat is to wear it.

I, at least, in my headrestless classic, could drive down Telegraph wearing my new fedora. Sure, whiplash could be a problem. But me and my fedora and my '53 Bel Air, we didn't give a damn.

Robert Duncan

A Poem Slow Beginning

remembering powers of love
   and of poetry,
the Berkeley we believed
   grove of Arcady—

that there might be
   potencies in common things,
"princely manipulations of the real"

the hard electric lights,
   filaments exposed
we loved by or studied by,
   romantic,
fused between glare and seraphic glow,
   old lamps of wisdom
   old lamps of suffering.

but that's not the way I saw.
   Crossd,
the sinister eye sees the near
   as clear fact,
         the far

blurs; the right eye
   fuses all that is
immediate to sight.

       There first I knew
the companions name themselves
   and move
in time of naming upward
   toward outward
forms of desire and enlightenment,

but intoxicated,
   only by longing
belonging to that first company
of named stars that in heaven
call attention to a tension
   in design,
         compel
as the letters by which we spell words compel
   magic refinements;

and sought from tree and sun, from night and sea,
old powers—Dionysus in wrath, Apollo in rapture,
Orpheus in song, and Eros secretly

four that Christ-crossd in one Nature
Plato named the First Beloved

that now I see
in all certain dear contributor
   to my being

has given me house, ghost,
image and color,   in whom I dwell
   past Arcady.

For tho Death is sweet and   veriest
   imitator of ecstasy

And there be a Great Lover,
  Salvator Mundi,
whose kingdom hangs above me;

tho the lamps strung among
   shadowy foliage are there;
tho all earlier ravishings,
   raptures,
happend, and sing melodies, moving thus
   when I touch them;

such sad lines they may have been
that now thou hast lifted to gladness.

Of all fearless happiness
from which reaches my life I sing—

   the years radiating

toward the so-calld first days,
toward the so-calld last days,

   inadequate boundaries

of the heart you hold to.

Jack Spicer

Berkeley in Time of Plague

Plague took us and the land from under us,
Rose like a boil, enclosing us within.
We waited and the blue skies writhed a while
Becoming black with death.

Plague took us and the chairs from under us,
Stepped cautiously while entering the room
(We were discussing Yeats); it paused a while
Then smiled and made us die.

Plague took us, laughed and reproportioned us
Swelled us to dizzy, unaccustomed size.
We died prodigiously; it hurt a while
But left a certain quiet in our eyes.

From *The Californians: Writings of Their Past and Present*, edited by Ursula Ericson and Robert Pearsall. "Berkeley in Time of Plague" copyright 1961 by Jack Spicer.

Jack Kerouac

from The Dharma Bums

IN BERKELEY I WAS LIVING WITH ALVAH GOLDBOOK IN HIS LITTLE ROSE-COVERED cottage in the backyard of a bigger house on Milvia Street. The old rotten porch slanted forward to the ground, among vines, with a nice old rocking chair that I sat in every morning to read my Diamond Sutra. The yard was full of tomato plants about to ripen, and mint, mint, everything smelling of mint, and one fine old tree that I loved to sit under and meditate on those cool perfect starry California October nights unmatched anywhere in the world. We had a perfect little kitchen with a gas stove, but no icebox, but no matter. We also had a perfect little bathroom with a tub and hot water, and one main room, covered with pillows and floor mats of straw and mattresses to sleep on, and books, books, hundreds of books everything from Catullus to Pound to Blyth to albums of Bach and Beethoven (and even one swinging Ella Fitzgerald album with Clark Terry very interesting on trumpet) and a good three-speed Webcor phonograph that played loud enough to blast the roof off: and the roof nothing but plywood, the walls too, through which one night in one of our Zen Lunatic drunks I put my fist in glee and Coughlin saw me and put his head through about three inches.

About a mile from there, way down Milvia and then upslope toward the campus of the University of California, behind another big old house on a quiet street (Hillegass), Japhy lived in his own shack which was infinitely smaller than ours, about twelve by twelve, with nothing in it but typical Japhy appurtenances that showed his belief in the simple monastic life—no chairs at all, not even one sentimental rocking chair, but just straw mats. In the corner was his famous rucksack with cleaned-up pots and pans all fitting into one another in a compact unit and all tied and put away inside a knotted-up blue bandana. Then his Japanese wooden pata shoes, which he never used, and a pair of black inside-pata socks to pad around softly in over his pretty straw mats, just room for your four toes on one side and your big toe on the other. He had a slew of orange crates all filled with beautiful scholarly books, some of them in Oriental languages, all the great sutras, comments on sutras, the complete works of D. T. Suzuki and a fine quadruple-volume edition of Japanese haikus. He also had an immense collection of valuable general poetry. In fact if a thief should have broken in there the only things of real value were the books. Japhy's clothes were all old hand-me-downs bought secondhand with a bemused and happy expression in Goodwill and Salvation Army stores: wool socks darned, colored undershirts, jeans, workshirts, moccasin shoes, and a few turtleneck sweaters that he wore one on top the other in the cold mountain nights of the High Sierras in California and the High Cascades of Washington and Oregon on the long incredible jaunts that sometimes lasted weeks and weeks with just a few pounds of dried food in his pack. A few orange crates made his table, on which, one late sunny afternoon as I arrived, was steaming a peaceful cup of tea at his side as he bent his serious head to the Chinese signs of the poet Han Shan. Coughlin had given me the address and I came there, seeing first Japhy's bicycle on the lawn in front of the big house out front (where his landlady lived) then the few odd boulders and rocks and funny little trees he'd brought back from mountain jaunts to set out in his own "Japanese tea garden" or "tea-house garden," as there was a convenient pine tree soughing over his little domicile.

A peacefuller scene I never saw than when, in that rather nippy late red afternoon, I simply opened his little door and looked in and saw him at the end of the little shack, sitting crosslegged on a Paisley pillow on a straw mat, with his spectacles on, making him look old and scholarly and wise, with book on lap and the little tin teapot and porcelain cup steaming at his side. He looked up very peacefully, saw who it was, said, "Ray, come in," and bent his eyes again to the script.

"What you doing?"

"Translating Han Shan's great poem called 'Cold Mountain' written a thousand years ago some of it scribbled on the sides of cliffs hundreds of miles away from any other living beings."

"Wow."

"When you come into this house though you've got to take your shoes off, see those straw mats, you can ruin 'em with shoes." So I took my softsoled blue cloth shoes off and laid them dutifully by the door and he threw me a pillow and I sat crosslegged along the little wooden board wall and he offered me a cup of hot tea. "Did you ever read the Book of Tea?" said he.

"No, what's that?"

"It's a scholarly treatise on how to make tea utilizing all the knowledge of two thousand years about tea-brewing. Some of the descriptions of the effect of the first sip of tea, and the second, and the third, are really wild and ecstatic."

"Those guys got high on nothing, hey?"

"Sip your tea and you'll see; this is good green tea." It was good and I immediately felt calm and warm. "Want me to read you parts of this Han Shan poem? Want me to tell you about Han Shan?"

"Yeah."

"Han Shan you see was a Chinese scholar who got sick of the big city and the world and took off to hide in the mountains."

"Say, that sounds like you."

"In those days you could really do that. He stayed in caves not far from a Buddhist monastery in the T'ang Hsing district of T'ien Tai and his only human friend was the funny Zen Lunatic Shih-te who had a job sweeping out the monastery with a straw broom. Shih-te was a poet too but he never wrote much down. Every now and then Han Shan would come down from Cold Mountain in his bark clothing and come into the warm kitchen and wait for food, but none of the monks would ever feed him because he didn't want to join the order and answer the meditation bell three times a day. You see why in some of his utterances, like—listen and I'll look here and read from the Chinese," and I bent over his shoulder and watched him read from big wild crowtracks of Chinese signs: "Climbing up Cold Mountain path, Cold Mountain path goes on and on, long gorge choked with scree and boulders, wide creek and mist-blurred grass, moss is slippery though there's been no rain, pine sings but there's no wind, who can leap the world's ties and sit with me among white clouds?"

"Wow."

"Course that's my own translation into English, you see there are five signs for each line and I have to put in Western prepositions and articles and such."

"Why don't you just translate it as it is, five signs, five words? What's those first five signs?"

"Sign for climbing, sign for up, sign for cold, sign for mountain, sign for path."

"Well then, translate it 'Climbing up Cold Mountain path.'"

"Yeah, but what do you do with the sign for long, sign for gorge, sign for choke, sign for avalanche, sign for boulders?"

"Where's that?"

"That's the third line, would have to read 'Long gorge choke avalanche boulders.'"

"Well that's even better!"

"Well yeah, I thought of that, but I have to have this pass the approval of Chinese scholars here at the university and have it clear in English."

"Boy what a great thing this is," I said looking around at the little shack, "and you sitting here so very quietly at this very quiet hour studying all alone with your glasses...."

"Ray what you got to do is go climb a mountain with me soon. How would you like to climb Matterhorn?"

"Great! Where's that?"

"Up in the High Sierras. We can go there with Henry Morley in his car and bring our packs and take off from the lake. I could carry all the food and stuff we need in my rucksack and you could borrow Alvah's small knapsack and carry extra socks and shoes and stuff."

"What's these signs mean?"

"These signs mean that Han Shan came down from the mountain after many years roaming around up there, to see his folks in town, says, 'Till recently I stayed at Cold Mountain, et cetera, yesterday I called on friends and family, more than half had gone to the Yellow Springs,' that means death, the Yellow Springs, 'now morning I face my lone shadow, I can't study with both eyes full of tears.'"

"That's like you too, Japhy, studying with eyes full of tears."

"My eyes aren't full of tears!"

"Aren't they going to be after a long long time?"

"They certainly will, Ray ... and look here, 'In the mountains it's cold, it's always been cold not just this year,' see, he's real high, maybe twelve thousand or thirteen thousand feet or more, way up there, and says, 'Jagged scarps always snowed in, woods in the dark ravines spitting mist, grass is still sprouting at the end of June, leaves begin to fall in early August, and here am I high as a junkey—'"

"As a junkey!"

"That's my own translation, he actually says here am I as high as the sensualist in the city below, but I made it modern and high translation."

"Great." I wondered why Han Shan was Japhy's hero.

"Because," said he, "he was a poet, a mountain man, a Buddhist dedicated to the principle of meditation on the essence of all things, a vegetarian too by the way though I haven't got on that kick from figuring maybe in this modern world to be a vegetarian is to split hairs a little since all sentient beings eat what they can. And he was a man of solitude who could take off by himself and live purely and true to himself."

"That sounds like you too."

"And like you too, Ray, I haven't forgotten what you told me about how you made it in the woods meditating in North Carolina and all." Japhy was very sad, subdued, I'd never seen him so quiet, melancholy, thoughtful his voice was as tender as a mother's, he seemed to be talking from far away to a poor yearning creature (me) who needed to hear his message he wasn't putting anything on he was in a bit of a trance.

"Have you been meditating today?"

"Yeah I meditate first thing in the morning before breakfast and I always meditate a long time in the afternoon unless I'm interrupted."

"Who interrupts you?"

"Oh, people. Coughlin sometimes, and Alvah came yesterday, and Rol Sturlason, and I got this girl comes over to play yabyum."

"Yabyum? What's that?"

"Don't you know about yabyum, Smith? I'll tell you later." He seemed to be too sad to talk about yabyum, which I found out about a couple of nights later. We talked a while longer about Han Shan and poems on cliffs and as I was going away his friend Rol Sturlason, a tall blond goodlooking kid, came in to discuss his coming trip to Japan with him. This Rol Sturlason was interested in the famous Ryoanji rock garden of Shokokuji monastery in Kyoto, which is nothing but old boulders placed in such a way, supposedly mystically aesthetic, as to cause thousands of tourists and monks every year to journey there to stare at the boulders in the sand and thereby gain peace of mind. I have never met such weird yet serious and earnest people. I never saw Rol Sturlason again, he went to Japan soon after, but I can't forget what he said about the boulders, to my question, "Well who placed them in that certain way that's so great?"

"Nobody knows, some monk, or monks, long ago. But there is a definite mysterious form in the arrangement of the rocks. It's only through form that we can realize emptiness." He showed me the picture of the boulders in well-raked sand, looking like islands in the sea, looking as though they had eyes (declivities) and surrounded by a neatly screened and architectural monastery patio. Then he showed me a diagram of the stone arrangement with the projection in silhouette and showed me the geometrical logics and all, and mentioned the phrases "lonely individuality" and the rocks as "bumps pushing into space," all meaning some kind of koan business I wasn't as much interested in as in him and especially in good kind Japhy who brewed more tea on his noisy gasoline primus and gave us added cups with almost a silent Oriental bow. It was quite different from the night of the poetry reading.

Allen Ginsberg

A Supermarket in California

What thoughts I have of you tonight, Walt Whitman, for I walked down the sidestreets under the trees with a headache self-conscious looking at the full moon.

In my hungry fatigue, and shopping for images, I went into the neon fruit supermarket, dreaming of your enumerations!

What peaches and what penumbras! Whole families shopping at night! Aisles full of husbands! Wives in the avocados, babies in the tomatoes!—and you, Garcia Lorca, what were you doing down by the watermelons?

I saw you, Walt Whitman, childless, lonely old grubber, poking among the meats in the refrigerator and eyeing the grocery boys.

I heard you asking questions of each: Who killed the pork chops? What price bananas? Are you my Angel?

I wandered in and out of the brilliant stacks of cans following you, and followed in my imagination by the store detective.

We strode down the open corridors together in our solitary fancy tasting artichokes, possessing every frozen delicacy, and never passing the cashier.

Where are we going, Walt Whitman? The doors close in an hour. Which way does your beard point tonight?

(I touch your book and dream of our odyssey in the supermarket and feel absurd.)

Will we walk all night through solitary streets? The trees add shade to shade, lights out in the houses, we'll both be lonely.

Will we stroll dreaming of the lost America of love past blue automobiles in driveways, home to our silent cottage?

Ah, dear father, graybeard, lonely old courage-teacher, what America did you have when Charon quit poling his ferry and you got out on a smoking bank and stood watching the boat disappear on the black waters of Lethe?

Berkeley 1955

Louis Simpson

🍃 There Is

1

Look! From my window there's a view
of city streets
where only lives as dry as tortoises
can crawl—the Galapagos of desire.

There is the day of Negroes with red hair
and the day of insane women on the subway;
there is the day of the word Trieste
and the night of the blind man with the electric guitar.

But I have no profession. Like a spy
I read the papers—Situations Wanted.
Surely there is a secret
which, if I knew it, would change everything!

2

I have the poor man's nerve-tic, irony.
I see through the illusions of the age!
The bell tolls, and the hearse advances,
and the mourners follow, for my entertainment.

I tread the burning pavement,
the streets where drunkards stretch

like photographs of civil death
and trumpets strangle in electric shelves.

The mannequins stare at me scornfully.
I know they are pretending
all day to be in earnest.
And can it be that love is an illusion?

When darkness falls on the enormous street
the air is filled with Eros, whispering.
Eyes, mouths, contrive to meet
in silence, fearing they may be prevented.

3

O businessmen like ruins,
bankers who are Bastilles,
widows, sadder than the shores of lakes,
then you were happy, when you still could tremble!

But all night long my window
sheds tears of light.
I seek the word. The word is not forthcoming.
O syllables of light ... O dark cathedral ...

Suzanne Lipsett

❧ Raw Material

DOORS SLAMMING ON DOORS.

You know how in hotel suites sometimes you open a door to the adjoining room only to find another door shut tight? After the debacle of the short story, my father slammed the door on our former life once more, and I slammed the door on that blessed world where the three Mikes and I had been looking for ways to dazzle each other with words. I slammed, wheeled, and dove into life on my own, off to college in Berkeley. Sounds brisk and well-scrubbed—"off to college." But it was the beginning of the sixties and, to complete the diving metaphor, I was lucky as I plunged in headfirst that there was water in the pool—not much, but some, and draining fast.

I learned to write academic English in the daytime. At night I went dancing in a place called the Steppenwolf—a name appropriate to the tenor of the times, considering Hermann Hesse's grip on students who were on their way to full-blown psychedelia. Each week by Thursday this narrow, stifling bar in the Berkeley badlands was jammed tight with people fiercely seeking a good time or something like it: oblivion with a twist.

The twist was racial tension, turned up a few notches at night and fueled by alcohol and music.

There is no way that place could have had a license for dancing. In the wasteland of San Pablo Avenue, stuck in among credit furniture warehouses, thrift shops, and a weird, cavernous market that sold dented canned goods, the Steppenwolf was a tinderbox waiting for a spark. But it was a tinderbox that a big, invisible hand could have been shaking from the outside, because everybody in it, cheek to jowl, butt to belly, thigh to thigh, hand to crotch, and front to backside, was jumping and dancing to the thundering music. An alien might have wondered what terrible affliction had trapped us all in that box, or perhaps would have recorded it as a religious rite because it looked—and felt—like an ecstatic frenzy, and it was.

I went there with friends, but you couldn't drink or talk together, you could only dance. Even if you didn't dance you danced—the place took you with it. I had never been much of a dancer before and haven't been one since, but I danced at the Steppenwolf, danced with strangers and danced alone and danced occasionally with the people I knew, sometimes kissing at the height of a record ones I would have been too shy to speak to in daylight. The place was usually so packed by midnight that people started dancing on tables, and even that higher level was so crowded it might have satisfied the hopes of any bar owner on its own.

I danced on tables too. I didn't know what I was doing or how to act—nobody knew how to act in those days, or what we were playing with. Perhaps if the place had been less crowded we all would have seen that the young black men and women from the Oakland neighborhoods and the white university students freshly released from the suburbs of America, their newly evolving identities as fragile and changeable as their clothes, were circling and staring at each other with distrust and curiosity, with ignorance and a thirst for experience, and with emotions boiling down under that haven't any names. Some of the feelings were idle, some mysterious and deeper than the deepest spoken thought. One night I came home from oblivion with a series of clean, nearly bloodless razor cuts laddering up my thigh.

My daylight hours could not have been more different. At the university I was wandering in a desert that just skirted an oasis, and the oasis was the few classes offered in writing. Here and there, without my control, the drumming passion of those nighttime forays merged with my studies, and an analytic paper became an all-night orgy of casting hot thoughts into words. Invariably, though, I'd be stung in those epiphanies by the arch marginal notes of a seedy teaching assistant—"Oh, *really*? Do we *care*?" Or the death sentence: "Subjective!" accompanied by an angry slash. Gradually I learned how to read so that books entered my head and stayed there, never sinking down to the place where I could savor their meaning. If books had been rooms for me before, now they were large, echoing public buildings, cold, hard-surfaced monuments full of strangers. The echoes of voices made such a racket that an authentic emotional response to the art housed there was impossible.

At work, on the Cal Berkeley campus, I wrote lazy professors' books for a clerk-typist's pay. I still can't look at a textbook without wondering what poor student, on subsistence pay, really wrote it. But I had a small office to myself, and the company was good. There was certainly more happening there than in my lonely little studio apartment, where the guy across the street and I often stared into each other's windows: we were both big readers and both read in bed, though we never spoke on the street. That guy, my books, and a wrong number who became a frequent caller made up a good percentage of my social life. The rest entailed a group house mired in marijuana and music: we had barbecues and then sank to the floor under the weight of our heads, floating as if at the bottom of the sea through the music of Bob Dylan, Jimi Hendrix, the Band, and the Rolling Stones.

One day, blasting suddenly out of a tunnel I had barely known was there, life came barreling at me like a freight train. The irony is, as I ponder it now, that train was to scoop me up and carry me even farther off my course than I had fallen on my own. The track eventually looped out of the country and completely around the world, but—so odd, so strangely lucky in a horrible way—eventually and perhaps inevitably that runaway train carried me home to myself, to my real life's work, to those doors upon doors in my mind.

The day was a Thursday, July 3. It was deathly hot. I was wearing a short dress of a synthetic silky fabric, flower-printed, and my thighs stuck to my chair. I wore patent leather shoes with no hose—too hot. This was nearly thirty years ago, and I can still remember how the four buttons at the top of the dress in back fitted through loops of fabric and left little gaps. At two or so in the sultry afternoon heat, I gave up on the article I was trying to create from my boss's single page of notes and left to go to the bathroom, outside the department lobby and down the hall.

When I emerged from the stall and stepped to the sink to wash my hands, I looked up to see a man—in his late twenties, early thirties, wearing black and standing straight up against the tile wall, staring at me in the mirror. Was he a workman, a plumber? Had he forgotten to put the yellow "closed" sign on the door and had I surprised him at his work? Embarrassed, I laughed—honestly, I can still hear my laughter ringing against the tiles.

Two strides and he stood behind me, breathing hotly on my neck. "Shut up," he said, and in the mirror I saw the muzzle of a gray-blue gun pushed into my hair just above my ear, saw it in the mirror and felt it, but—this was the beginning of the bizarre perceptual disjointedness that characterized the whole experience—as two separate events, remembered separately.

It had to be a toy, I thought. I don't believe I had ever seen a real gun before, except snapped into a policeman's holster. My mind told me, based on past experience, it *had* to be a toy.

"Shut up," he said again, though I couldn't have made a sound.

Behind us was a door. He pushed the gun harder into my head, not so it hurt, but so it nudged me in the direction of the door. He flung it open, and there was the cell we would occupy together for long, tangled hours—a tiny room with a bed: a state law required such amenities in all workplace women's rooms. It contained a cot for women with cramps and a cruel gray blanket.

The man put me in there at the end of his gun and closed the door behind him. "Down, down," he said, but then changed his mind and, signaling with his gun, had me take off my clothes. In a moment of pure comedy, if comedy is a burst of the unexpected that doesn't kill anybody, he had to help me take the dress off over my head and lay it down at the end of the bed. As if somebody had just shoved a baby into his arms and run away, the incongruity of my silky, flowery summer dress in his hands rendered him momentarily ridiculous—not that I was laughing now. I lay back down on the scratchy blanket, my legs straight out in front of me, and then flew up to the right-hand corner of the tiny little room to watch.

It was then that the man began to talk.

Thirty years, and I can remember how the buttons fastened on my dress, and I can remember that the man talked nonstop for as long as it took—which was long, which was long—I can remember that what he said made me know he was completely and permanently crazy, swinging in arcs from fantasy to reality and back again into some fully peopled scenario in his mind. I can remember the sound of his voice as he spoke, and how it worked its way into anger and then back to a kind of purring thoughtfulness, and I can remember how we both appeared from my odd vantage point on the ceiling as he poked me here and there and everywhere with his gun and told me what to do next. And I can even remember how I thought that the worst thing of all was that I still had on my patent leather shoes and how they seemed so sad. I can remember the up and down of his voice, its arcs, but I can't remember a thing that crazy man said.

It did take forever, so long in fact, requiring so many changing strategies and separate operations, that I had to assume that at the moment of climax he would shoot me. He said he would shoot me, he promised to shoot me, and the calm thing up in the corner of the room received the news with neutrality and patience.

But all of a sudden he was up and on his feet and full of warning: he warned me not to move for twenty minutes or or or—and then he was gone. The thing in the corner watched the thing on the bed comply—second followed second followed second until both things at once realized that he was gone, fled, probably out of the building and on the street by now, and the thing at the ceiling reentered the body and I was whole again.

The return was accomplished just as I was pondering how I might sense, without benefit of a watch, that the twenty minutes had passed. With my world rent, how was I to know whether twenty seconds, twenty minutes, twenty hours, or years, or eons had passed? I saw that it was impossible, and that it had been just a ruse anyway—he had conditioned me with that gun to obey, but the gun was gone now and I got up.

Back in my department, I found my friend Gina, the receptionist.

"Where *have* you been?" she drawled, high-pitched. She was from Texas, and screamed sometimes.

"Call the police," I commanded.

"What, what?"

"Call the police," I told her, and she did.

So that Thursday, before work, I had had no warning as I was slipping on my dress and my patent leather shoes that before the workday ended I was to have every imaginable form of sexual intercourse with one stranger, be grilled with the greatest rigor by another, be skewered in the hospital by several more with sharp metal instruments and finally made to cry, if briefly, before being shown the door to wind up alone and changed forever on the street. It was the back door of Herrick Hospital, near the emergency entrance, and if I had been aware of my loneliness night after night in my room, I was still unprepared for loneliness as it is experienced in the daylight by one who has been taken past the reach of human kindness.

Because I was. I stood and watched people walk past me. I felt the heat of the July afternoon pounding me so that my hair hung damp and lank into my eyes. I felt a slick of lubricant on the inside of my thighs and a burning— like soap!—in my poor handled and rehandled crotch.

I was lonelier than I'd ever been as an out-of-whack student lacking a clear direction. But as I stood outside the back door of Herrick Hospital, released into the street after a silent pelvic exam, I felt the compulsion to write, long out of use, kick in like a high-power gear. It would be ten years before I could even *say* the word *rape*, and by that time I would have lived—luckily— through an eerie double replay of the whole incident, when two women-hating "magazine salesmen" pushed into my house. This time the punishment for being in the wrong place (home) at the wrong time (two o'clock in the after- noon) came with a beating that left much of my body and especially my face the royal purple and yellow of an overripe plum. It took many years after that to recover from the dismay and peculiar embarrassment at having had such a thing happen to me *twice*. But now I wonder how many who were young and free in those crazy, hell-bent years reached thirty without having physically experienced the perils of the times.

If ever a writer had her first book pounded into her, I was it. In a cra- zy way, I told myself, I had been given a privileged view of something close to the heart of darkness. If only I could climb outside it to that calm observing place where I had floated at the time. Not as therapy, mind you. Not to exorcize, but to *make use*. The urge—the unspeakably *urgent* urge—was to transform these raw experiences into something other, something *more*, something that might even, in a way as yet unimaginable to me, flash with a kind of beauty.

But I couldn't do it. I must have tried fifty or sixty times to transform those terrible encounters into something they weren't, every failing time managing no more than a superficial rendering of an event seen far-off, as if through a paper tube. I found new meaning in the tired metaphor of life as an onion: these overfull life experiences I was trying to release onto the page seemed made up of layer upon layer of nearly transparent tissue, tissue that cracked and tore at a too-heavy touch. Writing and rewriting, my frustration grew at being unable to slice straight through to the heart, and the meaning, of the matter.

What I didn't know then was that the very events were growing new skins as fast as I could peel the old ones away. As to the meaning of these random events, the hidden heart within them that I could liberate and use, there was none—only random hatred, dressed up in city clothes.

Susan Griffin

On Cedar Street

On Cedar Street
in the rush hour
on our front porch
my daughter says,
"Mommy,
you wanna take
you clothes off?"
I lie to her,
"It's too cold
for me," I
say. What
truth could I
tell her.
Little daughter,
I will not be the one
to hurt
your ears.

Thomas Pynchon

from The Crying of Lot 49

THOUGH HER NEXT MOVE SHOULD HAVE BEEN TO CONTACT RANDOLPH DRIBLETTE again, she decided instead to drive up to Berkeley. She wanted to find out where Richard Wharfinger had got his information about Trystero. Possibly also take a look at how the inventor John Nefastis picked up his mail.

As with Mucho when she'd left Kinneret, Metzger did not seem desperate at her going. She debated, driving north, whether to stop off at home on the way to Berkeley or coming back. As it turned out she missed the exit for Kinneret and that solved it. She purred along up the east side of the bay, presently climbed into the Berkeley hills and arrived close to midnight at a sprawling, many-leveled, German-baroque hotel, carpeted in deep green, going in for curved corridors and ornamental chandeliers. A sign in the lobby said WELCOME CALIFORNIA CHAPTER AMERICAN DEAF-MUTE ASSEMBLY. Every light in the place burned, alarmingly bright; a truly ponderable silence occupied the building. A clerk popped up from behind the desk where he'd been sleeping and began making sign language at her. Oedipa considered giving him the finger to see what would happen. But she'd driven straight through, and all at once the fatigue of it had caught up with her. The clerk took her to a room with a reproduction of a Remedios Varo in it, through corridors gently curving as the streets of San Narciso, utterly silent. She fell asleep almost at once, but kept waking from a nightmare about something in the mirror, across from her bed. Nothing specific, only a possibility, nothing she could see. When she finally did settle into sleep, she dreamed that Mucho, her husband, was making love to her on a soft white beach that was not part of any California she knew. When she woke in the morning, she was sitting bolt upright, staring into the mirror at her own exhausted face.

She found the Lectern Press in a small office building on Shattuck Avenue. They didn't have *Plays of Ford, Webster, Tourneur and Wharfinger* on the premises, but did take her check for $12.50, gave her the address of their warehouse in Oakland and a receipt to show the people there. By the time she'd collected the book, it was afternoon. She skimmed through to find the line that had brought her all the way up here. And in the leaf-fractured sunlight, froze.

No hallowed skein of stars can ward, I trow, ran the couplet, *Who once has crossed the lusts of Angelo.*

"No," she protested aloud. "'Who's once been set his tryst with Trystero.'" The pencilled note in the paperback had mentioned a variant. But the paperback was supposed to be a straight reprint of the book she now held. Puzzled, she saw that this edition also had a footnote:

> According only to the Quarto edition (1687). The
> earlier Folio has a lead inserted where the closing
> line should have been. D'Amico has suggested that
> Wharfinger may have made a libellous comparison
> involving someone at court, and that the later
> 'restoration' was actually the work of the printer,
> Inigo Barfstable. The doubtful 'Whitechapel'
> version (c. 1670) has 'This tryst or odious awry, O
> Niccolò,' which besides bringing in a quite graceless
> Alexandrine, is difficult to make sense of syntac-
> tically, unless we accept the rather unorthodox
> though persuasive argument of J.-K. Sale that the
> line is really a pun on 'This trystero *dies irae....*'
> This, however, it must be pointed out, leaves the
> line nearly as corrupt as before, owing to no clear
> meaning for the word *trystero*, unless it be a
> pseudo-Italianate variant on *triste* (= wretched,
> depraved). But the 'Whitechapel' edition, besides

being a fragment, abounds in such corrupt and
probably spurious lines, as we have mentioned
elsewhere, and is hardly to be trusted.

Then where, Oedipa wondered, does the paperback I bought at Zapf's
get off with *its* "Trystero" line? Was there yet another edition, besides the
Quarto, Folio, and "Whitechapel" fragment? The editor's preface, signed
this time, by one Emory Bortz, professor of English at Cal, mentioned none.
She spent nearly an hour more, searching through all the footnotes, finding
nothing.

"Dammit," she yelled, started the car and headed for the Berkeley campus, to find Professor Bortz.

She should have remembered the date on the book—1957. Another
world. The girl in the English office informed Oedipa that Professor Bortz was
no longer with the faculty. He was teaching at San Narciso College, San Narciso, California.

Of course, Oedipa thought, wry, where else? She copied the address and
walked away trying to remember who'd put out the paperback. She couldn't.

It was summer, a weekday, and midafternoon; no time for any campus
Oedipa knew of to be jumping, yet this one was. She came downslope from
Wheeler Hall, through Sather Gate into a plaza teeming with corduroy, denim, bare legs, blonde hair, hornrims, bicycle spokes in the sun, bookbags,
swaying card tables, long paper petitions dangling to earth, posters for unde-
cipherable FSM's, YAF's, VDC's, suds in the fountain, students in nose-to-
nose dialogue. She moved through it carrying her fat book, attracted, unsure,
a stranger, wanting to feel relevant but knowing how much of a search among
alternate universes it would take. For she had undergone her own educating
at a time of nerves, blandness and retreat among not only her fellow students
but also most of the visible structure around and ahead of them, this having
been a national reflex to certain pathologies in high places only death had had
the power to cure, and this Berkeley was like no somnolent Siwash out of her
own past at all, but more akin to those Far Eastern or Latin American universities you read about, those autonomous culture media where the most beloved of folklores may be brought into doubt, cataclysmic of dissents voiced,
suicidal of commitments chosen—the sort that bring governments down. But

it was English she was hearing as she crossed Bancroft Way among the blonde children and the muttering Hondas and Suzukis; American English. Where were Secretaries James and Foster and Senator Joseph, those dear daft numina who'd mothered over Oedipa's so temperate youth? In another world. Along another pattern of track, another string of decisions taken, switches closed, the faceless pointsmen who'd thrown them now all transferred, deserted, in stir, fleeing the skip-tracers, out of their skull, on horse, alcoholic, fanatic, under aliases, dead, impossible to find ever again. Among them they had managed to turn the young Oedipa into a rare creature indeed, unfit perhaps for marches and sit-ins, but just a whiz at pursuing strange words in Jacobean texts.

She pulled the Impala into a gas station somewhere along a gray stretch of Telegraph Avenue and found in a phone book the address of John Nefastis. She then drove to a pseudo-Mexican apartment house, looked for his name among the U.S. mailboxes, ascended outside steps and walked down a row of draped windows till she found his door. He had a crewcut and the same underage look as Koteks, but wore a shirt on various Polynesian themes and dating from the Truman administration.

Introducing herself, she invoked the name of Stanley Koteks. "He said you could tell me whether or not I'm a 'sensitive'."

Nefastis had been watching on his TV set a bunch of kids dancing some kind of a Watusi. "I like to watch young stuff," he explained. "There's something about a little chick that age."

"So does my husband," she said. "I understand."

John Nefastis beamed at her, simpatico, and brought out his Machine from a workroom in back. It looked about the way the patent had described it. "You know how this works?"

"Stanley gave me a kind of rundown."

He began then, bewilderingly, to talk about something called entropy. The word bothered him as much as "Trystero" bothered Oedipa. But it was too technical for her. She did gather that there were two distinct kinds of this entropy. One having to do with heat-engines, the other to do with communication. The equation for one, back in the '30's, had looked very like the equation for the other. It was a coincidence. The two fields were entirely unconnected, except at one point: Maxwell's Demon. As the Demon sat and sorted his molecules into hot and cold, the system was said to lose entropy. But somehow the loss was offset by the information the Demon gained about what molecules were where.

"Communication is the key," cried Nefastis. "The Demon passes his data on to the sensitive, and the sensitive must reply in kind. There are untold billions of molecules in that box. The Demon collects data on each and every one. At some deep psychic level he must get through. The sensitive must receive that staggering set of energies, and feed back something like the same quantity of information. To keep it all cycling. On the secular level all we can see is one piston, hopefully moving. One little movement, against all that massive complex of information, destroyed over and over with each power stroke."

"Help," said Oedipa, "you're not reaching me."

"Entropy is a figure of speech, then," sighed Nefastis, "a metaphor. It connects the world of thermodynamics to the world of information flow. The Machine uses both. The Demon makes the metaphor not only verbally graceful, but also objectively true."

"But what," she felt like some kind of a heretic, "if the Demon exists only because the two equations look alike? Because of the metaphor?"

Nefastis smiled; impenetrable, calm, a believer. "He existed for Clerk Maxwell long before the days of the metaphor."

But had Clerk Maxwell been such a fanatic about his Demon's reality? She looked at the picture on the outside of the box. Clerk Maxwell was in profile and would not meet her eyes. The forehead was round and smooth, and there was a curious bump at the back of his head, covered by curling hair. His visible eye seemed mild and noncommittal, but Oedipa wondered what hangups, crises, spookings in the middle of the night might be developed from the shadowed subtleties of his mouth, hidden under a full beard.

"Watch the picture," said Nefastis, "and concentrate on a cylinder. Don't worry. If you're a sensitive you'll know which one. Leave your mind open, receptive to the Demon's message. I'll be back." He returned to his TV set, which was now showing cartoons. Oedipa sat through two Yogi Bears, one Magilla Gorilla and a Peter Potamus, staring at Clerk Maxwell's enigmatic profile, waiting for the Demon to communicate.

Are you there, little fellow, Oedipa asked the Demon, or is Nefastis putting me on. Unless a piston moved, she'd never know. Clerk Maxwell's hands were cropped out of the photograph. He might have been holding a book. He gazed away, into some vista of Victorian England whose light had been lost forever. Oedipa's anxiety grew. It seemed, behind the beard, he'd begun, ever so faintly, to smile. Something in his eyes, certainly, had changed...

And there. At the top edge of what she could see: hadn't the right-hand piston moved, a fraction? She couldn't look directly, the instructions were to keep her eyes on Clerk Maxwell. Minutes passed, pistons remained frozen in place. High-pitched, comic voices issued from the TV set. She had seen only a retinal twitch, a misfired nerve cell. Did the true sensitive see more? In her colon now she was afraid, growing more so, that nothing would happen. Why worry, she worried; Nefastis is a nut, forget it, a sincere nut. The true sensitive is the one that can share in the man's hallucinations, that's all.

How wonderful they might be to share. For fifteen minutes more she tried; repeating, if you are there, whatever you are, show yourself to me, I need you, show yourself. But nothing happened.

"I'm sorry," she called in, surprisingly about to cry with frustration, her voice breaking. "It's no use." Nefastis came to her and put an arm around her shoulders.

"It's OK," he said. "Please don't cry. Come on in on the couch. The news will be on any minute. We can do it there."

"It?" said Oedipal "Do it? What?"

"Have sexual intercourse," replied Nefastis. "Maybe there'll be something about China tonight. I like to do it while they talk about Viet Nam, but China is best of all. You think about all those Chinese. Teeming. That profusion of life. It makes it sexier, right?"

"Gah," Oedipa screamed, and fled, Nefastis snapping his fingers through the dark rooms behind her in a hippy-dippy, oh-go-ahead-then-chick fashion he had doubtless learned from watching the TV also.

"Say hello to old Stanley," he called as she pattered down the steps into the street, flung a babushka over her license plate and screeched away down Telegraph. She drove more or less automatically until a swift boy in a Mustang, perhaps unable to contain the new sense of virility his auto gave him, nearly killed her and she realized that she was on the freeway, heading irreversibly for the Bay Bridge.

Bobby Seale

from Seize the Time

ON THE EVENING OF AUGUST 19, 1969, WE WERE RETURNING FROM THE WEDDING OF Ray "Masai" Hewitt, our Minister of Education, and Shirley Needley, one of the sisters in the Party. The wedding had been held at the Berkeley Free Church, which is about half a mile from National Headquarters. After the ceremony was over, we all piled into Eldridge's car, the one with the telephone in it, and headed back toward the office. We were about three blocks from the office when a car sped up from our left, and swerved in front of us and stopped at the light. The people in the car all seemed to be looking at us through the rear-view mirror.

"Those cats look like ..." Masai was saying.

"Pigs!" June Hilliard finished the sentence for him. June was driving. I looked to the right and saw a Volkswagen blocking the entrance to the service station at the corner. Two other cars came up on our rear. "There's pigs all around us, in unmarked cars," June said. All of a sudden the doors of those cars opened, and agents and policemen began to flood out into the street from all directions. They were running toward our car yelling, "Get out of the car! Get out of the car!" They were holding .38 revolvers, .357 Magnums, and shotguns on us. There were at least fifteen cops surrounding us. "If they're going to shoot, they might as well start shooting, because we're just dead," I thought. They were still screaming, "Get out! Get out!" Then I thought they were just going to search the car for weapons, and thought it was good we didn't have any, if they weren't going to shoot us after all.

June had gotten out of the car, but the car began to roll, because the emergency brake wasn't on. Masai got out of the car also and I hollered to June to pull up the emergency brake. The door on the side where Shirley was, was snatched open and a cop pointed a gun in and said, "Get out! This is the FBI. Out of the car! Out of the car!"

"Well, they're going to harass us and arrest us, and that's what it's all about," I said to myself.

When June had gotten out of the car, he had been pushed around, away from the door. One of the agents reached in and grabbed the emergency brake. I watched him as he snatched it up. Then he pointed a gun at me and said, "All right, Seale, get out!" I pulled the lock latch off, opened the door, and stepped out, with my hands hanging down at my sides, palms open, looking at him, cursing him with everything I could think of, because at that point all I could see and think of was a form of general harassment. Readily, someone said, "Hands over your head," and "Turn around." They grabbed my shoulder, spun me around, and pushed me toward the car. They began to pat-search me and one cop snatched my right arm and pulled it back and put a handcuff on it. Another snatched my left arm and pulled it back from across the trunk of the car and twisted the back of my hands toward my back and said, "Let's go. Let's get out of here. Let's get out of here." They had guns in their hands and they were pushing me around. They didn't show me any identification. There must have been fifteen, twenty more police and plains-clothesmen there. They all had guns. Some were even dressed in blue jeans, T-shirts, and short sleeve shirts. I didn't see any uniforms.

I was rushed into a car and stuck in the back seat, an agent on each side of me. Three of them got in front with shotguns and they drove toward San Francisco. One agent said, "I'm informing you of your rights." He told me everything, except that I had a right to contact my lawyer. They asked me if I had anything to say. I didn't answer. They were talking to each other. They were giggling with each other saying, "This was so easy." In my estimation they were getting some sort of erotic sensation. They got on their radio and said, "All Berkeley Police Units and other units surrounding the Berkeley house [I assume they were referring to the house where I live] can leave. We have suspect in custody."

I was brought to the San Francisco City Jail and booked. Prior to the booking and after I took everything out of my pockets, the FBI took my little phone book away from me. That was my property. They didn't give it back to me at all. I don't know where it is now. I looked around at them and one of the FBI pigs said, "Now I've informed you of all your rights."

"You haven't informed me of all my rights!" I said.

"Yes, I did," he said. "I did it in the car."

"No, you didn't. You're a liar, and you know it. You haven't informed me of all my rights." I noticed another pig standing there. I'd seen his face before, a number of times at press conferences and speaking engagements. I know his face very well, because one time at a press conference I walked up to him and asked him if he was a government agent. "No," he had said. "I don't have anything to do with the government. I'm just a newsman. Can I come to this press conference?"

"Sure you can," I said. "I just wanted to expose you if you were an agent so that the rest of the newsmen can let people know that there are agents and provocateurs working for the government all around us, who want to take things out of context and tell lies." Well, he was one of those cats.

From everything I gathered, he must've been an FBI agent because he was there at the jail when they dropped me off. "Haven't I see you somewhere before?" I asked him.

He looked at me and just grinned. He really thought he was Superman. You can just look at a cat and see how he's psychologically goofed up with Superman notions, so brainwashed that he thinks he's defending the so-called "free world." There is no "free world." How in the world can America be free when somewhere between forty and fifty million poor, oppressed people are living at subsistence and below?

The dude was grinning and he said, "Yes, you might have seen me before."

"I've seen you at a couple of press conferences I've had," I told him, "and you got exposed by some of the legitimate members of the press. That's where I've seen you before—and then you denied that you were an agent for the FBI or that you were a member of any racist organization."

"Well, Bob, that's how it goes," he said, a shitty grin on his face. I guess he thought he was James Bond or some great white hunter.

They tried to get me to sign a statement. "No, I'm not signing it," I said. Then they tried to get me to sign something else. I don't know whether it was an attempt to get me to sign some stupid crap about waiving extradition rights or what it was. "I'm not signing anything," I told them. "I don't have to sign anything."

They took my fingerprints and a mug shot, and told me to go down the hall, and they would give me a cell. I walked down there and spoke to a black cop who said he was a member of the Officers for Justice. He told me to sit down, and I sat down in a little office there. He offered me a cup of coffee and I drank it. I was rather tired and wanted to go to sleep. I knew that I'd have to wait overnight before getting bailed out, so he gave me some blankets, put me in a cell, and I fell off to sleep.

The first indication I had that I was being railroaded on some trumped-up charges in connection with that Connecticut frame-up—what I call a criminal agent, Mission Impossible (Mission Imperialism—domestic) plot to try to try and destroy the Black Panther Party—was after I'd been handcuffed on Shattuck Avenue in Berkeley. They were walking me toward a car. They said, "You're under arrest for conspiracy to commit murder, and conspiracy to kidnap and murder, in connection with Connecticut."

"What are these damned fools doing now?" I thought right off. "Now these cats are out of their minds."

"And for unlawful flight to avoid prosecution," as they put it.

I lay on my bunk in jail, and I said to myself, "These damned fools! Trying to railroad me. They're trying to railroad everyone they can out of the Party. They're trying to stop the Party from functioning. We knew it was coming, but now they're gonna try and trump up something else, and of course on me. I expected to be attacked by the pigs and the government, because we know that where we're going is correct and will expose the power structure for its continued oppression of the people."

Charles Garry came in about an hour later and they woke me up. I had made a call to the Black Panther Party headquarters before I went down to the cell and told them that I was in the San Francisco City Jail, so they'd know where to send Charles. Charles Garry came in and we started smiling at each other because we knew that the racist cops had really gone overboard again in their attempts to try and destroy the Party and the Party leadership.

The next day I was taken over to the Federal Building. It was the day after the arrest. McTernan, Garry's partner, came in to see me and I said, "We'll have to post the bail, won't we?"

"Yes," he said.

"Well, let's just get a bail," I said. "We'll go from there." They really didn't have a warrant yet. The next day they still didn't have a warrant. I appeared in the federal court in front of a U.S. commissioner, and McTernan argued that bail of $25,000 was too high and that I hadn't fled anywhere to avoid prosecution.

McTernan said that I was watched twenty-four hours a day, that I'd been in the public eye continually, making speaking engagements, on TV in Los Angeles, speaking to 4,000 people at the National Committe to Combat Fascism convention, holding press conferences everywhere, even in that very building—so what did the government mean by claiming that I was fleeing to avoid prosecution.

The commissioner said he had no jurisdiction over that and could only set the bail, which he said would be $25,000. So I went back to the cell in the federal building.

I could see a whole crowd of San Francisco policemen and also what looked like plainclothesmen coming up with prisoners. At that point I couldn't tell whether they were local San Francisco plainclothesmen or federal marshals. They were running around in a frenzy and trying to look over at me every once in a while. They'd shake their heads and all this kind of stuff and run around.

Two hours after that first appearance in the federal court I was called back again and bail was posted—$25,000 in a cashier's check. And at that point I said, "Good, now can I get out of here and get this crap straight, and go talk to Garry and everything." Charles was in the middle of the Warren Wells shoot-out trial, so McTernan was substituting for him. When I got ready to leave the commissioner's court, the marshals said, "Will you step back here first?" I thought to myself, "Now, wait a minute. They have already booked me." They repeated, "Step back here!"

I remembered that the last time I was there (for the Chicago thing), when I posted bail I had to come back through there, and I thought that that was where they processed you out. But no sooner had I gone back than they said, "Well, you can wait in the cell right there." So I stepped back into the cell. The door was still open, and thirty seconds later, a cop in plainclothes walked back and said, "I'm from the San Francisco Police Department, and you're under arrest!"

"What kind of crap is this?" I said to myself. "These cats are really out to railroad me. I just got through posting bail. What the hell are they going to arrest me for now?"

They brought me back and put me in the city jail. They said they had a warrant from Connecticut on the trumped-up charges of murder, conspiracy to murder and kidnap, but they didn't actually get it until several days later. As soon as they had me in the county jail they dropped the phony "unlawful flight" charges. They just used that as a pretext to kidnap me.

Garry had put in a subpoena to get an assistant to Attorney General John Mitchell to appear but the judge revoked the subpoena, which I didn't dig. Here you are—you need to able to subpoena somebody and get some information and try to find out who's plotting what. But the power structure and the courts operate like that, they stick together against the individual who has certain rights. You have to have a right to subpoena a person. I don't give a darn if it's the President of the United States. He should be subpoenaed.

The reason we had subpoenaed one of Mitchell's assistants was that McTernan attempted to call the U.S. Department of Justice in Washington, D.C., and ask them some questions concerning the Chicago case that they had against me. They told him on the phone that this assistant attorney general, Victor Worheide, was in Connecticut. Worheide is the head of the special "Panther Unit" in the Justice Department. That was about a week before I was arrested, which puts the federal government there in Connecticut working in conjunction with the state and local officials of New Haven and Connecticut to plot this thing against me. So naturally we wanted to have him in court as a means of bringing out some of these erroneous charges. It also came to light in court the next day that there was no warrant out for me when I was arrested, but they had used this "unlawful flight to avoid prosecution" charge to hold me.

It didn't make any difference. They set a date for extradition and I was put in the San Francisco County Jail which is on the floor above the city jail. I sat up there for three weeks, and Garry visited me when he could, and McTernan would visit me and give me information. A few days after all this, McTernan came up and told me that it looked like Garry might have to go to the hospital. I'd have to send in a motion to Chicago that I wanted to have my lawyer, Garry, as the only lawyer to represent me. He was the one lawyer I had chosen, and the only one I had conferred with. I was to respectfully ask the court to postpone the date of the trial to a later date until my lawyer could appear. I also signed a document, by which I was informed that it was mandatory that Garry go into the hospital before he try another case, unless he wanted to risk his life.

Garry came to see me a couple of days later and told me that he had been in Chicago and that the judge had denied a postponement. He said the judge was going to try and choose a lawyer for me.

Dorothy Bryant

from Ella Price's Journal

Friday, no, I guess Saturday morning, 1 a.m., March 3

I STOOD ON THE CORNER OF BANCROFT AND ELSWORTH FOR ABOUT TWENTY MINUTES. I could hear the loudspeakers up on the university campus. People in twos and threes, sometimes in larger groups, brushed past me, going toward the sound of the loudspeakers. It was already dark. I didn't know what to do or even why I had come. Finally I started to walk, following the movement of larger and larger groups on both sides of the street, walking toward the sound of voices and applause, toward the lower plaza of the campus where the marchers would assemble.

The air was cold and damp, and most people had covered their heads with scarves or knitted caps. It was hard to see faces.

But on the campus the faces were all lit up by the bright lights above the playing field where the speeches were still going on. The faces looked happy, or at least calm and content. I don't know what I expected, but not so many smiles. People walked back and forth to keep warm and, I suppose, to look for familiar faces. The field was so crowded that I couldn't walk without brushing against people who constantly murmured, "Pardon me," or who just smiled as I brushed past. That was the first thing I noticed. I'd never been in a crowd of people who seemed so—is friendly the word? Not really, because no one spoke to me or tried to strike up an acquaintance. They were easy, relaxed, gentle. I can only think of the word "happy," and I know that's not right. I don't know a word to describe them. I don't think they were a special kind of people—they were just people. But maybe for tonight they had left behind their pettiness and discontent with the small details of life. They were all there for the same purpose, and each was glad that all the others were along. The larger the crowd, the more happy and polite they became, because each addition was more support and more reassurance. I was amazed. I didn't think there could be that many people against the war in the whole country.

The speakers stood on a platform surrounded by a few hundred people who stood still, listening. But beyond that cluster, many hundreds more walked back and forth, searching the faces of others, talking to friends, stopping occasionally to cock an ear toward the speakers' platform. Beyond them, on the edges of the moving crowd, were tables, a ring of tables labeled by various organizations, selling buttons and pamphlets and books. I went up close to the tables titled for communist groups. The young girls sitting behind them looked exactly like all the other young girls. Some boys walked around handing out leaflets; others carried cans, collecting money. A hot-dog stand was almost unidentifiable behind the mob that surrounded it. It was like a carnival, yet not like one. Here the atmosphere was warmer, closer.

I'd thought I might feel uncomfortable, but I didn't. I was completely anonymous—there was no chance of being seen by my family or neighbors; they wouldn't have been caught dead there. And there was the feeling of closeness. Everyone who was there belonged—the act of coming there made a person unquestionably a part of it all.

Inwardly I didn't quite feel a part of it. I didn't see how I could go through with it, especially alone—how I could actually get out into the street and march along with people looking at me, let alone heckling me. I couldn't do it, that was all, but maybe I could watch—and breathe in some of this unexpectedly good air, this free air. Was it the absence of fear that made the air so good?

Then people were moving out to the street, and I heard the speaker calling for monitors, the young people with ragged orange armbands. I followed one of them, knowing she would take me to where the march would start, where I could join spectators on the sidewalk and then decide what to do next.

The intersection at Bancroft and Telegraph was a thick mass of people, with policemen trying to clear a path for the escape of a couple of cars that had made the mistake of coming down Bancroft. The police were keeping all the people on the sidewalk and wouldn't let me cross the street. Finally I walked down Bancroft, threading my way through the crowds, went around the block and came up to Telegraph one block below the starting point of the march. The sidewalks were full of people. A boy crouched near a lamppost, beating on a long drum. A tall, long-haired boy making soft, reedy noises on wooden pipes was walking by. He stopped and stood leaning against the lamppost above the drummer and began improvising a melody to the rhythm of the drum. The drummer nodded without looking up. After a while the piper moved on. Then I saw people moving toward the curb and turning their heads toward the campus. It was starting. I moved forward and stood behind a brown-suited Negro policeman.

First came a red truck full of sound equipment. One boy drove, one sat with him in the cab and another hung on outside. Behind the red slats fencing the truck bed, young boys and girls stood, three or four of them, looking out at the people who looked at them from the curb. The only older person on the truck was a fat, bearded man in white shirt and pants. He was shaking bells and chanting.

"Who's that?" someone behind me said.

"Poet."

"What's he doing?"

"Getting rid of evil spirits, I think."

"But will it work on the Oakland cops?" I heard laughter.

About twenty feet behind the truck came the first line of marchers, five abreast, keeping to the right side of the street near the curb. They were all boys, one of them black. He looked at the Negro policeman and said, "Brother, what you doing in that uniform?" A few people laughed, including the policeman.

I began to look around at the people on the sidewalk, wondering why they were there. Most of them didn't look hostile, and I saw one of them move off the curb and join the march, then another and another. There were yells, "Hey, Jim" and "Lucy, wait up," as people recognized friends and moved into the march. I guess there were many people like me who had come alone and were looking for a familiar face before they joined in. I could wait until I saw someone I knew—that was one way of postponing action indefinitely.

In the meantime I began to enjoy watching the people go by, all kinds of people, moving in all kinds of ways and with all kinds of expressions on their faces. There were plenty of young people dripping with beads and hair, but even more families, middle-aged fathers and mothers with groups of young-sters who must have been their own children and those of their friends. A lot of older women alone, open-faced, matter-of-fact, intelligent-looking women. There were some quite old people, two or three in wheelchairs. Some of them talked among themselves, as if they were taking a casual stroll. Others walked silently, with a look of determination. A few of the younger people stared defiantly at those of us lining the curb. One little blonde girl (straight hair down to her hips) kept swinging her arms in a gathering gesture and saying to the spectators, "Come on, come on, what are you doing out there, come on along!" Most of the marchers didn't often look at the spectators and when they did, turned away quickly. There was a touch of embarrassment in it for most people. That comforted me. They seemed to feel just as I would in their places.

I began to envy them. I leaned over the curb, longing to step off and join them, but I could not quite do it. I began walking along the sidewalk, moving with the march but not in it, afraid to join it but wanting to be part of it. There were others doing the same thing, the ambivalent, drawn along the edges as if by a magnet.

I stopped behind some men who were arguing loudly. "Bunch of cow-ards, send them to Russia; go to China, traitors, draft dodgers!" one of them kept yelling.

"If you're so hot for this war," said the man next to him, "why aren't you over there? They'll take volunteers—even your age." A few people laughed, and the first man looked around as if he wanted to hit someone. Then he turned to me, sizing me up quickly and evidently deciding I was respectable.

"What do you think, lady, it's a disgrace, isn't it, what this country has come to?"

"Yes," I said. "I think it is."

Then I took a deep breath and stepped off the curb.

The little blonde girl was coming by again, and she cried, "Peace!" as her arm swept me into a place next to her. Then she floated off again, still exhorting people to join.

My first feeling as I walked along was fear, a deep, cold blast of panic chilling my insides while I asked myself, What are you doing, you idiot? Now you've done it, stupid!

Done what?

Gotten out in the middle of the street to make a fool of yourself as publicly as possible. Why are you doing this?

Because I'm against the war.

Why?

I'm not sure. I never even thought about it until a couple of months ago. I still don't know much about it. But I think it's wrong.

And you're marching in the street because you've tried everything else—letter to your congressman, etcetera—and none of it worked?

No, I didn't try anything else.

Nothing else?

No.

Never written a letter? Never worked to elect someone who'd change things? Never even licked a stamp?

Never.

Oh, those things weren't dramatic enough?

No, it wasn't that, it was just that I never thought much about such things.

Never thought. What makes you think you're thinking now?

I kept looking at the ground. I couldn't seem to raise my eyes; I just watched my own feet taking slow steps forward. Then I thought, Don't walk like you're ashamed of yourself. Straighten up, raise your head, look people in the eye. Now's no time to look sheepish. I raised my head and looked as steadily as I could at the people lining the streets. The faces were friendly, a little uncertain, a little sheepish as I looked at them, and a little envious. They were out, and I was in.

Someone handed me a candle and a paper cup. A man walking beside me showed me how to light the candle, drop a bit of wax in the bottom of the cup and make the candle stand up in the cup. I felt better carrying the candle. It seemed to add dignity to our shuffling along, bunching up behind red traffic lights, being herded close to the curb by monitors.

I noticed men running back and forth along our sides, snapping pictures as fast as they could. They didn't look like newspaper men, and they seemed to be photographing everyone and everything as fast as they could. The man next to me shrugged toward one of them. "You are now in the files of the F.B.I." I started turning away whenever I saw one of the men—there must have been dozens of them—snapping pictures. But then I saw it was futile and tried to ignore them.

"Candles out. Candles out," said a monitor. "We didn't issue those candles. Candles out."

"But I like carrying it anyway," I said.

"It lights up your face," said the man who had spoken before, "so they get a clearer picture of you."

"Don't be so paranoid," said a woman behind us.

But we all blew out our candles and walked silently for a few seconds until a girl on the end of my row said "Nobody'd better publish a picture of me—my mother doesn't know I smoke." We all burst into laughter, a loud release that took away my tension and made me see how funny it all was. At that point I stopped feeling afraid, and a whole new mood came over me, like the feeling I first had in the crowd, but different. I felt calm and peaceful. And pure. Pure in the sense of being concentrated, free of distractions and anxieties. I felt right—not self-righteous, not smugly correct, not right while others are wrong; I don't mean that. Just right, like a piece of tile dropped into place, perfectly fitting its place in a design. And warm with closeness to the people walking beside me, not physical closeness, something more. Something I had missed all my life without knowing it existed.

The crowds along the sides of the street thinned out as Telegraph Avenue widened into a thoroughfare and cars went by, slowing down briefly to look at us, then speeding up again. Now it was just a cold, dark walk on the side of the street near the gutter. We moved slowly. I could hear the sound truck up ahead but couldn't make out the words. I saw some people leaving the march and hurrying along the sidewalks, probably to rejoin it nearer the front. I decided to do the same thing. As I reached the sidewalk I looked back toward the campus. As far as I could see there were more and more coming, five abreast and thickly crowded.

I went back into the ranks of marchers about seven rows from the front.

"You don't think they'll let us through?"

"Hell, no, they'll stop us at the Oakland line. They say there's a hundred police up there."

"They can't do that, we got a right—"

"They still going to crack your head. Then three months from now some judge'll say you had a right. But you still got a cracked head."

"Anyone hits me going to get hit back, cop or no cop."

"I'm not afraid."

I am, I thought. I almost ran away then. I was still only a few blocks from my car and could have been home within a few minutes. I moved back onto the sidewalk, that step up the curb now separating me again from the demonstrators. I could be just a spectator, or an uninterested woman merely walking to her car. I moved toward a side street, but then I stopped and looked back. I didn't want to leave yet. People were starting to sing, some were walking arm in arm, some were clowning and showing off for the TV cameras. But underneath was a hum of fear as we got nearer to the Oakland line. Everyone had read the newspaper. Everyone knew the police would be waiting there. And nobody knew what would happen. I think that, except for the boys in the front, everyone felt the way I did.

I decided to move ahead, as I had before. I could walk on the sidewalk, up to the Oakland line, and see what was there. If it looked dangerous, I would turn off and go to my car. If not, I could rejoin the march. I began to walk fast, past the first line of marchers, past the red sound truck, past the television car moving slowly in front with cameramen perched on the trunk and facing back toward the marchers. I thought there would be fewer people up ahead, but the streets and sidewalks were becoming more and more crowded. After another block, I was moving from one side to the other, getting nowhere, picking my way around people on the sidewalk who were looking into the street. The street was packed with what looked like hundreds of boys—I couldn't figure out what they were doing there—just milling around. Finally I could hardly move at all, in any direction. I managed to get to the corner, went down a side street, then along a parallel street for two blocks; then I was in Oakland, and I turned back up toward Telegraph Avenue, beyond the Oakland line.

I came up behind the Oakland policemen, standing three deep in a row which stretched across the street where the sign said ENTERING OAKLAND, forming a human barrier. They stood with their hands behind their backs, grasping clubs and facing toward Berkeley. I could see nothing beyond those broad backs. All around me people were hanging out of windows. Some boys had climbed poles and clung, facing Berkeley. Others stood on top of cars. Everything was quite still as everyone watched.

"What's happening?" I asked.

"Fighting, I think," someone said.

Who fighting who? The police were just standing there, and the marchers were still two blocks back. I went up behind the police, but twenty feet from them I was stopped by a policeman who was walking back and forth, keeping everyone clear of the backs of the police.

"What's going on, officer?" I asked, with my most respectable suburban matron's manner. But he just gave me a disgusted look and waved me back. I didn't fool him. If I were a respectable suburban matron, his look said, I'd be home where I belonged.

I moved back again, looking at the rows of blue-shirted backs, unable to see a thing past them. Finally I saw someone slide down from the hood of a parked truck. I took off my shoes, scrambled up on it and stood up.

For a full block beyond the rows of policeman, the street was thick with boys and men. Some of them carried sticks, and others held objects in their hands that I couldn't see. They too faced toward Berkeley, toward the red truck which had stopped in the intersection just beyond them, facing them. Down nearer to the truck I saw hands raised as if the boys were waving or throwing things. All were shouting. Beyond the truck I saw the crowds of marchers, stopped and spreading out behind the truck, some shouting back. The police stood in a stolid line. The TV cameras had vanished.

I finally understood what was happening. Hundreds of boys and men, hecklers, filled the streets between the marchers and the police. The police watched them throwing things at the marchers but did nothing. They would let these rowdies attack the marchers. Their only concern was to hold the Oakland line. Boys were rushing toward the truck, throwing things and waving long sticks. The blue line never wavered. I could hear the sound truck now. "Hey, you guys, don't you know we're doing this for you?" This only brought on an angry shout and more throwing.

Then the sound truck began addressing the marchers. "We're going to turn. We're turning off." The roar from the front rows was as angry as the one that had come from the hecklers. The loudspeaker went on. "I don't care what you call me. You may be all ready for a fight, but we've got thousands of people behind us there, people who never hit the streets before; they're still leaving the campus. Still leaving the campus! You want a bloody mess or you want to build a movement? Build a movement? Turn off. This march is turning off here. If you cannot turn off here, you are no longer a part of this march. Turn. Turn off here. Turn." Then I could hear the poet chanting into the microphone.

The sound truck stayed where it was, repeating its message to turn off, shielding the marchers from the hecklers who were now moving on them. "All monitors up front. The march will turn off here. All monitors up front." The orange-armbanded boys and girls formed a line across the street, holding hands, to hold off the hecklers. They made a strange contrast to the blue line. I saw the little blonde girl in the midst of the line, her arms stretched outward in a position of crucifixion. A young heckler ran toward her and raised a club. "We love you!" she yelled, and I held my breath as he shook the club over her head, but he did not bring it down and finally walked off, swearing and shaking his club at the line of monitors.

I got down from the truck and walked back around the block, retracing my steps until I could rejoin the march, now turning west, down a dark side street, where windows opened and black faces appeared. All tension was gone. Even ranks had loosened, and marchers spread out, covering the entire street and sidewalks.

"Ella?"

I jumped at the sound of my name. It was Laura. She was smiling and said, "If I'd known you were coming ..."

"I didn't decide until the last minute."

"You alone?"

"Yes."

She put her arm through mine and we stepped back into the march together, walking along, saying nothing. Someone started singing "We Shall Overcome." Others joined in. Everyone sang softly, but the hundreds of soft voices combined filled the dark air. Timidly, I joined too, humming along, feeling again the closeness, the clear, pure rightness.

Anthony Boucher

🦋 The Compleat Werewolf

The Professor glanced at the note:

> Don't be silly—Gloria.

Wolfe Wolf crumpled the sheet of paper into a yellow ball and hurled it out the window into the sunshine of the bright campus spring. He made several choice and profane remarks in fluent Middle High German.

Emily looked up from typing the proposed budget for the departmental library. "I'm afraid I didn't understand that, Professor Wolf. I'm weak on Middle High."

"Just improvising," said Wolf, and sent a copy of the *Journal of English and Germanic Philology* to follow the telegram.

Emily rose from the typewriter. "There's something the matter. Did the committee reject your monograph on Hager?"

"That monumental contribution to human knowledge? Oh, no. Nothing so important as that."

"But you're so upset—"

"The office wife!" Wolf snorted. "And pretty damned polyandrous at that, with the whole department on your hands. Go away."

Emily's dark little face lit up with a flame of righteous anger that removed any trace of plainness. "Don't talk to me like that, Mr. Wolf. I'm simply trying to help you. And it isn't the whole department. It's—"

Professor Wolf picked up an inkwell, looked after the telegram and the *Journal*, then set the glass pot down again. "No. There are better ways of going to pieces. Sorrows drown easier than they smash. Get Herbrecht to take my two-o'clock, will you?"

"Where are you going?"

"To hell in sectors. So long."

"Wait. Maybe I can help you. Remember when the dean jumped you for serving drinks to students? Maybe I can—"

Wolf stood in the doorway and extended one arm impressively, pointing with that curious index which was as long as the middle finger. "Madam, academically you are indispensable. You are the prop and stay of the existence of this department. But at the moment this department can go to hell, where it will doubtless continue to need your invaluable services."

"But don't you see—" Emily's voice shook. "No. Of course not. You wouldn't see. You're just a man—no, not even a man. You're just Professor Wolf. You're Woof-woof."

Wolf staggered. "I'm what?"

"Woof-woof. That's what everybody calls you because your name's Wolfe Wolf. All your students, everybody. But you wouldn't notice a thing like that. Oh, no. Woof-woof, that's what you are."

"This," said Wolfe Wolf, "is the crowning blow. My heart is breaking, my world is shattered, I've got to walk a mile from the campus to find a bar; but all this isn't enough. I've got to be called Woof-woof. Goodbye!"

He turned, and in the doorway caromed into a vast and yielding bulk, which gave out with a noise that might have been either a greeting of "Wolf!" or more probably an inevitable grunt of "Oof!"

Wolf backed into the room and admitted Professor Fearing, paunch, pince-nez, cane and all. The older man waddled over to his desk, plumped himself down, and exhaled a long breath. "My dear boy," he gasped. "Such impetuosity."

"Sorry, Oscar."

"Ah, youth—" Professor Fearing fumbled about for a handkerchief, found none, and proceeded to polish his pince-nez on his somewhat stringy necktie. "But why such haste to depart? And why is Emily crying?"

"Is she?"

"You see?" said Emily hopelessly, and muttered "Woof-woof" into her damp handkerchief.

"And why do copies of the JEGP fly about my head as I harmlessly cross the campus? Do we have teleportation on our hands?"

"Sorry," Wolf repeated curtly. "Temper. Couldn't stand that ridiculous argument of Glocke's. Goodbye."

"One moment." Professor Fearing fished into one of his unnumbered handkerchiefless pockets and produced a sheet of yellow paper. "I believe this is yours?"

Wolf snatched at it and quickly converted it into confetti.

Fearing chuckled. "How well I remember when Gloria was a student here! I was thinking of it only last night when I saw her in *Moonbeams and Melody*. How she did upset this whole department! Heavens, my boy, if I'd been a younger man myself—"

"I'm going. You'll see about Herbrecht, Emily?"

Emily sniffled and nodded.

"Come, Wolfe." Fearing's voice had grown more serious. "I didn't mean to plague you. But you mustn't take these things too hard. There are better ways of finding consolation than in losing your temper or getting drunk."

"Who said anything about—"

"Did you need to say it? No, my boy, if you were to— You're not a religious man, are you?"

"Good God, no," said Wolf contradictorily.

"If only you were.... If I might make a suggestion, Wolfe, why don't you come over to the Temple tonight? We're having very special services. They might take your mind off Glo—off your troubles."

"Thanks, no. I've always meant to visit your Temple—I've heard the damnedest rumors about it—but not tonight. Some other time."

"Tonight would be especially interesting."

"Why? What's so special of a feast day about April thirtieth?"

Fearing shook his gray head. "It is shocking how ignorant a scholar can be outside of his chosen field.... But you know the place, Wolfe; I'll hope to see you there tonight."

"Thanks. But my troubles don't need any supernatural solutions. A couple of zombies will do nicely, and I do *not* mean serviceable stiffs. Good-bye, Oscar." He was halfway through the door before he added as an afterthought, "'Bye, Emily."

"Such rashness," Fearing murmured. "Such impetuosity. Youth is a wonderful thing to enjoy, is it not, Emily?"

Emily said nothing, but plunged into typing the proposed budget as though all the fiends of hell were after her, as indeed many of them were.

The sun was setting, and Wolf's tragic account of his troubles had laid an egg, too. The bartender had polished every glass in the joint and still the repetitive tale kept pouring forth. He was torn between a boredom new even in his experience and a professional admiration for a customer who could consume zombies indefinitely.

"Did I tell you about the time she flunked the mid-term?" Wolf demanded truculently.

"Only three times," said the bartender.

"All right, then; I'll tell you. Yunnerstand, I don't do things like this. Profeshical ethons, that's what's I've got. But this was different. This wasn't like somebody that doesn't know just because she doesn't know; this was a girl that didn't know because she wasn't the kind of girl that has to know the kind of things a girl has to know if she's the kind of girl that ought to know that kind of things. Yunnerstand?"

The bartender cast a calculating glance at the plump little man who sat alone at the end of the deserted bar, carefully nursing his gin-and-tonic.

"She made me see that. She made me see lossa things and I can still see the things she made me see the things. It wasn't just like a professor falls for a coed, yunnerstand? This was different. This was wunnaful. This was like a whole new life, like."

The bartender sidled down to the end of the bar. "Brother," he whispered softly.

The little man with the odd beard looked up from his gin-and-tonic. "Yes, colleague?"

"If I listen to that potted professor another five minutes, I'm going to start smashing up the joint. How's about slipping down there and standing in for me, huh?"

The little man looked Wolf over and fixed his gaze especially on the hand that clenched the tall zombie glass. "Gladly, colleague," he nodded.

The bartender sighed a gust of relief.

"She was Youth," Wolf was saying intently to where the bartender had stood. "But it wasn't just that. This was different. She was Life and Excitement and Joy and Ecstasy and stuff. Yunner—" He broke off and stared at the empty space. "*Uh*-mazing!" he observed. "Right before my very eyes. *Uh*-mazing!"

"You were saying, colleague?" the plump little man prompted from the adjacent stool.

Wolf turned. "So there you are. Did I tell you about the time I went to her house to check her term paper?"

"No. But I have a feeling you will."

"Howja know? Well, this night—"

The little man drank slowly; but his glass was empty by the time Wolf had finished the account of an evening of pointlessly tentative flirtation. Other customers were drifting in, and the bar was now about a third full.

"—and ever since then—" Wolf broke off sharply. "That isn't you," he objected.

"I think it is, colleague."

"But you're a bartender and *you* aren't a bartender."

"No. I'm a magician."

"Oh. That explains it. Now, like I was telling you— Hey! Your bald is beard."

"I beg your pardon?"

"Your bald is beard. Just like your head. It's all jussa fringe running around."

"I like it that way."

"And your glass is empty."

"That's all right too."

"Oh, no it isn't. It isn't every night you get to drink with a man that proposed to Gloria Garton and got turned down. This is an occasion for celebration." Wolf thumped loudly on the bar and held up his first two fingers.

The little man regarded their equal length. "No," he said softly. "I think I'd better not. I know my capacity. If I have another—well, things might start happening."

"Lettemappen!"

"No. Please, colleague. I'd rather—"

The bartender brought the drinks. "Go on, brother," he whispered. "Keep him quiet. I'll do you a favor sometime."

Reluctantly the little man sipped at his fresh gin-and-tonic.

The professor took a gulp of his nth zombie. "My name's Woof-woof," he proclaimed. "Lots of people call me Wolfe Wolf. They think that's funny. But it's really Woof-woof. Wazoors?"

The other paused a moment to decipher that Arabic-sounding word, then said, "Mine's Ozymandias the Great."

"That's a funny name."

"I told you, I'm a magician. Only I haven't worked for a long time. Theatrical managers are peculiar, colleague. They don't want a real magician. They won't even let me show 'em my best stuff. Why, I remember one night in Darjeeling—"

"Glad to meet you, Mr.... Mr.—"

"You can call me Ozzy. Most people do."

"Glad to meet you, Ozzy. Now, about this girl. This Gloria. Yunnerstand, donya?"

"Sure, colleague."

"She thinks being a professor of German is nothing. She wants something glamorous. She says if I was an actor, now, or a G-man—Yunnerstand?"

Ozymandias the Great nodded.

"Awright, then! So yunnerstand. Fine. But whatddayou want to keep talking about it for? Yunnerstand. That's that. To hell with it."

Ozymandias' round and fringed face brightened. "Sure," he said, and added recklessly, "Let's drink to that."

They clinked glasses and drank. Wolf carelessly tossed off a toast in Old Low Frankish, with an unpardonable error in the use of the genitive.

The two men next to them began singing "My Wild Irish Rose," but trailed off disconsolately. "What we need," said the one with the derby, "is a tenor."

"What I need," Wolf muttered, "is a cigarette."

"Sure," said Ozymandias the Great. The bartender was drawing beer directly in front of them. Ozymandias reached across the bar, removed a lighted cigarette from the barkeep's ear, and handed it to his companion.

"Where'd that come from?"

"I don't quite know. All I know is how to get them. I told you I was a magician."

"Oh. I see. Pressajijijation."

"No. Not a prestidigitator; I said a magician. Oh, blast it! I've done it again. More than one gin-and-tonic and I start showing off."

"I don't believe you," said Wolf flatly. "No such thing as magicians. That's just as silly as Oscar Fearing and his Temple and what's so special about April thirtieth anyway?"

The bearded man frowned. "Please, colleague. Let's forget it."

"No. I don't believe you. You pressajijijated that cigarette. You didn't magic it." His voice began to rise. "You're a fake."

"Please, brother," the barkeep whispered. "Keep him quiet."

"All right," said Ozymandias wearily. "I'll show you something that can't be prestidigitation." The couple adjoining had begun to sing again. "They need a tenor. All right; listen!"

And the sweetest, most ineffably Irish tenor ever heard joined in on the duet. The singers didn't worry about the source; they simply accepted the new voice gladly and were spurred on to their very best, with the result that the bar knew the finest harmony it had heard since the night the Glee Club was suspended en masse.

Wolf looked impressed, but shook his head. "That's not magic either. That's ventrocolism."

"As a matter of strict fact, that was a street singer who was killed in the Easter Rebellion. Fine fellow, too; never heard a better voice, unless it was that night in Darjeeling when—"

"Fake!" said Wolfe Wolf loudly and belligerently.

Ozymandias once more contemplated that long index finger. He looked at the professor's dark brows that met in a straight line over his nose. He picked his companion's limpish hand off the bar and scrutinized the palm. The growth of hair was not marked, but it was perceptible.

The magician chortled. "And you sneer at magic!"

"Whasso funny about me sneering at magic?"

Ozymandias lowered his voice. "Because, my fine furry friend, you are a werewolf."

The Irish martyr had begun "Rose of Tralee," and the two mortals were joining in valiantly.

"I'm what?"

"A werewolf."

"But there isn't any such thing. Any fool knows that."

"Fools," said Ozymandias, "know a great deal which the wise do not. There are werewolves. There always have been, and quite probably always will be." He spoke as calmly and assuredly as though he were mentioning that the earth was round. "And there are three infallible physical signs: the meeting of eyebrows, the long index finger, the hairy palms. You have all three. And even your name is an indication. Family names do not come from nowhere. Every Smith has an ancestor somewhere who was a smith. Every Fisher comes from a family that once fished. And your name is Wolf."

The statement was so quiet, so plausible, that Wolf faltered.

"But a werewolf is a man that changes into a wolf. I've never done that. Honest I haven't."

"A mammal," said Ozymandias, "is an animal that bears its young alive and suckles them. A virgin is nonetheless a mammal. Because you have never changed does not make you any the less a werewolf."

"But a werewolf—" Suddenly Wolf's eyes lit up. "A werewolf! But that's even better than a G-man! Now I can show Gloria!"

"What on earth do you mean, colleague?"

Wolf was climbing down from his stool. The intense excitement of this brilliant new idea seemed to have sobered him. He grabbed the little man by the sleeve. "Come on. We're going to find a nice quiet place. And you're going to prove you're a magician."

"But how?"

"You're going to show me how to change!"

Ozymandias finished his gin-and-tonic, and with it drowned his last regretful hesitation. "Colleague," he announced, "you're on!"

Professor Oscar Fearing, standing behind the curiously carved lectern of the Temple of the Dark Truth, concluded the reading of the prayer with mumbling sonority. "And on this night of all nights, in the name of the black light that glows in the darkness, we give thanks!" He closed the parchment-bound book and faced the small congregation, calling out with fierce intensity, "Who wishes to give his thanks to the Lower Lord?"

A cushioned dowager rose. "I give thanks!" she shrilled excitedly. "My

Ming Choy was sick, even unto death. I took of her blood and offered it to the Lower Lord, and he had mercy and restored her to me!"

Behind the altar an electrician checked his switches and spat disgustedly. "Bugs! Every last one of 'em!"

The man who was struggling into a grotesque and horrible costume paused and shrugged. "They pay good money. What's it to us if they're bugs?"

A tall, thin old man had risen uncertainly to his feet. "I give thanks!" he cried. "I give thanks to the Lower Lord that I have finished my great work. My protective screen against magnetic bombs is a tried and proven success, to the glory of our country and science and the Lord."

"Crackpot," the electrician muttered.

The man in costume peered around the altar. "Crackpot, hell. That's Chiswick from the physics department. Think of a man like that falling for this stuff! And listen to him: He's even telling about the government's plans for installation. You know, I'll bet you one of these fifth columnists could pick up something around here."

There was silence in the Temple when the congregation had finished its thanksgiving. Professor Fearing leaned over the lectern and spoke quietly and impressively. "As you know, brothers in Darkness, tonight is May Eve, the thirtieth of April, the night consecrated by the Church to that martyr missionary St. Walpurgis, and by us to other and deeper purposes. It is on this night, and this night only, that we may directly give our thanks to the Lower Lord himself. Not in wanton orgy and obscenity, as the Middle Ages misconceived his desires, but in praise and in the deep, dark joy that issues forth from Blackness."

"Hold your hats, boys," said the man in the costume. "Here I go again."

"*Eka!*" Fearing thundered. "*Dva yri chatur! Pancha! Shas sapta! Ashta nava dasha ekadasha!*" He paused. There was always the danger that at this moment some scholar in this university town might recognize that the invocation, though perfect Sanskrit, consisted solely of the numbers from one to eleven. But no one stirred, and he launched forth in more apposite Latin: "*Per vota nostra ipse nunc surgat nobis dicatus Baal Zebub!*"

"Baal Zebub!" the congregation chorused.

"Cue," said the electrician, and pulled a switch.

The lights flickered and went out. Lightning played across the sanctuary. Suddenly out of the darkness came a sharp bark, a yelp of pain, and a long-drawn howl of triumph.

A blue light now began to glow dimly. In its faint reflection, the electrician was amazed to see his costumed friend at his side, nursing his bleeding hand.

"What the hell—" the electrician whispered.

"Hanged if I know. I go out there on cue, all ready to make my terrifying appearance, and what happens? Great big hell of a dog up and nips my hand. Why didn't they tell me they'd switched the script?"

In the glow of the blue light the congregation reverently contemplated the plump little man with the fringe of beard and the splendid gray wolf that stood beside him. "Hail, O Lower Lord!" resounded the chorus, drowning out one spinster's murmur of "But my *dear*, I swear he was *much* handsomer last year."

"Colleagues!" said Ozymandias the Great, and there was utter silence, a dread hush awaiting the momentous words of the Lower Lord. Ozymandias took one step forward, placed his tongue carefully between his lips, uttered the ripest, juiciest raspberry of his career, and vanished, wolf and all.

Wolfe Wolf opened his eyes and shut them again hastily. He had never expected the quiet and sedate Berkeley Inn to install centrifugal rooms. It wasn't fair. He lay in darkness, waiting for the whirling to stop and trying to reconstruct the past night.

He remembered the bar all right, and the zombies. And the bartender. Very sympathetic chap that, up until he suddenly changed into a little man with a fringe of beard. That was where things began getting strange. There was something about a cigarette and an Irish tenor and a werewolf. Fantastic idea, that. Any fool knows—

Wolf sat up suddenly. He *was* the werewolf. He threw back the bedclothes and stared down at his legs. Then he sighed relief. They were long legs. They were hairy enough. They were brown from much tennis. But they were indisputably human.

He got up, resolutely stifling his qualms, and began to pick up the clothing that was scattered nonchalantly about the floor. A crew of gnomes was excavating his skull, but he hoped they might go away if he didn't pay too much attention to them. One thing was certain: he was going to be good from now on. Gloria or no Gloria, heartbreak or no heartbreak, drowning your sorrows wasn't good enough. If you felt like this and could imagine you'd been a werewolf—

But why should he have imagined it in such detail? So many fragmentary memories seemed to come back as he dressed. Going up Strawberry Canyon with the fringed beard, finding a desolate and isolated spot for magic, learning the words—

Hell, he could even remember the words. The word that changed you and the one that changed you back.

Had he made up those words, too, in his drunken imaginings? And had he made up what he could only barely recall—the wonderful, magical freedom of changing, the single, sharp pang of alteration and then the boundless happiness of being lithe and fleet and free?

He surveyed himself in the mirror. Save for the unwonted wrinkles in his conservative single-breasted gray suit, he looked exactly what he was: a quiet academician; a little better built, a little more impulsive, a little more romantic than most, perhaps, but still just that—Professor Wolf.

The rest was nonsense. But there was, that impulsive side of him suggested, only one way of proving the fact. And that was to say The Word.

"All right," said Wolfe Wolf to his reflection. "I'll show you." And he said it.

The pang was sharper and stronger than he'd remembered. Alcohol numbs you to pain. It tore him for a moment with an anguish like the descriptions of childbirth. Then it was gone, and he flexed his limbs in happy amazement. But he was not a lithe, fleet, free beast. He was a helplessly trapped wolf, irrevocably entangled in a conservative single-breasted gray suit.

He tried to rise and walk, but the long sleeves and legs tripped him over flat on his muzzle. He kicked with his paws, trying to tear his way out, and then stopped. Werewolf or no werewolf, he was likewise still Professor Wolf, and this suit had cost thirty-five dollars. There must be some cheaper way of securing freedom than tearing the suit to shreds.

He used several good, round Low German expletives. This was a complication that wasn't in any of the werewolf legends he'd ever read. There, people just—boom!—became wolves or—bang!—became men again. When they were men, they wore clothes; when they were wolves, they wore fur. Just like Hyperman becoming Bark Lent again on top of the Empire State Building

132

and finding his street clothes right there. Most misleading. He began to re-member now how Ozymandias the Great had made him strip before teaching him the words—

The words! That was it. All he had to do was say the word that changed you back—*Absarka!*—and he'd be a man again, comfortably fitted inside his suit. Then he could strip and play what games he wished. You see? Reason solves all. "*Absarka!*" he said.

Or thought he said. He went through all the proper mental processes for saying *Absarka!* but all that came out of his muzzle was a sort of clicking whine. And he was still a conservatively dressed and helpless wolf.

This was worse than the clothes problem. If he could be released only by saying *Absarka!* and if, being a wolf, he could say nothing, why, there he was. Indefinitely. He could go find Ozzy and ask—but how could a wolf wrapped up in a gray suit get safely out of a hotel and set out hunting for an unknown address?

He was trapped. He was lost. He was—

"*Absarka!*"

Professor Wolfe Wolf stood up in his grievously rumpled gray suit and beamed on the beard-fringed face of Ozymandias the Great.

"You see, colleague," the little magician explained, "I figured you'd want to try it again as soon as you got up, and I knew darned well you'd have your troubles. Thought I'd come over and straighten things out for you."

Wolf lit a cigarette in silence and handed the pack to Ozymandias. "When you came in just now," he said at last, "what did you see?"

"You as a wolf."

"Then it really— I actually—"

"Sure. You're a full-fledged werewolf, all right."

Wolf sat down on the rumpled bed. "I guess," he ventured slowly, "I've got to believe it. And if I believe that— But it means I've got to believe everything I've always scorned. I've got to believe in gods and devils and hells and—"

"You needn't be so pluralistic. But there is a God." Ozymandias said this as calmly and convincingly as he had stated last night that there were werewolves.

"And if there's a God, then I've got a soul?"

"Sure."

"And if I'm a werewolf— Hey!"

"What's the trouble, colleague?"

"All right, Ozzy. You know everything. Tell me this: Am I damned?"

"For what? Just for being a werewolf? Shucks, no; let me explain. There's two kinds of werewolves. There's the cursed kind that can't help themselves, that just go turning into wolves without any say in the matter; and there's the voluntary kind like you. Now, most of the voluntary kind are damned, sure, because they're wicked men who lust for blood and eat innocent people. But they aren't damnably wicked because they're werewolves; they became werewolves because they are damnably wicked. Now, you changed yourself just for the hell of it and because it looked like a good way to impress a gal; that's an innocent-enough motive, and being a werewolf doesn't make it any less so. Werewolves don't have to be monsters; it's just that we hear about only the ones that are."

"But how can I be voluntary when you told me I was a werewolf before I ever changed?"

"Not everybody can change. It's like being able to roll your tongue or wiggle your ears. You can, or you can't; and that's that. And as with those abilities, there's probably a genetic factor involved, though nobody's done any serious research on it. You were a werewolf *in posse*; now you're one *in esse*."

"Then it's all right? I can be a werewolf just for having fun, and it's safe?"

"Absolutely."

Wolf chortled. "Will I show Gloria! Dull and unglamorous indeed! Anybody can marry an actor or a G-man; but a werewolf—"

"Your children probably will be, too," said Ozymandias cheerfully.

Wolf shut his eyes dreamily, then opened them with a start. "You know what?"

"What?"

"I haven't got a hangover anymore! This is marvelous. This is— Why, this is practical. At last the perfect hangover cure. Shuffle yourself into a wolf and back and— Oh, that reminds me. How do I get back?"

"*Absarka.*"

"I know. But when I'm a wolf I can't say it."

"That," said Ozymandias sadly, "is the curse of being a white magician. You keep having to use the second-best form of spells, because the best would be black. Sure, a black-magic werebeast can turn himself back whenever he wants to. I remember in Darjeeling—"

"But how about me?"

"That's the trouble. You have to have somebody to say *Absarka!* for you. That's what I did last night, or do you remember? After we broke up the party at your friend's Temple— Tell you what, I'm retired now, and I've got enough to live on modestly because I can always magic up a little— Are you going to take up werewolfing seriously?"

"For a while, anyway. Till I get Gloria."

"Then why shouldn't I come and live here in your hotel? Then I'll always be handy to *Absarka!* you. After you get the girl, you can teach her."

Wolf extended his hand. "Noble of you. Shake." And then his eye caught his wrist watch. "Good Lord! I've missed two classes this morning. Werewolfing's all very well, but a man's got to work for his living."

"Most men." Ozymandias calmly reached his hand into the air and plucked a coin. He looked at it ruefully; it was a gold moidore. "Hang these spirits; I simply cannot explain to them about gold being illegal."

From Los Angeles, Wolf thought, with the habitual contempt of the northern Californian, as he surveyed the careless sport coat and the bright-yellow shirt of his visitor.

This young man rose politely as the professor entered the office. His green eyes gleamed cordially and his red hair glowed in the spring sunlight. "Professor Wolf?" he asked.

Wolf glanced impatiently at his desk. "Yes."

"O'Breen's the name. I'd like to talk to you a minute."

"My office hours are from three to four Tuesdays and Thursdays. I'm afraid I'm rather busy now."

"This isn't faculty business. And it's important." The young man's attitude was affable and casual, but he managed nonetheless to convey a sense of urgency that piqued Wolf's curiosity. The all-important letter to Gloria had waited while he took two classes; it could wait another five minutes.

"Very well, Mr. O'Breen."

"And alone, if you please."

Wolf himself hadn't noticed that Emily was in the room. He now turned to the secretary and said, "All right. If you don't mind, Emily—"

Emily shrugged and went out.

"Now, sir. What is this important and secret business?"

"Just a question or two. To start with, how well do you know Gloria Garton?"

Wolf paused. You could hardly say, "Young man, I am about to re-propose to her in view of my becoming a werewolf." Instead he simply said—the truth, if not the whole truth—"She was a pupil of mine a few years ago."

"I said *do*, not *did*. How well do you know her now?"

"And why should I bother to answer such a question?" The young man handed over a card. Wolf read:

FERGUS O'BREEN

Private Inquiry Agent

Licensed by the State of California

Wolf smiled. "And what does this mean? Divorce evidence? Isn't that the usual field of private inquiry agents?"

"Miss Garton isn't married, as you probably know very well. I'm just asking if you've been in touch with her much lately."

"And I'm simply asking why you should want to know."

O'Breen rose and began to pace around the office. "We don't seem to be getting very far, do we? I'm to take it that you refuse to state the nature of your relations with Gloria Garton?"

"I see no reason why I should do otherwise." Wolf was beginning to be annoyed.

To his surprise, the detective relaxed into a broad grin. "OK. Let it ride. Tell me about your department. How long have the various faculty members been here?"

"Instructors and all?"

"Just the professors."

"I've been here for seven years. All the others at least a good ten, probably more. If you want exact figures, you can probably get them from the dean, unless, as I hope"—Wolf smiled cordially—"he throws you out flat on your red pate."

O'Breen laughed. "Professor, I think we could get on. One more question, and you can do some pate-tossing yourself. Are you an American citizen?"

"Of course."

"And the rest of the department?"

"All of them. And now would you have the common decency to give me some explanation of this fantastic farrago of questions?"

"No," said O'Breen casually. "Goodbye, professor." His alert green eyes had been roaming about the room, sharply noticing everything. Now, as he left, they rested on Wolf's long index finger, moved up to his heavy meeting eyebrows, and returned to the finger. There was a suspicion of a startled realization in those eyes as he left the office.

But that was nonsense, Wolf told himself. A private detective, no matter how shrewd his eyes, no matter how apparently meaningless his inquiries, would surely be the last man on earth to notice the signs of lycanthropy.

Funny. "Werewolf" was a word you could accept. You could say, "I'm a werewolf," and it was all right. But say "I am a lycanthrope" and your flesh crawled. Odd. Possibly material for a paper on the influence of etymology on connotation for one of the learned periodicals.

But, hell! Wolfe Wolf was no longer primarily a scholar. He was a werewolf now, a white-magic werewolf, a werewolf-for-fun; and fun he was going to have. He lit his pipe, stared at the blank paper on his desk, and tried desperately to draft a letter to Gloria. It should hint at just enough to fascinate her and hold her interest until he could go south when the term ended and reveal to her the whole wonderful new truth. It—

Professor Oscar Fearing grunted his ponderous way into the office. "Good afternoon, Wolfe. Hard at it, my boy?"

"Afternoon," Wolf replied distractedly, and continued to stare at the paper.

"Great events coming, eh? Are you looking forward to seeing the glorious Gloria?"

Wolf started. "How— What do you mean?"

Fearing handed him a folded newspaper. "You hadn't heard?"

Wolf read with growing amazement and delight:

GLORIA GARTON TO ARRIVE FRIDAY
Local Girl Returns to Berkeley

As part of the most spectacular talent hunt since the search for Scarlett O'Hara, Gloria Garton, glamorous Metropolis starlet, will visit Berkeley Friday.

Friday afternoon at the Campus Theater, Berkeley canines will have their chance to compete in the nation-wide quest for a dog to play Tookah the wolf dog in the great Metropolis epic "Fangs of the Forest," and Gloria Garton herself will be present at the auditions.

"I owe so much to Berkeley," Miss Garton said. "It will mean so much to me to see the campus and the city again." Miss Garton has the starring human role in "Fangs of the Forest."

Miss Garton was a student at the University of California when she received her first chance in films. She is a member of Mask and Dagger, honorary dramatic society, and Rho Rho Rho Sorority.

Wolfe Wolf glowed. This was perfect. No need now to wait till term was over. He could see Gloria now and claim her in all his wolfish vigor. Friday—today was Wednesday; that gave him two nights to practice and perfect the technique of werewolfry. And then—

He noticed the dejected look on the older professor's face, and a small remorse smote him. "How did things go last night, Oscar?" he asked sympathetically. "How were your big Walpurgis Night services?"

Fearing regarded him oddly. "You know that now? Yesterday April thirtieth meant nothing to you."

"I got curious and looked it up. But how did it go?"

"Well enough," Fearing lied feebly. "Do you know, Wolfe," he demanded after a moment's silence, "what is the real curse of every man interested in the occult?"

"No. What?"

"That true power is never enough. Enough for yourself, perhaps, but never enough for others. So that no matter what your true abilities, you must forge on beyond them into charlatanry to convince the others. Look at St.

Germain. Look at Francis Stuart. Look at Cagliostro. But the worst tragedy is the next stage: when you realize that your powers were greater than you supposed and that the charlatanry was needless. When you realize that you have no notion of the extent of your powers. Then—"

"Then, Oscar?"

"Then, my boy, you are a badly frightened man."

Wolf wanted to say something consoling. He wanted to say, "Look, Oscar. It was just me. Go back to your halfhearted charlatanry and be happy." But he couldn't do that. Only Ozzy could know the truth of that splendid gray wolf. Only Ozzy and Gloria.

The moon was bright on that hidden spot in the canyon. The night was still. And Wolfe Wolf had a severe case of stage fright. Now that it came to the real thing—for this morning's clothes-complicated fiasco hardly counted and last night he could not truly remember—he was afraid to plunge cleanly into wolfdom and anxious to stall and talk as long as possible.

"Do you think," he asked the magician nervously, "that I could teach Gloria to change, too?"

Ozymandias pondered. "Maybe, colleague. It'd depend. She might have the natural ability, and she might not. And, of course, there's no telling what she might change into."

"You mean she wouldn't necessarily be a wolf?"

"Of course not. The people who can change, change into all sorts of things. And every folk knows best the kind that most interests it. We've got an English and Central European tradition, so we know mostly about werewolves. But take Scandinavia and you'll hear chiefly about werebears, only they call 'em berserkers. And Orientals, now, they're apt to know about weretigers. Trouble is, we've thought so much about were*wolves* that that's all we know the signs for; I wouldn't know how to spot a weretiger just offhand."

"Then there's no telling what might happen if I taught her The Word?"

"Not the least. Of course, there's some werethings that just aren't much use being. Take like being a wereant. You change and somebody steps on you and that's that. Or like a fella I knew once in Madagascar. Taught him The Word, and know what? Hanged if he wasn't a werediplodocus. Shattered the whole house into little pieces when he changed and damned near trampled me under hoof before I could say *Absarka!* He decided not to make a career of

139

it. Or then there was that time in Darjeeling— But, look, colleague, are you going to stand around here naked all night?"

"No," said Wolf. "I'm going to change now. You'll take my clothes back to the hotel?"

"Sure. They'll be there for you. And I've put a very small spell on the night clerk, just enough for him not to notice wolves wandering in. Oh, and by the way—anything missing from your room?"

"Not that I noticed. Why?"

"Because I thought I saw somebody come out of it this afternoon. Couldn't be sure, but I think he came from there. Young fella with red hair and Hollywood clothes."

Wolfe Wolf frowned. That didn't make sense. Pointless questions from a detective were bad enough, but searching your hotel room— But what were detectives to a full-fledged werewolf? He grinned, nodded a friendly goodbye to Ozymandias the Great, and said The Word.

The pain wasn't so sharp as this morning, though still quite bad enough. But it passed almost at once, and his whole body filled with a sense of limitless freedom. He lifted his snout and sniffed deep at the keen freshness of this night air. A whole new realm of pleasure opened up for him through this acute new nose alone. He wagged his tail amicably at Ozzy and set off up the canyon on a long, easy lope.

For hours, loping was enough—simply and purely enjoying one's wolfness was the finest pleasure one could ask. Wolf left the canyon and turned up into the hills, past the Big C and on into noble wildness that seemed far remote from all campus civilization. His brave new legs were stanch and tireless, his wind seemingly inexhaustible. Every turning brought fresh and vivid scents of soil and leaves and air, and life was shimmering and beautiful.

But a few hours of this, and Wolf realized that he was damned lonely. All this grand exhilaration was very well, but if his mate Gloria were loping by his side— And what fun was it to be something as splendid as a wolf if no one admired you? He began to want people, and he turned back to the city.

Berkeley goes to bed early. The streets were deserted. Here and there a light burned in a rooming house where some solid grind was plodding on his almost-due term paper. Wolf had done that himself. He couldn't laugh in this shape, but his tail twitched with amusement at the thought.

He paused along the tree-lined street. There was a fresh human scent here, though the street seemed empty. Then he heard a soft whimpering, and trotted off toward the noise.

Behind the shrubbery fronting an apartment house sat a disconsolate two-year-old, shivering in his sunsuit and obviously lost for hours on hours. Wolf put a paw on the child's shoulder and shook him gently.

The boy looked around and was not in the least afraid. "He'o," he said, brightening up.

Wolf growled a cordial greeting, and wagged his tail and pawed at the ground to indicate that he'd take the lost infant wherever it wanted to go.

The child stood up and wiped away its tears with a dirty fist which left wide black smudges. "Tootootootoo!" he said.

Games, thought Wolf. He wants to play choo-choo. He took the child by the sleeve and tugged gently.

"Tootootootoo!" the boy repeated firmly. "Die way."

The sound of a railway whistle, to be sure, does die away; but this seemed a poetic expression for such a toddler. Wolf thought, and then abruptly would have snapped his fingers if he'd had them. The child was saying "2222 Dwight Way," having been carefully brought up to tell his address when lost. Wolf glanced up at the street sign. Bowditch and Hillegas; 2222 Dwight would be just a couple of blocks.

Wolf tried to nod his head, but the muscles didn't seem to work that way. Instead he wagged his tail in what he hoped indicated comprehension, and started off leading the child.

The infant beamed and said, "Nice woof-woof."

For an instant Wolf felt like a spy suddenly addressed by his right name, then realized that if some say "bow-wow" others might well say "woof-woof."

He led the child for two blocks without event. It felt good, having an innocent human being like this. There was something about children; he hoped Gloria felt the same. He wondered what would happen if he could teach this confiding infant The Word. It would be swell to have a pup that would—

He paused. His nose twitched and the hair on the back of his neck rose. Ahead of them stood a dog: a huge mongrel, seemingly a mixture of St.

Bernard and Husky. But the growl that issued from his throat indicated that carrying brandy kegs or rushing serum was not for him. He was a bandit, an outlaw, an enemy of man and dog. And they had to pass him.

Wolf had no desire to fight. He was as big as this monster and certainly, with his human brain, much cleverer; but scars from a dog fight would not look well on the human body of Professor Wolf, and there was, moreover, the danger of hurting the toddler in the fracas. It would be wiser to cross the street. But before he could steer the child that way, the mongrel brute had charged at them, yapping and snarling.

Wolf placed himself in front of the boy, poised and ready to leap in defense. The scar problem was secondary to the fact that this baby had trusted him. He was ready to face this cur and teach him a lesson, at whatever cost to his own human body. But halfway to him the huge dog stopped. His growls died away to a piteous whimper. His great flanks trembled in the moonlight. His tail curled craven between his legs. And abruptly he turned and fled.

The child crowed delightedly. "Bad woof-woof go away." He put his little arms around Wolf's neck. "*Nice* woof-woof." Then he straightened up and said insistently, "Tootootootoo. Die way," and Wolf led on, his strong wolf's heart pounding as it had never pounded at the embrace of a woman.

"Tootootootoo" was a small frame house set back from the street in a large yard. The lights were still on, and even from the sidewalk Wolf could hear a woman's shrill voice.

"—since five o'clock this afternoon, and you've got to find him, Officer. You simply must. We've hunted all over the neighborhood and—"

Wolf stood up against the wall on his hind legs and rang the doorbell with his front right paw.

"Oh! Maybe that's somebody now. The neighbors said they'd— Come, Officer, and let's see— Oh!"

At the same moment Wolf barked politely, the toddler yelled "Mamma!" and his thin and worn-looking young mother let out a scream—half delight at finding her child and half terror of this large gray canine shape that loomed behind him. She snatched up the infant protectively and turned to the large man in uniform. "Officer! Look! That big dreadful thing! It stole my Robby!"

"No," Robby protested firmly. "Nice woof-woof."

The officer laughed. "The lad's probably right, ma'am. It *is* a nice woof-

woof. Found your boy wandering around and helped him home. You haven't maybe got a bone for him?"

"Let that big, nasty brute into my home? Never! Come on, Robby."

"Want my nice woof-woof."

"I'll woof-woof you, staying out till all hours and giving your father and me the fright of our lives. Just wait till your father sees you, young man; he'll—Oh, good night, Officer!" And she shut the door on the yowls of Robby.

The policeman patted Wolf's head. "Never mind about the bone, Rover. She didn't so much as offer me a glass of beer, either. My, you're a husky specimen, aren't you, boy? Look almost like a wolf. Who do you belong to, and what are you doing wandering about alone? Huh?" He turned on his flash and bent over to look at the nonexistent collar.

He straightened up and whistled. "No license. Rover, that's bad. You know what I ought to do? I ought to turn you in. If you weren't a hero that just got cheated out of his bone, I'd— Hell, I ought to do it, anyway. Laws are laws, even for heroes. Come on, Rover. We're going for a walk."

Wolf thought quickly. The pound was the last place on earth he wanted to wind up. Even Ozzy would never think of looking for him there. Nobody'd claim him, nobody'd say *Absarka!* and in the end a dose of chloroform— He wrenched loose from the officer's grasp on his hair and with one prodigious leap cleared the yard, landed on the sidewalk, and started hell for leather up the street. But the instant he was out of the officer's sight he stopped dead and slipped behind a hedge.

He scented the policeman's approach even before he heard it. The man was running with the lumbering haste of two hundred pounds. But opposite the hedge, he too stopped. For a moment Wolf wondered if his ruse had failed; but the officer had paused only to scratch his head and mutter, "Say! There's something screwy here. *Who rang that doorbell?* The kid couldn't reach it, and the dog— Oh, well," he concluded. "Nuts," and seemed to find in that monosyllabic summation the solution to all his problems.

As his footsteps and smell died away, Wolf became aware of another scent. He had only just identified it as cat when someone said, "You're were, aren't you?"

Wolf started up, lips drawn back and muscles tense. There was nothing human in sight, but someone had spoken to him. Unthinkingly, he tried to say "Where are you?" but all that came out was a growl.

"Right behind you. Here in the shadows. You can scent me, can't you?"

"But you're a cat," Wolf thought in his snarls. "And you're talking."

"Of course. But I'm not talking human language. It's just your brain that takes it that way. If you had your human body, you'd think I was just going *meowrr*. But you are were, aren't you?"

"How do you ... why do you think so?"

"Because you didn't try to jump me, as any normal dog would have. And besides, unless Confucius taught me all wrong, you're a wolf, not a dog; and we don't have wolves around here unless they're were."

"How do you know all this? Are you—"

"Oh, no. I'm just a cat. But I used to live next door to a werechow named Confucius. He taught me things."

Wolf was amazed. "You mean he was a man who changed to chow and stayed that way? Lived as a pet?"

"Certainly. This was back at the worst of the depression. He said a dog was more apt to be fed and looked after than a man. I thought it was a smart idea."

"But how terrible! Could a man so debase himself as—"

"Men don't debase themselves. They debase each other. That's the way of most weres. Some change to keep from being debased, others to do a little more effective debasing. Which are you?"

"Why, you see, I—"

"*Sh!* Look. This is going to be fun. Holdup."

Wolf peered around the hedge. A well-dressed, middle-aged man was walking along briskly, apparently enjoying a night constitutional. Behind him moved a thin, silent figure. Even as Wolf watched, the figure caught up with him and whispered harshly, "Up with 'em, buddy!"

The quiet pomposity of the stroller melted away. He was ashen and aspen as the figure slipped a hand around into his breast pocket and removed an impressive wallet.

And what, thought Wolf, was the good of his fine, vigorous body if it merely crouched behind hedges as a spectator? In one fine bound, to the shocked amazement of the were-wise cat, he had crossed the hedge and landed with his forepaws full in the figure's face. It went over backward with him on top, and then there came a loud noise, a flash of light, and a frightful sharp smell. For a moment Wolf felt an acute pang in his shoulder, like the jab of a long needle, and then the pain was gone.

But his momentary recoil had been enough to let the figure get to its feet. "Missed you, huh?" it muttered. "Let's see how you like a slug in the belly, you interfering—" and he applied an epithet that would have been purely literal description if Wolf had not been were.

There were three quick shots in succession even as Wolf sprang. For a second he experienced the most acute stomachache of his life. Then he landed again. The figure's head hit the concrete sidewalk and he was still.

Lights were leaping into brightness everywhere. Among all the confused noises, Wolf could hear the shrill complaints of Robby's mother, and among all the compounded smells, he could distinguish scent of the policeman who wanted to impound him. That meant getting the hell out, and quick.

The city meant trouble, Wolf decided as he loped off. He could endure loneliness while he practiced his wolfry, until he had Gloria. Though just as a precaution he must arrange with Ozzy about a plausible-looking collar, and—

The most astounding realization yet suddenly struck him! He had received four bullets, three of them square in the stomach, and he hadn't a wound to show for it! Being a werewolf certainly offered its practical advantages. Think what a criminal could do with such bullet-proofing. Or— But no. He was a werewolf for fun, and that was that.

But even for a werewolf, being shot, though relatively painless, is tiring. A great deal of nervous energy is absorbed in the magical and instantaneous knitting of those wounds. And when Wolfe Wolf reached the peace and calm of the uncivilized hills, he no longer felt like reveling in freedom. Instead he stretched out to his full length, nuzzled his head down between his forepaws, and slept.

"Now, the essence of magic," said Heliophagus of Smyrna, "is deceit; and that deceit is of two kinds. By magic, the magician deceives others; but magic deceives the magician himself."

So far the lycanthropic magic of Wolfe Wolf had worked smoothly and pleasantly, but now it was to show him the second trickery that lurks behind every magic trick. And the first step was that he slept.

He woke in confusion. His dreams had been human—and of Gloria—despite the body in which he dreamed them, and it took several full minutes for him to reconstruct just how he happened to be in that body. For a moment the dream, even that episode in which he and Gloria had been eating blueberry waffles on a roller coaster, seemed more sanely plausible than the reality.

But he readjusted quickly, and glanced up at the sky. The sun looked as though it had been up at least an hour, which meant in May that the time was somewhere between six and seven. Today was Thursday, which meant that he was saddled with an eight-o'clock class. That left plenty of time to change back, shave, dress, breakfast, and resume the normal life of Professor Wolf—which was, after all, important if he intended to support a wife.

He tried, as he trotted through the streets, to look as tame and un-wolflike as possible, and apparently succeeded. No one paid him any mind save children, who wanted to play, and dogs, who began by snarling and ended by cowering away terrified. His friend the cat might be curiously tolerant of weres, but not so dogs.

He trotted up the steps of the Berkeley Inn confidently. The clerk was under a slight spell and would not notice wolves. There was nothing to do but rouse Ozzy, be *Absarka!*'d, and—

"Hey! Where are you going? Get out of here! Shoo!"

It was the clerk, a stanch and brawny young man, who straddled the stairway and vigorously waved him off.

"No dogs in here! Go on now. Scoot!"

Quite obviously this man was under no spell, and equally obviously there was no way of getting up that staircase short of using a wolf's strength to tear the clerk apart. For a second Wolf hesitated. He had to get changed back. It would be a damnable pity to use his powers to injure another human being. If only he had not slept, and arrived before this unmagicked day clerk came on duty; but necessity knows no—

Then the solution hit him. Wolf turned and loped off just as the clerk hurled an ash tray at him. Bullets may be relatively painless, but even a werewolf's rump, he learned promptly, is sensitive to flying glass.

The solution was foolproof. The only trouble was that it meant an hour's wait, and he was hungry. Damnably hungry. He found himself even display-ing a certain shocking interest in the plump occupant of a baby carriage. You do get different appetites with a different body. He could understand how some originally well-intentioned werewolves might in time become monsters. But he was stronger in will, and much smarter. His stomach could hold out until this plan worked.

The janitor had already opened the front door of Wheeler Hall, but the building was deserted. Wolf had no trouble reaching the second floor unnoticed or finding his classroom. He had a little more trouble holding the chalk between his teeth and a slight tendency to gag on the dust; but by balancing his forepaws on the eraser trough, he could manage quite nicely. It took three springs to catch the ring of the chart in his teeth, but once that was pulled down there was nothing to do but crouch under the desk and pray that he would not starve quite to death.

The students of German 31B, as they assembled reluctantly for their eight-o'clock, were a little puzzled at being confronted by a chart dealing with the influence of the gold standard on world economy, but they decided simply that the janitor had been forgetful.

The wolf under the desk listened unseen to their gathering murmurs, overheard that cute blonde in the front row make dates with three different men for that same night, and finally decided that enough had assembled to make his chances plausible. He slipped out from under the desk far enough to reach the ring of the chart, tugged at it, and let go.

The chart flew up with a rolling crash. The students broke off their chatter, looked up at the blackboard, and beheld in a huge and shaky scrawl the mysterious letters

ABSARKA

It worked. With enough people, it was an almost mathematical certainty that one of them in his puzzlement—for the race of subtitle readers, though handicapped by the talkies, still exists—would read the mysterious word aloud. It was the much-bedated blonde who did it.

"*Absarka,*" she said wonderingly.

And there was Professor Wolfe Wolf, beaming cordially at his class.

The only flaw was this: He had forgotten that he was only a werewolf, and not Hyperman. His clothes were still at the Berkeley Inn, and here on the lecture platform he was stark naked.

Two of his best pupils screamed and one fainted. The blonde only giggled appreciatively.

Emily was incredulous but pitying.

Professor Fearing was sympathetic but reserved.

The chairman of the department was cool.

The dean of letters was chilly.

The president of the university was frigid.

Wolfe Wolf was unemployed.

And Heliophagus of Smyrna was right. "The essence of magic is deceit."

"But what can I do?" Wolf moaned into his zombie glass. "I'm stuck. I'm stymied. Gloria arrives in Berkeley tomorrow, and here I am—nothing. Nothing but a futile, worthless werewolf. You can't support a wife on that. You can't raise a family. You can't— Hell, you can't even propose.... I want another. Sure you won't have one?"

Ozymandias the Great shook his round, fringed head. "The last time I took two drinks I started all this. I've got to behave if I want to stop it. But you're an able-bodied, strapping young man; surely, colleague, you can get work?"

"Where? All I'm trained for is academic work, and this scandal has put the kibosh on that forever. What university is going to hire a man who showed up naked in front of his class without even the excuse of being drunk? And supposing I try something else—say one of these jobs in defense that all my students seem to be getting—I'd have to give references, say something about what I'd been doing with my thirty-odd years. And once these references were checked— Ozzy, I'm a lost man."

"Never despair, colleague. I've learned that magic gets you into some tight squeezes, but there's always a way of getting out. Now, take that time in Darjeeling—"

"But what can I do? I'll wind up like Confucius the werechow and live off charity, if you'll find me somebody who wants a pet wolf."

"You know," Ozymandias reflected, "you may have something there, colleague."

"Nuts! That was a joke. I can at least retain my self-respect, even if I go on relief doing it. And I'll bet they don't like naked men on relief, either."

"No. I don't mean just being a pet wolf. But look at it this way: What are your assets? You have only two outstanding abilities. One of them is to teach German, and that is now completely out."

"Check."

"And the other is to change yourself into a wolf. All right, colleague. There must be some commercial possibilities in that. Let's look into them."

"Nonsense."

"Not quite. For every kind of merchandise there's a market. The trick is to find it. And you, colleague, are going to be the first practical commercial werewolf on record."

"I could— They say Ripley's Odditorium pays good money. Supposing I changed six times a day regular for delighted audiences?"

Ozymandias shook his head sorrowfully. "It's no good. People don't want to see real magic. It makes 'em uncomfortable—starts 'em wondering what else might be loose in the world. They've got to feel sure it's all done with mirrors. I know. I had to quit vaudeville because I wasn't smart enough at faking it; all I could do was the real thing."

"I could be a Seeing Eye dog, maybe?"

"They have to be female."

"When I'm changed I can understand animal language. Maybe I could be a dog trainer and— No, that's out. I forgot: they're scared to death of me."

But Ozymandias' pale-blue eyes had lit up at the suggestion. "Colleague, you're warm. Oh, are you warm! Tell me: why did you say your fabulous Gloria was coming to Berkeley?"

"Publicity for a talent hunt."

"For what?"

"A dog to star in *Fangs of the Forest*."

"And what kind of a dog?"

"A—" Wolf's eyes widened and his jaw sagged. "A wolf dog," he said softly.

And the two men looked at each other with a wild surmise—silent, beside a bar in Berkeley.

"It's all the fault of that damned Disney dog," the trainer complained. "Pluto does anything. Everything. So our poor mutts are expected to do likewise. Listen to that dope! 'The dog should come into the room, give one paw to the baby, indicate that he recognizes the hero in his Eskimo disguise, go over to the table, find the bone, and clap his paws gleefully!' Now, who's got a set of signals to cover stuff like that? Pluto!" he snorted.

Gloria Garton said, "Oh." By that one sound she managed to convey that she sympathized deeply, that the trainer was a nice-looking young man whom she'd just as soon see again, and that no dog star was going to steal *Fangs of the Forest* from her. She adjusted her skirt slightly, leaned back, and made the plain wooden chair on the bare theater stage seem more than ever like a throne.

"All right." The man in the violet beret waved away the last unsuccessful applicant and read from a card: "'Dog: Wopsy. Owner: Mrs. Channing Galbraith. Trainer: Luther Newby.' Bring it in."

An assistant scurried offstage, and there was a sound of whines and whimpers as a door opened.

"What's got into those dogs today?" the man in the violet beret demanded. "They all seem scared to death and beyond."

"I think," said Fergus O'Breen, "that it's that big, gray wolf dog. Somehow, the others just don't like him."

Gloria Garton lowered her bepurpled lids and cast a queenly stare of suspicion on the young detective. There was nothing wrong with his being there. His sister was head of publicity for Metropolis, and he'd handled several confidential cases for the studio; even one for her, that time her chauffeur had decided to try his hand at blackmail. Fergus O'Breen was a Metropolis fixture; but still it bothered her.

The assistant brought in Mrs. Galbraith's Wopsy. The man in the violet beret took one look and screamed. The scream bounced back from every wall of the theater in the ensuing minute of silence. At last he found words. "A wolf dog! Tookah is the greatest role ever written for a wolf dog! And what do they bring us? A terrier, yet! So if we wanted a terrier we could cast Asta!"

"But if you'd only let us show you—" Wopsy's tall young trainer started to protest.

"Get out!" the man in the violet beret shrieked. "Get out before I lose my temper!"

Wopsy and her trainer slunk off.

"In El Paso," the casting director lamented, "they bring me a Mexican hairless. In St. Louis it's a Pekinese yet! And if I do find a wolf dog, it sits in a corner and waits for somebody to bring it a sled to pull."

"Maybe," said Fergus, "you should try a real wolf."

"Wolf, *schmolf!* We'll end up wrapping John Barrymore in a wolf-skin." He picked up the next card. "'Dog: Yoggoth. Owner and trainer: Mr. O. Z. Manders.' Bring it in."

The whining noise offstage ceased as Yoggoth was brought out to be tested. The man in the violet beret hardly glanced at the fringe-bearded owner and trainer. He had eyes only for that splendid gray wolf. "If you can only act ..." he prayed, with the same fervor with which many a man has thought, If you could only cook ...

He pulled the beret to an even more unlikely angle and snapped, "All right, Mr. Manders. The dog should come into the room, give one paw to the baby, indicate that he recognizes the hero in his Eskimo disguise, go over to the table, find the bone, and clap his paws joyfully. Baby here, hero here, table here. Got that?"

Mr. Manders looked at his wolf dog and repeated, "Got that?"

Yoggoth wagged his tail.

"Very well, colleague," said Mr. Manders. "Do it."

Yoggoth did it.

The violet beret sailed into the flies, on the wings of its owner's triumphal scream of joy. "He did it!" he kept burbling. "He did it!"

"Of course, colleague," said Mr. Manders calmly.

The trainer who hated Pluto had a face as blank as a vampire's mirror. Fergus O'Breen was speechless with wonderment. Even Gloria Garton permitted surprise and interest to cross her regal mask.

"You mean he can do anything?" gurgled the man who used to have a violet beret.

"Anything," said Mr. Manders.

"Can he— Let's see, in the dance-hall sequence ... can he knock a man down, roll him over, and frisk his back pocket?"

Even before Mr. Manders could say "Of course," Yoggoth had demonstrated, using Fergus O'Breen as a convenient dummy.

"Peace!" the casting director sighed. "Peace.... Charley!" he yelled to his assistant. "Send 'em all away. No more tryouts. We've found Tookah! It's wonderful."

The trainer stepped up to Mr. Manders. "It's more than that, sir. It's positively superhuman. I'll swear I couldn't detect the slightest signal, and for such complicated operations, too. Tell me, Mr. Manders, what system do you use?"

Mr. Manders made a Hoople-ish *kaff-kaff* noise. "Professional secret, you understand, young man. I'm planning on opening a school when I retire, but obviously until then—"

"Of course, sir. I understand. But I've never seen anything like it in all my born days."

"I wonder," Fergus O'Breen observed abstractly from the floor, "if your marvel dog can get off of people, too?"

Mr. Manders stifled a grin. "Of course! Yoggoth!"

Fergus picked himself up and dusted from his clothes the grime of the stage, which is the most clinging grime on earth. "I'd swear," he muttered, "that beast of yours enjoyed that."

"No hard feelings, I trust, Mr.—"

"O'Breen. None at all. In fact, I'd suggest a little celebration in honor of this great event. I know you can't buy a drink this near the campus, so I brought along a bottle just in case."

"Oh," said Gloria Garton, implying that carousals were ordinarily beneath her; that this, however, was a special occasion; and that possibly there was something to be said for the green-eyed detective after all.

This was all too easy, Wolfe Wolf-Yoggoth kept thinking. There was a catch to it somewhere. This was certainly the ideal solution to the problem of how to earn money as a werewolf. Bring an understanding of human speech and instructions into a fine animal body, and you are the answer to a director's prayer. It was perfect as long as it lasted; and if *Fangs of the Forest* was a smash hit, there were bound to be other Yoggoth pictures. Look at Rin-Tin-Tin. But it was too easy....

His ears caught a familiar "Oh," and his attention reverted to Gloria. This "Oh" had meant that she really shouldn't have another drink, but since liquor didn't affect her anyway and this was a special occasion, she might as well.

She was even more beautiful than he had remembered. Her golden hair was shoulder-length now, and flowed with such rippling perfection that it was all he could do to keep from reaching out a paw to it. Her body had ripened, too; was even more warm and promising than his memories of her. And in his new shape he found her greatest charm in something he had not been able to appreciate fully as a human being: the deep, heady scent of her flesh.

"To *Fangs of the Forest!*" Fergus O'Breen was toasting. "And may that pretty-boy hero of yours get a worse mauling than I did."

Wolf-Yoggoth grinned to himself. That had been fun. That'd teach the detective to go crawling around hotel rooms.

"And while we're celebrating, colleagues," said Ozymandias the Great, "why should we neglect our star? Here, Yoggoth." And he held out the bottle.

"He drinks, yet!" the casting director exclaimed delightedly.

"Sure. He was weaned on it."

Wolf took a sizable gulp. It felt good. Warm and rich—almost the way Gloria smelled.

"But how about you, Mr. Manders?" the detective insisted for the fifth time. "It's your celebration really. The poor beast won't get the four-figure checks from Metropolis. And you've taken only one drink."

"Never take two, colleague. I know my danger point. Two drinks in me and things start happening."

"More should happen yet than training miracle dogs? Go on, O'Breen. Make him drink. We should see what happens."

Fergus took another long drink himself. "Go on. There's another bottle in the car, and I've gone far enough to be resolved not to leave here sober. And I don't want sober companions, either." His green eyes were already beginning to glow with a new wildness.

"No, thank you, colleague."

Gloria Garton left her throne, walked over to the plump man, and stood close, her soft hand resting on his arm. "Oh," she said, implying that dogs were dogs, but still that the party was unquestionably in her honor and his refusal to drink was a personal insult.

Ozymandias the Great looked at Gloria, sighed, shrugged, resigned himself to fate, and drank.

"Have you trained many dogs?" the casting director asked.

"Sorry, colleague. This is my first."

"All the more wonderful! But what's your profession otherwise?"

"Well, you see, I'm a magician."

"Oh," said Gloria Garton, implying delight, and went so far as to add, "I have a friend who does black magic."

"I'm afraid, ma'am, mine's simply white. That's tricky enough. With the black you're in for some real dangers."

"Hold on!" Fergus interposed. "You mean really a magician? Not just presti ... sleight of hand?"

"Of course, colleague."

"Good theater," said the casting director. "Never let 'em see the mirrors."

"Uh-huh," Fergus nodded. "But look, Mr. Manders. What can you do, for instance?"

"Well, I can change—"

Yoggoth barked loudly.

"Oh, no," Ozymandias covered hastily, "that's really a little beyond me. But I can—"

"Can you do the Indian rope trick?" Gloria asked languidly. "My friend says that's terribly hard."

"Hard? Why, ma'am, there's nothing to it. I can remember that time in Darjeeling—"

Fergus took another long drink. "I," he announced defiantly, "want to see the Indian rope trick. I have met people who've met people who've met people who've seen it, but that's as close as I ever get. And I don't believe it."

"But, colleague, it's so simple."

"I don't believe it."

Ozymandias the Great drew himself up to his full lack of height. "Colleague, you are about to see it!" Yoggoth tugged warningly at his coattails. "Leave me alone, Wolf. An aspersion has been cast!"

Fergus returned from the wings dragging a soiled length of rope. "This do?"

"Admirably."

"What goes?" the casting director demanded.

"*Shh!*" said Gloria. "Oh—"

She beamed worshipfully on Ozymandias, whose chest swelled to the point of threatening the security of his buttons. "Ladies and gentlemen!" he announced, in the manner of one prepared to fill a vast amphitheater with his voice. "You are about to behold Ozymandias the Great in—The Indian Rope Trick! Of course," he added conversationally, "I haven't got a small boy to chop into mincemeat, unless perhaps one of you— No? Well, we'll try it without. Not quite so impressive, though. And will you stop yapping, Wolf?"

"I thought his name was Yogi," said Fergus.

"Yoggoth. But since he's part wolf on his mother's side— Now, quiet, all of you!"

He had been coiling the rope as he spoke. Now he placed the coil in the center of the stage, where it lurked like a threatening rattler. He stood beside it and deftly, professionally, went through a series of passes and mumblings so rapidly that even the superhumanly sharp eyes and ears of Wolf-Yoggoth could not follow them.

The end of the rope detached itself from the coil, reared in the air, turned for a moment like a head uncertain where to strike, then shot straight up until all the rope was uncoiled. The lower end rested a good inch above the stage.

Gloria gasped. The casting director drank hurriedly. Fergus, for some reason, stared curiously at the wolf.

"And now, ladies and gentlemen—oh, hang it, I do wish I had a boy to carve—Ozymandias the Great will ascend this rope into that land which only the users of the rope may know. Onward and upward! Be right back," he added reassuringly to Wolf.

His plump hands grasped the rope above his head and gave a little jerk. His knees swung up and clasped about the hempen pillar. And up he went, like a monkey on a stick, up and up and up—until suddenly he was gone.

Just gone. That was all there was to it. Gloria was beyond even saying "Oh." The casting director sat his beautiful flannels down on the filthy floor and gaped. Fergus swore softly and melodiously. And Wolf felt a premonitory prickling in his spine.

The stage door opened, admitting two men in denim pants and work shirts. "Hey!" said the first. "Where do you think you are?"

"We're from Metropolis Pictures," the casting director started to explain, scrambling to his feet.

"I don't care if you're from Washington, we gotta clear this stage. There's movies here tonight. Come on, Joe, help me get 'em out. And that pooch, too."

"You can't, Fred," said Joe reverently, and pointed. His voice sank to an awed whisper. "That's Gloria Garton—"

"So it is. Hi, Miss Garton. Cripes, wasn't that last one of yours a stinkeroo!"

"Your public, darling," Fergus murmured.

"Come on!" Fred shouted. "Out of here. We gotta clean up. And you, Joe! Strike that rope!"

Before Fergus could move, before Wolf could leap to the rescue, the efficient stagehand had struck the rope and was coiling it up.

Wolf stared up into the flies. There was nothing up there. Nothing at all. Someplace beyond the end of that rope was the only man on earth he could trust to say *Absarka!* for him; and the way down was cut off forever.

Wolfe Wolf sprawled on the floor of Gloria Garton's boudoir and watched that vision of volupty change into her most fetching negligee.

The situation was perfect. It was the fulfillment of all his dearest dreams. The only flaw was that he was still in a wolf's body.

Gloria turned, leaned over, and chucked him under the snout. "Wuzzum a cute wolf dog, wuzzum?"

Wolf could not restrain a snarl.

"Doesn't um like Gloria to talk baby talk? Um was a naughty wolf, yes, um was."

It was torture. Here you are in your best-beloved's hotel room, all her beauty revealed to your hungry eyes, and she talks baby talk to you! Wolf had been happy at first when Gloria suggested that she might take over the care of her co-star pending the reappearance of his trainer—for none of them was quite willing to admit that "Mr. O. Z. Manders" might truly and definitely have vanished—but he was beginning to realize that the situation might bring on more torment than pleasure.

"Wolves are funny," Gloria observed. She was more talkative when alone, with no need to be cryptically fascinating. "I knew a Wolfe once, only that was his name. He was a man. And he was a funny one."

Wolf felt his heart beating fast under his gray fur. To hear his own name on Gloria's warm lips … But before she could go on to tell her pet how funny Wolfe was, her maid rapped on the door.

"A Mr. O'Breen to see you, madam."

"Tell him to go 'way."

"He says it's important, and he does look, madam, as though he might make trouble."

"Oh, all right." Gloria rose and wrapped her negligee more respectably about her. "Come on, Yog— No, that's a silly name; I'm going to call you Wolfie. That's cute. Come on, Wolfie, and protect me from the big, bad detective."

Fergus O'Breen was pacing the sitting room with a certain vicious deliberateness in his strides. He broke off and stood still as Gloria and the wolf entered.

"So?" he observed tersely. "Reinforcements?"

"Will I need them?" Gloria cooed.

"Look, light of my love life." The glint in the green eyes was cold and deadly. "You've been playing games, and whatever their nature, there's one thing they're not. And that's cricket."

Gloria gave him a languid smile. "You're amusing, Fergus."

"Thanks. I doubt, however, if your activities are."

"You're still a little boy playing cops and robbers. And what boogyman are you after now?"

"Ha-ha," said Fergus politely. "And you know the answer to that question better than I do. That's why I'm here."

Wolf was puzzled. This conversation meant nothing to him. And yet he sensed a tension of danger in the air as clearly as though he could smell it.

"Go on," Gloria snapped impatiently. "And remember how dearly Metropolis Pictures will thank you for annoying one of its best box-office attractions."

"Some things, my sweeting, are more important than pictures, though you mightn't think it where you come from. One of them is a certain federation of forty-eight units. Another is an abstract concept called democracy."

"And so?"

"And so I want to ask you one question: Why did you come to Berkeley?"

"For publicity on *Fangs*, of course. It was your sister's idea."

"You've gone temperamental and turned down better ones. Why leap at this?"

"You don't haunt publicity stunts yourself, Fergus. Why are *you* here?"

Fergus was pacing again. "And why was your first act in Berkeley a visit to the office of the German department?"

"Isn't that natural enough? I used to be a student here."

"Majoring in dramatics, and you didn't go near the Little Theater. Why the German department?" He paused and stood straight in front of her, fixing her with his green gaze.

Gloria assumed the attitude of a captured queen defying the barbarian conqueror. "Very well. If you must know—I went to the German department to see the man I love."

Wolf held his breath, and tried to keep his tail from thrashing.

"Yes," she went on impassionedly, "you strip the last veil from me, and force me to confess to you what he alone should have heard first. This man proposed to me by mail. I foolishly rejected his proposal. But I thought and thought—and at last I knew. When I came to Berkeley I had to see him—"

"And did you?"

"The little mouse of a secretary told me he wasn't there. But I shall see him yet. And when I do—"

Fergus bowed stiffly. "My congratulations to you both, my sweeting. And the name of this more than fortunate gentleman?"

"Professor Wolfe Wolf."

"Who is doubtless the individual referred to in this?" He whipped a piece of paper from his sport coat and thrust it at Gloria. She paled and was silent. But Wolfe Wolf did not wait for her reply. He did not care. He knew the solution to his problem now, and he was streaking unobserved for her boudoir.

Gloria Garton entered the boudoir a minute later, a shaken and wretched woman. She unstoppered one of the delicate perfume bottles on her dresser and poured herself a stiff tot of whiskey. Then her eyebrows lifted in surprise as she stared at her mirror. Scrawlingly lettered across the glass in her own deep-crimson lipstick was the mysterious word

ABSARKA

Frowning, she said it aloud. *"Absarka—"*

From behind a screen stepped Professor Wolfe Wolf, incongruously wrapped in one of Gloria's lushest dressing robes. "Gloria dearest—" he cried.

"Wolfe!" she exclaimed. "What on earth are you doing here in my room?"

"I love you. I've always loved you since you couldn't tell a strong from a weak verb. And now that I know that you love me—"

"This is terrible. Please get out of here!"

"Gloria—"

"Get out of here, or I'll sick my dog on you. Wolfie— Here, nice Wolfie!"

"I'm sorry, Gloria. But Wolfie won't answer you."

"Oh, you beast! Have you hurt Wolfie? Have you—"

"I wouldn't touch a hair on his pelt. Because, you see, Gloria darling, I am Wolfie."

"What on earth do you—" Gloria stared around the room. It was undeniable that there was no trace of the presence of a wolf dog. And here was a man dressed only in one of her robes and no sign of his own clothes. And after that funny little man and the rope …

"You thought I was drab and dull," Wolf went on. "You thought I'd sunk into an academic rut. You'd sooner have an actor or a G-man. But I, Gloria, am something more exciting than you've ever dreamed of. There's not another soul on earth I'd tell this to, but I, Gloria, am a werewolf."

Gloria gasped. "That isn't possible! But it does all fit in. What I heard about you on campus, and your friend with the funny beard and how he vanished, and, of course, it explains how you did tricks that any real dog couldn't possibly do—"

"Don't you believe me, darling?"

Gloria rose from the dresser chair and went into his arms. "I believe you, dear. And it's wonderful! I'll bet there's not another woman in all Hollywood that was ever married to a werewolf!"

"Then you will—"

"But of course, dear. We can work it out beautifully. We'll hire a stooge to be your trainer on the lot. You can work daytimes, and come home at night and I'll say that word for you. It'll be perfect."

"Gloria …" Wolf murmured with tender reverence.

"One thing, dear. Just a little thing. Would you do Gloria a favor?"

"Anything!"

"Show me how you change. Change for me now. Then I'll change you back right away."

Wolf said The Word. He was in such ecstatic bliss that he hardly felt the pang this time. He capered about the room with all the litheness of his fine wolfish legs, and ended up before Gloria, wagging his tail and looking for approval.

Gloria patted his head. "Good boy, Wolfie. And now, darling, you can just damned well stay that way."

Wolf let out a yelp of amazement.

"You heard me, Wolfie. You're staying that way. You didn't happen to believe any of that guff I was feeding the detective, did you? Love you? I should waste my time! But this way you can be very useful to me. With your trainer gone, I can take charge of you and pick up an extra thousand a week or so. I won't mind that. And Professor Wolfe Wolf will have vanished forever, which fits right in with my plans."

Wolf snarled.

"Now, don't try to get nasty, Wolfie darling. Um wouldn't threaten ums darling Gloria, would ums? Remember what I can do for you. I'm the only person that can turn you into a man again. You wouldn't dare teach anyone else that. You wouldn't dare let people know what you really are. An ignorant person would kill you. A smart one would have you locked up as a lunatic."

Wolf still advanced threateningly.

"Oh, no. You can't hurt me. Because all I'd have to do would be to say the word on the mirror. Then you wouldn't be a dangerous wolf any more. You'd just be a man here in my room, and I'd scream. And after what happened on the campus yesterday, how long do you think you'd stay out of the madhouse?"

Wolf backed away and let his tail droop.

"You see, Wolfie darling? Gloria has ums just where she wants ums. And ums is damned well going to be a good boy."

There was a rap on the boudoir door, and Gloria called, "Come in."

"A gentleman to see you, madam," the maid announced. "A Professor Fearing."

Gloria smiled her best cruel and queenly smile. "Come along, Wolfie. This may interest you."

Professor Oscar Fearing, overflowing one of the graceful chairs of the sitting room, beamed benevolently as Gloria and the wolf entered. "Ah, my dear! A new pet. Touching."

"And what a pet, Oscar. Wait till you hear."

Professor Fearing buffed his pince-nez against his sleeve. "And wait, my dear, until you hear all that I have learned. Chiswick has perfected his protective screen against magnetic bombs, and the official trial is set for next week. And Farnsworth has all but completed his researches on a new process for obtaining osmium. Gas warfare may start any day, and the power that can command a plentiful supply of—"

"Fine, Oscar," Gloria broke in. "But we can go over all this later. We've got other worries right now."

"What do you mean, my dear?"

"Have you run onto a red-headed young Irishman in a yellow shirt?"

"No, I— Why, yes. I did see such an individual leaving the office yesterday. I believe he had been to see Wolfe."

"He's on to us. He's a detective from Los Angeles, and he's tracking us down. Someplace he got hold of a scrap of record that should have been destroyed. He knows I'm in it, and he knows I'm tied up with somebody here in the German department."

Professor Fearing scrutinized his pince-nez, approved of their cleanness, and set them on his nose. "Not so much excitement, my dear. No hysteria. Let us approach this calmly. Does he know about the Temple of the Dark Truth?"

"Not yet. Nor about you. He just knows it's somebody in the department."

"Then what could be simpler? You have heard of the strange conduct of Wolfe Wolf?"

"Have I!" Gloria laughed harshly.

"Everyone knows of Wolfe's infatuation with you. Throw the blame onto him. It should be easy to clear yourself and make you appear an innocent tool. Direct all attention to him and the organization will be safe. The Temple of the Dark Truth can go its mystic way and extract even more invaluable information from weary scientists who need the emotional release of a false religion."

"That's what I've tried to do. I gave O'Breen a long song and dance about my devotion to Wolfe, so obviously phony he'd be bound to think it was a cover-up for something else. And I think he bit. But the situation's a damned sight trickier than you guess. Do you know where Wolfe Wolf is?"

"No one knows. After the president … ah … rebuked him, he seems to have vanished."

Gloria laughed again. "He's right here. In this room."

"My dear! Secret panels and such? You take your espionage too seriously. Where?"

"There!"

Professor Fearing gaped. "Are you serious?"

"As serious as you are about the future of Fascism. That is Wolfe Wolf."

Fearing approached the wolf incredulously and extended his hand.

"He might bite," Gloria warned him a second too late.

Fearing stared at his bleeding hand. "That, at least," he observed, "is undeniably true." And he raised his foot to deliver a sharp kick.

"No, Oscar! Don't! Leave him alone. And you'll have to take my word for it—it's way too complicated. But the wolf is Wolfe Wolf, and I've got him absolutely under control. He's perfectly in our hands. We'll switch suspicion to him, and I'll keep him this way while Fergus and his friends the G-men go off hotfoot on his trail."

"My dear!" Fearing ejaculated. "You're mad. You're more hopelessly mad than the devout members of the Temple." He took off his pince-nez and stared again at the wolf. "And yet Tuesday night— Tell me one thing: From whom did you get this … this wolf dog?"

"From a funny plump little man with a fringy beard."

Fearing gasped. Obviously he remembered the furor in the Temple, and the wolf and the fringe-beard. "Very well, my dear. I believe you. Don't ask me why, but I believe you. And now—"

"Now, it's all set, isn't it? We keep him here helpless and we use him to…"

"The wolf as scapegoat. Yes. Very pretty."

"Oh! One thing—" She was suddenly frightened.

Wolfe Wolf was considering the possibilities of a sudden attack on Fearing. He could probably get out of the room before Gloria could say *Absarka!* But after that? Whom could he trust to restore him? Especially if G-men were to be set on his trail ...

"What is it?" Fearing asked.

"That secretary. That little mouse in the department office. She knows it was you I asked for, not Wolf. Fergus can't have talked to her yet, because he swallowed my story; but he will. He's thorough."

"Hm-m-m. Then, in that case—"

"Yes, Oscar?"

"She must be attended to." Professor Oscar Fearing beamed genially and reached for the phone.

Wolf acted instantly, on inspiration and impulse. His teeth were strong, quite strong enough to jerk the phone cord from the wall. That took only a second, and in the next second he was out of the room and into the hall before Gloria could open her mouth to speak that word that would convert him from a powerful and dangerous wolf to a futile man.

There were shrill screams and a shout or two of "Mad dog!" as he dashed through the hotel lobby, but he paid no heed to them. The main thing was to reach Emily's house before she could be "attended to." Her evidence was essential. That could swing the balance, show Fergus and his G-men where the true guilt lay. And, besides, he admitted to himself, Emily was a damned nice kid....

His rate of collision was about one point six six per block, and the curses heaped upon him, if theologically valid, would have been more than enough to damn him forever. But he was making time, and that was all that counted. He dashed through traffic signals, cut into the path of trucks, swerved from under streetcars, and once even leaped over a stalled car that was obstructing him. Everything was going fine, he was halfway there, when two hundred pounds of human flesh landed on him in a flying tackle.

He looked up through the brilliant lighting effects of smashing his head on the sidewalk and saw his old nemesis, the policeman who had been cheated of his beer.

"So, Rover!" said the officer. "Got you at last, did I? Now we'll see if you'll wear a proper license tag. Didn't know I used to play football, did you?"

The officer's grip on his hair was painfully tight. A gleeful crowd was gathering and heckling the policeman with fantastic advice.

"Get along, boys," he admonished. "This is a private matter between me and Rover here. Come on," and he tugged even harder.

Wolf left a large tuft of fur and skin in the officer's grasp and felt the blood ooze out of the bare patch on his neck. He heard a ripe oath and a pistol shot simultaneously, and felt the needlelike sting through his shoulder. The awestruck crowd thawed before him. Two more bullets hied after him, but he was gone, leaving the most dazed policeman in Berkeley.

"I hit him," the officer kept muttering blankly. "I hit the—"

Wolfe Wolf coursed along Dwight Way. Two more blocks and he'd be at the little bungalow that Emily shared with a teaching assistant in something or other. Ripping out that telephone had stopped Fearing only momentarily; the orders would have been given by now, the henchmen would be on their way. But he was almost there....

"He'o!" a child's light voice called to him. "Nice woof-woof come back!"

Across the street was the modest frame dwelling of Robby and his shrewish mother. The child had been playing on the sidewalk. Now he saw his idol and deliverer and started across the street at a lurching toddle. "Nice woof-woof!" he kept calling. "Wait for Robby!"

Wolf kept on. This was no time for playing games with even the most delightful of cubs. And then he saw the car. It was an ancient jalopy, plastered with wisecracks even older than itself; and the high school youth driving was obviously showing his girl friend how it could make time on this deserted residential street. The girl was a cute dish, and who could be bothered watching out for children?

Robby was directly in front of the car. Wolf leaped straight as a bullet. His trajectory carried him so close to the car that he could feel the heat of the radiator on his flank. His forepaws struck Robby and thrust him out of danger. They fell to the ground together, just as the car ground over the last of Wolf's caudal vertebrae.

The cute dish screamed. "Homer! Did we hit them?"

Homer said nothing, and the jalopy zoomed on.

Robby's screams were louder. "You hurt me! You hurt me! *Baaaad woof-woof!*"

His mother appeared on the porch and joined in with her own howls of rage. The cacophony was terrific. Wolf let out one wailing yelp of his own, to make it perfect and to lament his crushed tail, and dashed on. This was no time to clear up misunderstandings.

But the two delays had been enough. Robby and the policeman had proved the perfect unwitting tools of Oscar Fearing. As Wolf approached Emily's little bungalow, he saw a gray sedan drive off. In the rear was a small, slim girl, and she was struggling.

Even a werewolf's lithe speed cannot equal that of a motor car. After a block of pursuit, Wolf gave up and sat back on his haunches panting. It felt funny, he thought even in that tense moment, not to be able to sweat, to have to open your mouth and stick out your tongue and ...

"Trouble?" inquired a solicitous voice.

This time Wolf recognized the cat. "Heavens, yes," he assented wholeheartedly. "More than you ever dreamed of."

"Food shortage?" the cat asked. "But that toddler back there is nice and plump."

"Shut up," Wolf snarled.

"Sorry; I was just judging from what Confucius told me about werewolves. You don't mean to tell me that you're an altruistic were?"

"I guess I am. I know werewolves are supposed to go around slaughtering, but right now I've got to save a life."

"You expect me to believe that?"

"It's the truth."

"Ah," the cat reflected philosophically. "Truth is a dark and deceitful thing."

Wolfe Wolf was on his feet. "Thanks," he barked. "You've done it."

"Done what?"

"See you later." And Wolf was off at top speed for the Temple of the Dark Truth.

That was the best chance. That was Fearing's headquarters. The odds were at least even that when it wasn't being used for services it was the hangout of his ring, especially since the consulate had been closed in San Francisco. Again the wild running and leaping, the narrow escapes; and where Wolf had not taken these too seriously before, he knew now that he might be immune to bullets, but certainly not to being run over. His tail still stung and ached tormentingly. But he had to get there. He had to clear his own reputation, he kept reminding himself; but what he really thought was, I have to save Emily.

A block from the Temple he heard the crackle of gunfire. Pistol shots and, he'd swear, machine guns, too. He couldn't figure what it meant, but he pressed on. Then a bright-yellow roadster passed him and a vivid flash came from its window. Instinctively he ducked. You might be immune to bullets, but you still didn't just stand still for them.

The roadster was gone and he was about to follow when a glint of bright metal caught his eye. The bullet that had missed him had hit a brick wall and ricocheted back onto the sidewalk. It glittered there in front of him—pure silver!

This, he realized abruptly, meant the end of his immunity. Fearing had believed Gloria's story, and with his smattering of occult lore he had known the successful counterweapon. A bullet, from now on, might mean no more needle sting, but instant death.

And so Wolfe Wolf went straight on.

He approached the Temple cautiously, lurking behind shrubbery. And he was not the only lurker. Before the Temple, crouching in the shelter of a car every window of which was shattered, were Fergus O'Breen and a moon-faced giant. Each held an automatic, and they were taking pot shots at the steeple.

Wolf's keen lupine hearing could catch their words even above the firing. "Gabe's around back," Moonface was explaining. "But it's no use. Know what that damned steeple is? It's a revolving machine-gun turret. They've been ready for something like this. Only two men in there, far as we can tell, but that turret covers all the approaches."

"Only two?" Fergus muttered.

"And the girl. They brought a girl here with them. If she's still alive."

Fergus took careful aim at the steeple, fired, and ducked back behind the car as a bullet missed him by millimeters. "Missed him again! By all the kings that ever ruled Tara, Moon, there's got to be a way in there. How about tear gas?"

Moon snorted. "Think you can reach the firing gap in that armored turret at this angle?"

"That girl ..." said Fergus.

Wolf waited no longer. As he sprang forward, the gunner noticed him and shifted his fire. It was like a needle shower in which all the spray is solid steel. Wolf's nerves ached with the pain of reknitting. But at least machine guns apparently didn't fire silver.

The front door was locked, but the force of his drive carried him through and added a throbbing ache in his shoulder to his other comforts. The lower-floor guard, a pasty-faced individual with a jutting Adam's apple, sprang up, pistol in hand. Behind him, in the midst of the litter of the cult, ceremonial robes, incense burners, curious books, even a Ouija board, lay Emily.

Pasty-face fired. The bullet struck Wolf full in the chest and for an instant he expected death. But this, too, was lead, and he jumped forward. It was not his usual powerful leap. His strength was almost spent by now. He needed to lie on cool earth and let his nerves knit. And this spring was only enough to grapple with his foe, not to throw him.

The man reversed his useless automatic and brought its butt thudding down on the beast's skull. Wolf reeled back, lost his balance, and fell to the floor. For a moment he could not rise. The temptation was so strong just to lie there and ...

The girl moved. Her bound hands grasped a corner of the Ouija board. Somehow, she stumbled to her rope-tied feet and raised her arms. Just as Pasty-face rushed for the prostrate wolf, she brought the heavy board down.

Wolf was on his feet now. There was an instant of temptation. His eyes fixed themselves to the jut of that Adam's apple, and his long tongue licked his jowls. Then he heard the machine-gun fire from the turret, and tore himself from Pasty-face's unconscious form.

Ladders are hard on a wolf, damned near impossible. But if you use your jaws to grasp the rung above you and pull up, it can be done. He was halfway up the ladder when the gunner heard him. The firing stopped, and Wolf heard a rich German oath in what he automatically recognized as an East Prussian dialect with possible Lithuanian influences. Then he saw the man himself, a broken-nosed blond, staring down the ladder well.

The other man's bullets had been lead. So this must be the one with the silver. But it was too late to turn back now. Wolf bit the next rung and hauled up as the bullet struck his snout and stung through. The blond's eyes widened as he fired again and Wolf climbed another rung. After the third shot he withdrew precipitately from the opening.

Shots still sounded from below, but the gunner did not return them. He stood frozen against the wall of the turret watching in horror as the wolf emerged from the well. Wolf halted and tried to get his breath. He was dead with fatigue and stress, but this man must be vanquished.

The blond raised his pistol, sighted carefully, and fired once more. He stood for one terrible instant, gazing at this deathless wolf and knowing from his grandmother's stories what it must be. Then deliberately he clamped his teeth on the muzzle of the automatic and fired again.

Wolf had not yet eaten in his wolf's body, but food must have been transferred from the human stomach to the lupine. There was at least enough for him to be extensively sick.

Getting down the ladder was impossible. He jumped. He had never heard anything about a wolf's landing on its feet, but it seemed to work. He dragged his weary and bruised body along to where Emily sat by the still un-conscious Pasty-face, his discarded pistol in her hand. She wavered as the wolf approached her, as though uncertain yet as to whether he was friend or foe.

Time was short. With the machine gun silenced, Fergus and his compan-ions would be invading the Temple at any minute. Wolf hurriedly nosed about and found the planchette of the Ouija board. He pushed the heart-shaped bit of wood onto the board and began to shove it around with his paw.

Emily watched, intent and puzzled. "A," she said aloud. "B—S—"

Wolf finished the word and edged around so that he stood directly beside one of the ceremonial robes. "Are you trying to say something?" Emily frowned.

Wolf wagged his tail in vehement affirmation and began again.

"A—" Emily repeated. "B—S—A—R—"

He could already hear approaching footsteps.

"—K—A— What on earth does that mean? *Absarka—*"

Ex-professor Wolfe Wolf hastily wrapped his naked human body in the cloak of the Dark Truth. Before either he or Emily knew quite what was happening, he had folded her in his arms, kissed her in a most thorough expression of gratitude, and fainted.

Even Wolf's human nose could tell, when he awakened, that he was in a hospital. His body was still limp and exhausted. The bare patch on his neck, where the policeman had pulled out the hair, still stung, and there was a lump where the butt of the automatic had connected. His tail, or where his tail had been, sent twinges through him if he moved. But the sheets were cool and he was at rest and Emily was safe.

"I don't know how you got in there, Mr. Wolf, or what you did; but I want you to know you've done your country a signal service." It was the moonfaced giant speaking.

Fergus O'Breen was sitting beside the bed too. "Congratulations, Wolf. And I don't know if the doctor would approve, but here."

Wolfe Wolf drank the whiskey gratefully and looked a question at the huge man.

"This is Moon Lafferty," said Fergus. "FBI man. He's been helping me track down this ring of spies ever since I first got wind of them."

"You got them—all?" Wolf asked.

"Picked up Fearing and Garton at the hotel," Lafferty rumbled.

"But how— I thought—"

"You thought we were out for you?" Fergus answered. "That was the Garton's idea, but I didn't quite tumble. You see, I'd already talked to your secretary. I knew it was Fearing she'd wanted to see. And when I asked around about Fearing, and learned of the Temple and the defense researches of some of its members, the whole picture cleared up."

"Wonderful work, Mr. Wolf," said Lafferty. "Any time we can do anything for you— And how you got into that machine-gun turret— Well, O'Breen, I'll see you later. Got to check up on the rest of this roundup. Pleasant convalescence to you, Wolf."

Fergus waited until the G-man had left the room. Then he leaned over the bed and asked confidentially, "How about it, Wolf? Going back to your acting career?"

Wolf gasped. "What acting career?"

"Still going to play Tookah? If Metropolis makes *Fangs* with Miss

Garton in a Federal prison."

Wolf fumbled for words. "What sort of nonsense—"

"Come on, Wolf. It's pretty clear I know that much. Might as well tell me the whole story."

Still dazed, Wolf told it. "But how in heaven's name did you know it?" he concluded.

Fergus grinned. "Look. Dorothy Sayers said someplace that in a detective story the supernatural may be introduced only to be dispelled. Sure, that's swell. Only in real life there come times when it won't be dispelled. And this was one. There was too damned much. There were your eyebrows and fingers, there were the obviously real magical powers of your friend, there were the tricks which no dog could possibly do without signals, there was the way the other dogs whimpered and cringed— I'm pretty hardheaded, Wolf, but I'm Irish. I'll string along only so far with the materialistic, but too much coincidence is too much."

"Fearing believed it too," Wolf reflected. "But one thing that worries me: if they used a silver bullet on me once, why were all the rest of them lead? Why was I safe from then on?"

"Well," said Fergus, "I'll tell you. Because it wasn't 'they' who fired the silver bullet. You see, Wolf, up till the last minute I thought you were on 'their' side. I somehow didn't associate good will with a werewolf. So I got a mold from a gunsmith and paid a visit to a jeweler and— I'm damned glad I missed," he added sincerely.

"*You're* glad!"

"But look. Previous question stands. Are you going back to acting? Because if not, I've got a suggestion."

"Which is?"

"You say you fretted about how to be a practical, commercial werewolf. All right. You're strong and fast. You can terrify people even to commit suicide. You can overhear conversations that no human being could get in on. You're invulnerable to bullets. Can you tell me better qualifications for a G-man?"

Wolf goggled. "Me? A G-man?"

"Moon's been telling me how badly they need new men. They've changed the qualifications lately so that your language knowledge'll do instead of the law or accounting they used to require. And after what you did today, there won't be any trouble about a little academic scandal in your past. Moon's pretty sold on you."

Wolf was speechless. Only three days ago he had been in torment because he was not an actor or a G-man. Now—

"Think it over," said Fergus.

"I will. Indeed I will. Oh, and one other thing. Has there been any trace of Ozzy?"

"Nary a sign."

"I like that man. I've got to try to find him and—"

"If he's the magician I think he is, he's staying up there only because he's decided he likes it."

"I don't know. Magic's tricky. Heavens knows I've learned that. I'm going to try to do my damnedest for that fringe-bearded old colleague."

"Wish you luck. Shall I send in your other guest?"

"Who's that?"

"Your secretary. Here on business, no doubt."

Fergus disappeared discreetly as he admitted Emily. She walked over to the bed and took Wolf's hand. His eyes drank in her quiet, charming simplicity, and his mind wondered what freak of belated adolescence had made him succumb to the blatant glamour of Gloria.

They were silent for a long time. Then at once they both said, "How can I thank you? You saved my life."

Wolf laughed. "Let's not argue. Let's say we saved our life."

"You mean that?" Emily asked gravely.

Wolf pressed her hand. "Aren't you tired of being an office wife?"

In the bazaar of Darjeeling, Chulundra Lingasuta stared at his rope in numb amazement. Young Ali had climbed up only five minutes ago, but now as he descended he was a hundred pounds heavier and wore a curious fringe of beard.

Glenn Myles

Berkeley Beat: Tales from a Private Investigator

Once upon a time in Berkeley
before—

One way streets
Before wrecking crews
Before Heroin
Before Telegraph Avenue pulled off the
    Eisenhower jacket
Before Herrick Horsefiddle's rude concert
Before acupuncture came to the rescue
Before money brokers with wrecking cranes
    for minds
Before mixedup liberals flamed out
Before the rightwing grabbed their whining armor
Before sickhoods raped girls with
    lovely asses
Before ministers reached for their magic
And before Chicken Little yelled to all of us—
    git out!
The sky is falling—

Ray Charles and Mariachi could hitch you to the
Red Mountain and there was nothing the 70's
    could do about it.

Dale Pendell

The City Is So Beautiful from the Roof

Over the tree tops, lying
Like a silver wolf—
Warm wind has blown away the smog; sun
Is just behind Tamalpais.

What a unique place to live!

The Feather River burns here—
Hetch-hetchy whirrs, complains ...
An old-one climbs over the crest
Of the hills, gathering acorns
With the women—

He pauses, sees it:
The span of the bridge,
The towers, the buildings, the lights,
A brief moment,
    Shudders to himself;
Thinks it must be his great age—
Says nothing to the women.

Ishmael Reed

🍃 *from* The Last Days of Louisiana Red

California, named for the negro
Queen Califia
California, The Out-Yonder State
California, refuge for survivors
of the ancient continent of
Lemuria
California, Who, one day, prophets
say will also sink

THE STORY BEGINS IN BERKELEY, CALIFORNIA. THE CITY OF UNFINISHED ATTICS AND
stairs leading to strange towers.

Berkeley, California, was incorporated on April Fools' Day, 1878; it is
an Aries town: Fire, Cardinal, Head (brain children who gamble with life,
according to Carl Payne Tobey, author of *Astrology of Inner Space*).

Aries: activity, exaltation. PROPAGANDA. Self Assertiveness. Now,
that would characterize Ed Yellings.

Ed Yellings was an american negro itinerant who popped into Berkeley
during the age of Nat King Cole. People looked around one day and there he
was.

When Osiris entered Egypt, cannibalism was in vogue. He stopped men
from eating men. Thousands of years later when Ed Yellings entered Berkeley, there was a plague too, but not as savage. After centuries of learning how

to be subtle, the scheming beast that is man had acquired the ability to cover up.

When Ed Yellings entered Berkeley "men were not eating men"; men were inflicting psychological stress on one another. Driving one another to high blood pressure, hardening of the arteries, which only made it worse, since the stabbings, rapings, muggings went on as usual. Ed Yellings, being a Worker, decided he would find some way to end Louisiana Red, which is what all of this activity was called. The only future Louisiana Red has is a stroke.

Ed gained a reputation for being not only a Worker but a worker too. No one could say that this loner didn't pay his way. He worked at odd jobs: selling tacos on University Avenue across the street from the former Santa Fe passenger station, now a steak joint; during the Christmas season peddling Christmas trees in a lot on San Pablo across the street from the Lucky Dog pet shop and the V.I.P. massage parlor.

He even worked in an outdoor beer joint on Euclid Street a few doors above the U.C. Corner.

Since he worked with workers, he gained a knowledge of the workers' lot. He knew that their lives were bitter. He experienced their surliness, their downtroddenness, their spitefulness and the hatred they had for one another and for their wives and their kids. He saw them repeatedly go against their own best interests as they were swayed and bedazzled by modern subliminal techniques, manipulated by politicians and corporate tycoons, who posed as their friends while sapping their energy. Whose political campaigns amounted to: "Get the Nigger."

Louisiana Red was the way they related to one another, oppressed one another, maimed and murdered one another, carving one another while above their heads, fifty thousand feet, billionaires flew in custom-made jet planes equipped with saunas tennis courts swimming pools discotheques and meeting rooms decorated like a Merv Griffin Show set. Like J. P. Morgan, who once made Millard Fillmore cool his heels, these men stood up powerful senators of the United States—made them wait and fidget in the lobby of the Mayflower Hotel.

The miserable workers were anti-negro, anti-chicano, anti-puerto rican, anti-asian, anti-native american, had forgotten their guild oaths, disrespected craftsmanship; produced badly made cars and appliances and were stimulated by gangster-controlled entertainment; turned out worms in the tuna fish, spiders in the soup, inflammatory toys, tumorous chickens, d.d.t. in fish and the brand new condominium built on quicksand.

What would you expect from innocent victims caught by the american tendency towards standardization, who monotonously were assigned to churning out fragments instead of the whole thing?

Sherwood Anderson, the prophet, had warned of the consequences of standardization and left Herbert Hoover's presence when he found that Hoover was a leveler: I don't care if my car looks like the other fellow's, as long as it gets me to where I'm going was how Hoover saw it.

Ed wanted to free the worker from Louisiana Red because Louisiana Red was killing the worker. It would be a holy occupation to give Louisiana Red the Business, Ed thought. Ed thought about these things a lot. Ed was a thinker and a Worker. After working at his odd jobs Ed would go to his cottage on Milvia Street and read up on botany theology music poetry corporation law american Business practices, and it was this reading as well as his own good instincts and experiences that led him to believe that he would help the worker by entering Business and recruiting fellow Workers. Not the primitive and gross businessmen of old who introduced the late movies on television, but the kind of Business people who made the circuit of 1890s America, contributing mystery and keeping their Business to themselves.

His reading directed him to an old company that was supposed to be the best in the Business. Their Board of Directors was very stringent; cruel, some would say. Ed passed their test and received his certificate from Blue Coal, the Chairman of the Board. Shortly afterwards he received an assignment from his new employers; they sent him to New Orleans on a mission to collect the effects of a certain astrologer, diviner and herbalist who had been done in by some pretty rough industrial spies working for the competition. Ed's assignment was to collect this man's bookkeeping and records and to continue this Businessman's Work. (His Board of Directors had distributed franchises all over the world; the New Orleans branch was one.)

Some say that it was after Ed returned from New Orleans that he abandoned the rarefied world of ideals and put his roots to Business; gave up being a short-order cook and handyman and became instead the head of a thriving "Gumbo" Business: Solid Gumbo Works.

He chose a very small staff of Workers—very small, because Ed had learned through bitter experience that if you go over a secret number you will run into an informer who leaks industrial secrets to industrial spies, or even worse a maniac who not only wishes to self-destruct but to bring down the whole corporation as well.

Ed rented an office on the Berkeley Marina and started making his Gumbo. He was deliberately cryptic about the kind of Gumbo he was into; it certainly wasn't "Soul Food."

Ed's Gumbo became the talk of the town, though people could only guess what Ed was up to in this city named for Bishop George Berkeley, the philosopher, who coined the phrase "Westward The Course Of Empire Takes Its Way."

When asked his purpose, Ed would merely answer that he had gone into the Gumbo Business.

Though no one could testify to having seen it or tasted it, Ed's Gumbo began making waves; though ordinary salesmen hated it, distributors wouldn't touch it and phony cuisinières gave it a bad name, no one could deny that, however unexplained, there was some kind of operation going on at Ed's Gumbo premises: cars could be seen arriving and departing; others got theirs through subscription.

Whatever Ed was selling, the people were buying, and rather than put his product on the shelves next to the synthetic wares of a poisonous noxious time, Ed catered to a sophisticated elite. In a town like Berkeley, as in any other American small town, superstitiousness and primitive beliefs were rife and so was their hideous Sister, gossip.

Ghosts too. The computer isn't to blame; the problems of The Bay Area Rapid Transit are due to the burial grounds of the Costanoan indians it disturbs as it speeds through the East Bay.

David Lodge

🌿 *from* Changing Places

AT ABOUT 12:30, THE VIGIL CAME TO AN UNEVENTFUL END, AND THE DEMONSTRATORS dispersed, chattering, for lunch. Philip had a shrimp salad sandwich with Sy Gootblatt in the Silver Steer restaurant on campus. Afterwards, Sy went back to his office to pound out another Hooker article on his electric typewriter. Philip, too restless to work (he hadn't read a book, not a real book, right through, for weeks) took the air. He strolled across Howle Plaza, soaking up the sunshine, past the booths and stalls of student political groups—a kind of ideological fair, this, at which you could join SDS, buy the literature of the Black Panthers, contribute to the Garden Bail Fund, pledge yourself to Save the Bay, give blood to the Viet Cong, obtain leaflets on first-aid in gas attacks, sign a petition to legalize pot, and express yourself in a hundred other interesting ways. On the street side of the plaza, a fundamentalist preacher and a group of chanting Buddhist monks vied with each other for the souls of those too committed to the things of this world. It was a relatively quiet day in Plotinus. Although there were State Troopers stationed on every intersection along Cable Avenue, directing the traffic, keeping the pavements clear, preventing people from congregating, there was little tension in the air, and the crowds were patient and good-humoured. It was a kind of hiatus between the violence, gassing and bloodshed of the recent past and the unpredictable future of the Great March. The Gardeners were busy with their preparations for that event; and the police, having had some bad publicity for their role in the Garden riots, were keeping a low profile. It was business as usual along

Cable Avenue, though several windows were shattered and boarded up, and there was a strong, peppery smell of gas in the Beta Bookshop, a favourite gathering-place for radicals into which the police had lobbed so many gas grenades it was said you could tell which students in your class had bought their books there by the tears streaming down their faces. The more wholesome and appetizing fumes of hamburger, toasted cheese and pastrami, coffee and cigars, seeped into the street from crowded bars and cafés, the record shops were playing the latest rock-gospel hit *Oh Happy Day* through their external speakers, the bead curtains rattled in the breeze outside Indian novelty shops reeking of joss-sticks, and the strains of taped sitar music mingled with the sounds of radios tuned to twenty-five possible stations in the Bay area coming from the open windows of cars jammed nose to tail in the narrow roadway.

Philip snapped up a tiny vacant table at the open window of Pierre's café, ordered himself an ice-cream and Irish coffee, and sat back to observe the passing parade: the young bearded Jesuses and their barefoot Magdalenes in cotton maxis, Negroes with Afro haircuts like mushroom clouds and metallic-lensed sunglasses flashing heliographed messages of revolution to their brothers across the street, junkies and potheads stoned out of their minds groping their way along the kerb or sitting on the pavement with their backs to a sunny wall, ghetto kids and huckleberry runaways hustling the parking meters, begging dimes from drivers who paid up for fear of getting their fenders scratched, priests and policemen, bill-posters and garbage collectors, a young man distributing, without conviction, leaflets about courses in Scientology, hippies in scarred and tattered leather jackets toting guitars, and girls, girls of every shape and size and description, girls with long straight hair to their waists, girls in plaits, girls in curls, girls in short skirts, girls in long skirts, girls in jeans, girls in flared trousers, girls in Bermuda shorts, girls without bras, girls very probably without panties, girls white, brown, yellow, black, girls in kaftans, saris, skinny sweaters, bloomers, shifts, muu-muus, granny-gowns, combat jackets, sandals, sneakers, boots, Persian slippers, bare feet, girls with beads, flowers, slave bangles, ankle bracelets, earrings, straw boaters, coolie hats, sombreros, Castro caps, girls fat and thin, short and tall, clean and dirty, girls with big breasts and girls with flat chests, girls with tight, supple, arrogant buttocks and girls with loose globes of pendant flesh wobbling at every step and one girl who particularly caught Philip's attention as she waited at the kerb to cross the street, dressed in a crotch-high

179

mini with long bare white legs and high up one thigh a perfect, mouth-shaped bruise.

Sitting there, taking it all in with the same leisurely relish as he sucked the fortified black coffee through its filter of whipped cream, Philip felt himself finally converted to expatriation; and he saw himself, too, as part of a great historical process—a reversal of that cultural Gulf Stream which had in the past swept so many Americans to Europe in search of Experience. Now it was not Europe but the West Coast of America that was the furthest rim of experiment in life and art, to which one made one's pilgrimage in search of liberation and enlightenment; and so it was to American literature that the European now looked for a mirror-image of his quest. He thought of James's *The Ambassadors* and Strether's injunction to Little Bilham, in the Paris garden, to 'Live ... live all you can; it's a mistake not to,' feeling himself to partake of both characters, the speaker who had discovered this insight too late, and the young man who might still profit by it. He thought of Henry Miller sitting over a beer in some scruffy Parisian café with his notebook on his knee and the smell of cunt still lingering on his fingers and he felt some distant kinship with that coarse, uneven, priapic imagination. He understood American Literature for the first time in his life that afternoon, sitting in Pierre's on Cable Avenue as the river of Plotinus life flowed past, understood its prodigality and indecorum, its yea-saying heterogeneity, understood Walt Whitman who laid end to end words never seen in each other's company before outside of a dictionary, and Herman Melville who split the atom of the traditional novel in the effort to make whaling a universal metaphor and smuggled into a book addressed to the most puritanical reading public the world has ever known a chapter on the whale's foreskin and got away with it; understood why Mark Twain nearly wrote a sequel to *Huckleberry Finn* in which Tom Sawyer was to sell Huck into slavery, and why Stephen Crane wrote his great war-novel first and experienced war afterwards, and what Gertrude Stein meant when she said that 'anything one is remembering is a repetition, but existing as a human being, that is being, listening and hearing is never repetition'; understood all that, though he couldn't have explained it to his students, some thoughts do often lie too deep for seminars, and understood, too, at last, what it was that he wanted to tell Hilary.

Robert Hass

Adhesive: For Earlene

How often we overslept
those grey enormous mornings
in the first year of marriage
and found that rain and wind
had scattered palm nuts,
palm leaves, and sweet rotting crabapples
across our wildered lawn.

By spring your belly was immense
and your coloring a high rosy almond.

We were so broke
we debated buying thumbtacks
at the Elmwood Dime Store
knowing cellophane tape would do.
Berkeley seemed more innocent
in those flush days
when we skipped lunch
to have the price of *Les Enfants de Paradis.*

From *Field Guide*, copyright 1973 by Robert Hass. Reprinted by permission of Yale University Press.

C. L. Babcock

The Bancroft Way

Plopped plump as an Easter egg
on the curling green grass.

I've got coffee running in
my veins running in
my veins running in
my veins running in
my veins.
I've got coffee running in my veins,
oh lordy, nothing like it.

Dancing

       among

             and on by

                   the hare krishna.

I was selective this morning about the coffeehouse in which I would alight.
Passed by five or six after floating through their interiors like a curious mer-
ry breeze. Found the right combination (croissant and cappuccino), and was
immediately found myself by Big Blonde Meg whom I didn't recognize at first
as the woman so naked and rolling fat at the pond last Saturday. I didn't tell
her that, but I did admit that I had been thinking of her friend Louis (who had
been with her Saturday) as I had rounded the corner to the cafe, because I
smelled the Kretak Krakatoa Turkish cigarettes he smoked.

She was with Ralph, photographer and painter from NYC (who reminded me of Andy of Mayberry character ... Howard?), but is married to Chester who "works." She said she was going to school "for the first time," studying French in a summer class also attended by a man who walked by our table with his coffee cup.

A young long frizzy blondhaired man with guitar began to scream outside the cafe. Customers grimaced in embarrassment. Meg recalled discussing an oceanic dream at a gestalt session and her leader had suggested she become the ocean, making the sounds of the waves breaking, and she couldn't allow herself the noise. It never came, she said: "It was blocked." Sometimes, she said, she and her husband retire to their bedroom, climb under the covers, count to three, and scream together. It makes them feel good.

A policeman arrived to talk to the young screamer who sang and played a guitar response.

Authority and insanity walked away together.

Czeslaw Milosz

The Evangelical Emissary

SLOWLY, INDIRECTLY, I AM APPROACHING THE PROPER THEME OF MY BOOK. BUT BE-
fore I proceed to gather and tie up the various strands, let Holy Hubert appear
on these pages. For several years this small, freckled man has stood every day
at his post by the entrance to the university campus in Berkeley. He is an
evangelist, a preacher of the teachings of Jesus. I have practically never seen
him speak calmly. He is usually thrashing about in something like a trance,
red-faced, with swollen veins and drops of sweat on his dandruff-covered
forehead; his noisy exhortations and thunderings against sin do not carry
very far because hoarseness makes his voice break in a choked falsetto. He is
such a part of the colorful carnival atmosphere that practically no one stops
for him, never more than four or five listeners, who regard him with mellow
smiles and sometimes amuse themselves by asking him questions if his enthusiasm slackens and he has to be reexcited. He is a popular figure, a part
of the local folklore like the boys in their saffron robes chanting "Rama
Krishna, Krishna Rama" over and over, and the students treat him with the
benevolence one shows the harmlessly insane.

Despite certain psychopathic traits, Holy Hubert is not mentally ill,
even though the complete uselessness of his dogged ministerings (for it is
doubtful whether he has convinced even a single student) could prompt such
suspicions. His mistake was that, instead of addressing the citizens in small
towns in Arkansas or Kentucky, who would have listened to him with respect,

he decided to become a missionary among people whose way of thinking is not accessible to him, so that even the religious students remain indifferent to his cries. Perhaps he wishes to imitate St. Paul preaching in pagan Athens, but he is completely unaware of any of the historical changes occurring now. He is an unwilling example of the aging of certain mental formations which continue to exist along with other fresher ones and which, in Arkansas, for example, are still taken completely seriously, while elsewhere, in Berkeley, they seem like parodies. If the supporters of Ho Chi Minh or members of the Black Panthers begin speaking on the steps of Sproul Hall near the spot on the sidewalk Holy Hubert works, a fervent, excited crowd forms at once, and that alone ought to cause Hubert to reflect, though obviously he could explain all that to himself in his own way.

The absurdity of behavior like Hubert's, playfully nicknamed "Holy" by the students, may deserve sympathy, although he is not devoid of humor and he clearly needs to blow off steam by yelling for his own health. My theme, which I am approaching indirectly, is the erosion of the system of ideas and customs which form the American way of life. Hubert, in some sense, is a delegate from the traditional morality sent out among the apostates and sinners. The battle of the police against marijuana in the vicinity of the campus is another example of such holding actions.

Describing his states after taking hashish in his treatise *Les Paradis Artificiels*, Baudelaire contributed to a new variety of tale about witches and ghosts. The heroes of those tales were bohemian artists appalling the philistines with their readiness to make pacts with the devil. The paintings and literary works of these bohemians were finally recognized as precursors and included in "culture," but their customs were thought of as characteristic of a certain epoch forever past. In the Europe of my youth, impressed by the seriousness of political upheavals, no one would have believed that bohemia, by its very way of life, was an augury of mass phenomena with social and political significance and that a time would come when Baudelaires, though not necessarily talented ones, would number in the hundreds of thousands or millions. Those who read Stanislaw Ignacy Witkiewicz's novels about the future thought there was something to his prophecies, but not when he predicted the great role narcotics would play (this was considered a private eccentricity on his part).

Taking a logical approach, there is no reason not to sentence people to death for smoking tobacco or to long prison sentences for drinking alcohol; those are dangerous drugs. But, although in certain countries tobacco had its martyrs who were hanged, the strict edicts against it have passed into oblivion, and after the failure of Prohibition in America, drinking has become a ritual that proves one a normal, decent, loyal citizen. Taking into account the fact that *Cannabis sativa* is, in comparison with tobacco and alcohol, a rather innocent substance, much ado about nothing, the stubbornness with which the police pursued marijuana throughout the sixties had the mark of an obsession like Hubert's zealous rantings. The searching of pockets, the handcuffs, the prison sentences can only be explained by a sense of threat from "others," and not without basis. It is doubtful whether the use of marijuana would have become so widespread had it not also served as a sort of tribal insignia for all those who questioned the established order.

I do not mean to slight the political potential of marijuana, if only because, like jazz, it came from the underground culture, the colored peoples. Black activists are trying to wipe out heroin, the plague of the ghetto, but everyone smokes marijuana. Moreover, the police ban on marijuana is causing the whites to draw nearer the blacks because of the similarity of their situations: to be a criminal means to look at society from the bottom, from underground, the way it is seen by blacks, who know the color of their skin makes them suspicious to the police.

Hubert's missionary zeal: unfortunately, while observing him, I cannot understand what makes him tick, and for me he is a sort of living puppet, not a pleasant way to think about another human being.

But at least, thanks to him, I can puzzle out how the two systems of ideas and customs, the old and the new, relate to each other. If it were up to me, I would prefer not to be forced to choose between them.

Al Young

The Robbie's Dance

Years later
I fall back in.
The jukebox is new
but the music is dated
the talk is dated
even the beer is dated
but the people are the same;
a black & tan bohemia
that never was,
Miss Brown Baby in a getup
that defines her squareness
right up to the hip,
Mrs Lager Belly
Mr Fare Thee Well &
Mr Ne'er Do Well
walk in
for the thousandth time that day
& stage a talk-in
up near the exit.
I keep trying to grin sincerely
like a liberated bore

but the game's too quick
to be played back
successfully
by my facial muscles.
The chinese jew
who scoops the gravied rice
to go with turkey
or chow mein
has been jaded so long
he's taken to hiding out
backstage in the kitchen
between I.D. checks
to keep his eyelid from atrophying.
The dancers here
are all string-operated
but even the thread is worn & dated.
The john is a living little magazine
a sort of piss wall review
that takes the story up
wherever you leave off.
On my way back out
I'm busy picturing
the illustrious canned hippie
who sticks it out in here for years
before finally typing up &
getting his thesis published on
Current Trends in California

Herrick Hospital, Fifth Floor

for a musician friend who
finally OD'd on Blackness

Well, so youve gone & overdone it again,
overdosed yourself this time on Blackness;
locked between Blue Cross nurse-padded walls,
the unreliable air outside & beyond
shot up with softening Berkeley sunshine

Phrasing fails you, diction cramps,
words are a loss & reflection too costly
What color were you ever but infamous blue?

If your music werent sound & its realness
didnt cleanse, I know you could never walk
much less dance out of this white room again

Philip K. Dick

🍃 *from* The Transmigration of Timothy Archer

BAREFOOT CONDUCTS HIS SEMINARS ON HIS HOUSEBOAT IN SAUSALITO. IT COSTS A hundred dollars to find out why we are on this Earth. You also get a sandwich, but I wasn't hungry that day. John Lennon had just been killed and I think I know why we are on this Earth; it's to find out that what you love the most will be taken away from you, probably due to an error in high places rather than by design.

After I parked my Honda Civic in the metered slot I sat listening to the radio. Already all the Beatles songs ever written could be heard on every frequency. Shit, I thought. I feel like I'm back in the Sixties, still married to Jefferson Archer.

"Where's Gate Five?" I asked two hippies going by.

They didn't answer. I wondered if they'd heard the news about John Lennon. I wondered, then, what the hell I cared about Arabic mysticism, about the Sufis and all that other stuff that Edgar Barefoot talked about on his weekly radio program on KPFA in Berkeley. The Sufis are a happy lot. They teach that the essence of God isn't power or wisdom or love but beauty. That's a totally new idea in the world, unknown to Jews and Christians. I am neither. I still work at the Musik Shop on Telegraph Avenue in Berkeley and I'm trying to make the payments on the house that Jeff and I bought when we were married. I got the house and Jeff got nothing. That was the story of his life.

Why would anybody in their right mind care about Arabic mysticism? I asked myself as I locked up my Honda and started toward the line of boats. Especially on a nice day. But what the fuck; I had already made the drive over the Richardson Bridge, through Richmond, which is tawdry, and then past the refineries. The bay is beautiful. The police clock you on the Richardson Bridge; they time when you pay your toll and when you leave the bridge on the Marin side. If you arrive in Marin County too soon, it costs you big bucks.

I never cared for the Beatles. Jeff brought home *Rubber Soul* and I told him it was insipid. Our marriage was breaking up and I date it from hearing "Michelle" one billion times, day after day. That would be roughly around 1966, I guess. A lot of people in the Bay Area date events by the release of Beatles records. Paul McCartney's first solo album came out the year before Jeff and I separated. If I hear "Teddy Boy," I start crying. That was the year I lived in our house alone. Don't do it. Don't live alone. Right up to the end, Jeff had his antiwar activity to keep him company. I withdrew and listened to KPFA playing baroque music better left forgotten. That was how I first heard Edgar Barefoot, who impressed me initially as a jerk-off, with his little voice and that tone of savoring his own cerebral activity immensely, delighting like a two-year-old in each successive *satori*. There is evidence that I was the only person in the Bay Area who felt that way. I changed my mind later; KPFA started broadcasting Barefoot's taped lectures late at night, and I would listen while I tried to get to sleep. When you're half asleep, all that monotonous intoning makes sense. Several people explained to me once that subliminal messages had been inserted in all the programs aired in the Bay Area around 1973, almost certainly by Martians. The message I got from listening to Barefoot seemed to be: You are actually a good person and you shouldn't let anyone else determine your life. Anyhow I got to sleep more and more readily as time passed; I forgot Jeff and the light that had gone out when he died, except that now and then an incident would pop into existence in my mind, usually regarding some crisis in the Co-op on University Avenue. Jeff used to get into fights in the Co-op. I thought it was funny.

So now, I realized as I walked up the gangplank onto Edgar Barefoot's cushy houseboat, I will date my going to this seminar by John Lennon's murder; the two events are for me of a seamless whole. What a way to start understanding, I thought. Go back home and smoke a number. Forget the wimpy voice of enlightenment; this is a time of guns; you can do nothing, enlightened or otherwise; you are a record clerk with a degree in liberal arts from Cal. *"The best lack all conviction"* ... something like that. *"What rough beast ... slouches towards Bethlehem to be born."* A creature with bad posture, nightmare of the world. We had a test on Yeats. I got an A-minus. I was good. I used to be able to sit on the floor all day eating cheese and drinking goat's milk, figuring out the longest novel ... I have read all the long novels. I graduated from Cal. I live in Berkeley. I read *The Remembrance of Things Past* and I remember nothing: I came out the door I went in, as the saying goes. It did me no good, all those years in the library waiting for my number to light up, signifying that my book had been carried to the desk. That's true for a lot of people, most likely.

But those remain in my mind as good years in which we had more cunning than is generally recognized; we knew exactly what we had to do: the Nixon regime had to go; we did what we did deliberately, and none of us regrets it. Jeff Archer is dead, now; John Lennon is dead as of today. Other dead people lie along the path, as if something fairly large passed by. Maybe the Sufis with their conviction about God's innate beauty can make me happy; maybe this is why I am marching up the gangplank to this plush houseboat: a plan is fulfilled in which all the sad deaths add up to something instead of nothing, somehow get converted to joy.

A terribly thin kid who resembled our friend Joe the junkie stopped me, saying, "Ticket?"

"You mean this thing?" From my purse I got out the printed card that Barefoot had mailed me upon receipt of my hundred dollars. In California you buy enlightenment the way you buy peas at the supermarket, by size and by weight. I'd like four pounds of enlightenment, I said to myself. No, better make that ten pounds. I'm really running short.

"Go to the rear of the boat," the skinny youth said.

"And you have a nice day," I said.

When one catches sight of Edgar Barefoot for the first time one says: He fixes car transmissions. He stands about five-six and because he weighs so much you get the impression that he survives on junk food, by and large hamburgers. He is bald. For this area of the world at this time in human civilization, he dresses all wrong; he wears a long wool coat and the most ordinary brown pants and blue cotton shirt ... but his shoes appear to be expensive. I don't know if you can call that thing around his neck a tie. They tried to hang him, perhaps, and he proved too heavy; he broke the rope and continued on about his business. Enlightenment and survival are intermingled, I said to myself as I took a seat—cheap folding chairs, and already a few people here and there, mostly young. My husband is dead and his father is dead; his father's mistress ate a mason jar of barbiturates and is in the grave, perpetually asleep, which was the whole point of doing it. It sounds like a chess game: the bishop is dead, and with him the blond Norwegian woman who he supported by means of the Bishop's Discretionary Fund, according to Jeff; a chess game and a racket. These are strange times now, but those were far stranger.

Edgar Barefoot, standing before us, motioned us to change seats, to sit up front. I wondered what would happen if I lit a cigarette. I once lit a cigarette in an *ashram*, after a lecture on the Vedas. Mass loathing descended on me, plus a sharp dig in the ribs. I had outraged the lofty. The strange thing about the lofty is that they die just like the common. Bishop Timothy Archer owned a whole lot of loftiness, by weight and by size, and it did him no good; he lies like the rest, underground. So much for spiritual things. So much for aspirations. He sought Jesus. Moreover, he sought what lies behind Jesus: the real truth. Had he been content with the phony he would still be alive. That is something to ponder. Lesser people, accepting falsehood, are alive to tell about it; they did not perish in the Dead Sea Desert. The most famous bishop of modern times bit the big one because he mistrusted Jesus. There is a lesson there. So perhaps I have enlightenment; I know not to doubt. I know, also, to take more than two bottles of Coca-Cola with me when I drive out into the wastelands, ten thousand miles from home. Using a gas station map as if I am still in downtown San Francisco. It's fine for locating Portsmouth Square but not so fine for locating the genuine source of Christianity, hidden from the world these twenty-two hundred years.

I will go home and smoke a number, I said to myself. This is a waste of time; from the moment John Lennon died everything has been a waste of time, including mourning over it. I have given up mourning for Lent ... that is, I cease to grieve.

Raising his hands to us, Barefoot began to talk. I little noted what he said; neither did I long remember, as the expression goes. The horse's ass was me, for paying a hundred dollars to listen to this; the man before us was the smart one because he got to keep the money: we got to give it. That is how you calculate wisdom: by who pays. I teach this. I should instruct the Sufis, and the Christians as well, especially the Episcopalian bishops with their funds. Front me a hundred bucks, Tim. Imagine calling the bishop "Tim." Like calling the pope "George" or "Bill" like the lizard in *Alice*. I think Bill descended the chimney, as I recall. It is an obscure reference; like what Barefoot is saying it is little noted, and no one remembers it.

"Death in life," Barefoot said, "and life in death; two modalities, like *yin* and *yang*, of one underlying continuum. Two faces—a 'holon,' as Arthur Koestler terms it. You should read *Janus*. Each passes into the other as a joyous dance. It is Lord Krishna who dances in us and through us; we are all Sri Krishna, who, if you remember, comes in the form of time. That is his real, universal shape. Ultimate form, destroyer of all people ... of everything that is." He smiled at us all, with beatific pleasure.

Only in the Bay Area, I thought, would this nonsense be tolerated. A two-year-old addresses us. Christ, how foolish it all is! I feel my old distaste, the angry aversion we cultivate in Berkeley, that Jeff enjoyed so. His pleasure was to get angry at every trifle. Mine is to endure nonsense. At financial cost.

I am terribly frightened of death, I thought. Death has destroyed me; it isn't Sri Krishna, destroyer of all people; it is death, destroyer of my friends. It singled them out and left everyone else undisturbed. Fucking death, I thought. You homed in on those I love. You utilized their folly and prevailed. You took advantage of foolish people, which is truly unkind. Emily Dickinson was full of shit when she prattled about "kindly Death"; that's an abominable thought, that death is kind. She never saw a six-car pile-up on the Eastshore Freeway. Art, like theology, a packaged fraud. Downstairs the people are fighting while I look for God in a reference book. God, ontological arguments for. Better yet: practical arguments against. There is no such listing. It would have helped a lot if it had come in time: arguments against being foolish, ontological and empirical, ancient and modern (see common sense). The trouble with being educated is that it takes a long time; it uses up the better part of your life and when you are finished what you know is that you would have benefited more by going into banking. I wonder if bankers ask such questions. They ask what the prime rate is up to today. If a banker goes out on the Dead Sea Desert he probably takes a flare pistol and canteens and C-rations and a knife. Not a crucifix displaying a previous idiocy that was intended to remind him. Destroyer of the people on the Eastshore Freeway, and my hopes besides; Sri Krishna, you got us all. Good luck in your other endeavors. Insofar as they are equally commendable in the eyes of other gods.

I am faking it, I thought. These passions are bilge. I have become in-bred, from hanging around the Bay Area intellectual community; I think as I talk: pompously, and in riddles; I am not a person but a self-admonishing voice. Worse, I talk as I hear. Garbage in (as the computer science majors say); garbage out. I should stand up and ask Mr. Barefoot a meaningless question and then go home while he is phrasing the perfect answer. That way he wins and I get to leave. We both gain. He does not know me; I do not know him, except as a sententious voice. It ricochets in my head, I thought, already, and it's just begun; this is the first lecture of many. Sententious twaddle ... the name of the Archer family's black retainer in, perhaps, a TV sitcom. "Sententious, you get your black ass in here, you hear me?" What this droll little man is saying is important; he is discussing Sri Krishna and how men die. This is a topic that I from personal experience deem significant. I should know, because it is familiar to me; it showed up in my life years ago and will not go away.

Once we owned a little old farm house. The wiring shorted out when someone plugged in a toaster. During rainy weather, water dripped from the light bulb in the kitchen ceiling. Jeff every now and then poured a coffee can of black tarlike stuff onto the roof to stop it from leaking; we could not afford the ninety-weight paper. The tar did no good. Our house belonged with others like it in the flat part of Berkeley on San Pablo Avenue, near Dwight Way. The good part was that Jeff and I could walk to the Bad Luck Restaurant and look at Fred Hill, the KGB agent (some said) who fixed the salads and owned the place and decided whose pictures got hung up for free exhibition. When Fred came to town years ago, all the Party members in the Bay Area froze solid, out of fear; this was the tip-off that a Soviet hatchetman was in the vicinity. It also told you who belonged to the Party and who did not. Fear reigned among the dedicated but no one else cared. It was like the eschatological judge sorting the sheep, the faithful, from among the ordinary others, except in this case it was the sheep who quaked.

Dreams of poverty excited universal enjoyment in Berkeley, coupled with the hope that the political and economic situation would worsen, throwing the country into ruin: this was the theory of the activists. Misfortune so vast that it would wreck everyone, responsible and not responsible alike sinking into defeat. We were then and we are now totally crazy. It's literate to be crazy. For example, you would have to be crazy to name your daughter Goneril. Like they taught us at the English Department at Cal, madness was funny to the patrons of the Globe Theater. It is not funny now. At home you are a great artist, but here you are just the author of a difficult book about Here Comes Everybody. Big deal, I thought. With a drawing in the margin of someone thumbing his nose. And for that, like this speech now, we paid good money. You'd think having been poor so long would have taught me better, sharpened my wits, as it were. My instinct for self-preservation.

I am the last living person who knew Bishop Timothy Archer of the Diocese of California, his mistress, his son my husband the homeowner and wage earner *pro forma*. Somebody should—well, it would be nice if no one went the way they collectively went, volunteering to die, each of them, like Parsifal, a perfect fool.

Larry Eigner

April 17–22 81

roll and

Rock rock rock all over Berkeley

stars, sky

but what's to be seen

trees, yes, hills, light

window reflection
air wavering
more nights   stars
and you push out the light

this something new a
piano somewhere
maybe over the town
like a church bell once

Laura Chester

❧ Last Breath

When the petals of the plum tree
swirl Up
before my headlights
I turn the car downhill and Drive.

Because I can't see
the way the apple flower
snows the air

the way the fever
of the plum
is brooding everywhere in Berkeley

I drive and I am driven.
Tightly smooth   and
forward in my black compartment.

Thinking things
that make me know   my
heart still beats.

Loving in a way
that will not get there.

So if I weep   behind this steering wheel

I say that it's ok
here in my privacy.

I can allow myself   one luxury.

Let it go now

as behind
the petals from the plum   turn brown
and blow
Down the dark driveway.

Valerie Miner

from Movement

SUSAN SLID THE ROMAINE LEAF AROUND THE FADED PARQUET BOWL. IT WAS TOO
heavy with oil to curl through her fork. Larry Blake's special salad had
more garlic than she remembered and the Coke tasted oversweet. Still,
everything had a certain pungency compared to the stewed tea on which
she had been surviving in London for years. A jock sat down in the opposite booth. Varsity most likely. He wore a pin-striped shirt under the
Vaughn maroon sweater. Fraternities were popular again, she had heard,
and everybody went to football games.

Susan felt personally offended, as if the last ten years hadn't happened.
What did the 70's reap but an excuse for apathy? They hadn't "overcome"
anything except their own idealism. Not completely true. But Berkeley
seemed the same as before the Revolution—right down to these sunset scapes
of San Francisco Bay on the restaurant walls. Her first year at Berkeley, she
thought this was what you called an art exhibit. Some things *had* changed. She
used to like Larry Blake's restaurant for the art exhibits.

Larry Blake's. What could you expect? Of course Guy would insist on
meeting here, where they used to come for salads after studying. His con-
science was a compass, always drawing them back around. Guy, her ex-
husband, her first lover. None of the labels were either indelible or ephemeral
enough. He was a ghost in her life; he would always be there, somewhere in the
shadow of her former self. She looked at her watch and worried. It wasn't like
Guy to be late.

Occasionally, Susan still wondered if she should have stayed with him. She might have been saner, safer in their academic coterie, drinking more gin and less tonic, serving cottage cheese and mandarin oranges on Centura unbreakable side plates. But the whole marriage stretched between "what-ifs" and "might-have-beens." And Susan was getting too old for abstractions.

She used to fantasize about what image she would bring back for him—successful critic, laid back vagabond, mad politico, artiste—and she used to worry about what he would choose to see. The six years since their divorce had spun as dizzily as a projector on rewind: *Liberation*, reel one. Now she wanted to tell him all she had learned about their marriage, him and herself. All that she had discovered about being a woman, about coming from an immigrant, unschooled, working class family. Although they had been married for seven years they had, like most proper Americans, ignored the delicate issues of class. She wanted to tell him about her failed contributions to the Mozambican revolution. About how she learned over and over that America was not the center of the world. And there was so much that was hard to speak in anecdotes. How she had moved from being a good Catholic girl to being a radical feminist. She wanted to tell him how she discovered she had a decent mind and then that she had deep feelings and fervent commitments and how she was just beginning to believe again that she had a soul. Even this morning she debated about wearing her Zanzibarian dress or her jeans and workshirt. Now, realizing how loud was the sameness around her, she understood that she didn't have to *project* any image. It didn't matter what he thought. It didn't matter if he showed up. And knowing this, she could wait a while longer.

Of course he would come back to the States when Carter pardoned the draft dodgers. Although it should have been amnesty rather than pardon, although deserters should have been included, although Guy and Susan had both sworn futures to Canada, the land of the possible, they would each come back. Guy had written to her: "Life is not a moral gymnasium." Susan had been able to appreciate Shaw only after the divorce. Yes, she had long known they would come back in different ways to different places in Berkeley.

The waiter deposited thick, bloody steaks in front of the jock and his girlfriend. Extra rare. She and Guy would have had just enough money now to order sirloin, to buy an el toro and paddle around the Bay. As it was, she could barely afford this salad. If nothing else, money marked the solid distinction between what might have been and what actually was.

Susan looked down at her notebook, pretending to read. The proposal for her next book. Had she brought it to save time or to show Guy or to hide behind at a solitary lunch?

They had been the ideal couple, much admired, often envied. Young, dedicated, vigorous. With a certain stylish earnestness. A handsome intelligence—they were the kind of couple who would be photographed for marijuana magazine ads in a few years. Political, unneurotic, talented, professional without being careerist. Comfortable in the funky apartment they shared with another couple above an Italian grocery in a West Indian district of Toronto. Even Guy's mother—after she had made her way through the neighbors—had to admit that the giant paisley cushions and the macrographics were "kind of cute and so resourceful." Guy was doing well in graduate school and Susan was making enough money from the magazine to buy a new sound system. Everything that might have been was happening.

So why was she unhappy? Her therapist told her she wasn't ready to grow up. Her Marx teacher told her she was tied to bourgeois gratifications. Her CR group told her she was confined by the patriarchal family. And everybody, despite their caveat, thought she and Guy had an open or healthy or growing relationship. Their friends were surprised when they split up: "Of all people." Susan was surprised that they were surprised.

She reached deep into her scarred leather purse and pulled out Guy's note. One o'clock. He said one o'clock. Now it was nearly 2:00 p.m.

In college, she would daydream about meeting her lover at an Italian restaurant with red-checked tablecloths and with Chianti bottles hanging from the ceiling. He would be a rather 50's Jack Lemmon lover. She never dreamed about her lover arriving, just about the waiting, about savoring his arrival. Now, she returned to her notebook, absently spooning the ice from her water glass to dilute the sweetness of the Coke. She used to do this with rum.

She remembered one stunning Bacardi afternoon during the last month of their marriage. She sat on the giant paisley cushion with page proofs strewn around her. *Appalachian Spring* was spinning on the Gerrard. She nibbled from a plate of carrots and raisins, sipping her third rum and Coke. For half an hour she had sat, staring blankly. There was something she had to figure out. Something about Guy's motivation for ... now, what was it? Guy's motivation for....

She had sat for another twenty minutes groping for the idea and re-leasing it just as it filed back into her head. Maybe she didn't want to settle the "marriage thing" after all. Maybe she had always known it would break down. No, the scary part was that there was nothing she had always known. This marriage was her fault, she realized, adding the rest of the rum to her Coke. When they were at Berkeley, she wanted to get married; he just wanted to live together. He said he needed a lot more backpacking, a lot more political work and, to be up front, a lot more screwing around before he settled into any-thing. But she won. They were married because, if nothing else, it was necessary for crossing borders.

The whole summer before the divorce had continued like that—phasing in and out, days sunk to the bottom of her glass. She switched to sherry, because it was cheaper, more convenient—for some reason. Everything was paced to possible depressions. Could she rationalize a drink for this? A little extra sleep for that? What the hell had happened to her? To them? It wasn't *his* fault. He was faithful. Now he was talking about kids and a communal house. Just what she had asked for. Why did she get herself into the labyrinth of drinking and sleeping that desultory summer?

Guy's note, she read it again. Yes, one o'clock. This was his first com-munication in three years, despite a dozen letters from her. He used to be the prolific one. He had maintained the correspondence with their families. He was the sentimental one. And now?

Often in those last days he had tried to relieve her spells of depression. On their seventh anniversary he suggested a good dinner at Damarco's. They both tried to enjoy the vignette. Red-checked tablecloths. Chianti bottles. (But she had no one to wait for. They had come together.) Guy ordered them the second most expensive thing on the menu. The talked about plans for the summer and about a friend from Berkeley who would visit the next week. He said he wanted to tell her something and he hoped it wouldn't sound too sop-py. He rather liked being married to a frizzy radical. Of course he wasn't politically impotent just because he was intellectual. His work in the dialec-tical influences on Freud was important for the Movement too. He wasn't go-ing to apologize. Anyway, he knew *she* wasn't judgmental; that was one of the reasons he would always love her.

After that meal at Damarco's, she really craved a liqueur. Kahlua or Tia Maria. No, she had promised herself—only three drinks a night. What the hell was wrong with her anyway? Why was she constricted by his good will? Guilty. Yes, she had used this marriage for her own ends, for support and confidence. Now she needed to stand alone. Maybe not completely guilty. "A mortal sin is a knowing offense against...." She sipped her coffee slowly, trying not to conjure the soothing qualities of Kahlua. The change had come naturally, least imperceptibly. They had both changed. They weren't the same people. God, it all sounded so trite, so hollow, boring. No, this couldn't—wouldn't—happen to them, she told herself. They would talk when they got to bed. This air was too close with smoke and parmesan for sense. Once they got out of this place, they would be all right.

Neither of them felt like going to bed. Guy suggested Scrabble. She agreed. Her first word was "cache."

"That's a double word score," he smiled, "twenty-four points."

From that moment, that move, Susan never again doubted that they would separate. And understanding so, she didn't have much left to figure out.

She did wonder, now as she waited at Larry Blake's, whether Guy still played Scrabble.

Alice Kahn
✿ Berkeley Explained

I AM WALKING NORTH ON SHATTUCK AVENUE—MAIN STREET—BERKELEY, CALIFOR-
nia. In my head I hear Elvis, the late King, singing "In the ghet-*toe* ..." I
improvise his back-up, the Mighty Clouds of Joy, adding, "the gourmet ghetto ..."

A young man comes up to me on the corner of Cedar and Shattuck and
asks, "Do you know where I can get any food around here? I'm new in town."
I brace myself against a lamppost because the question is staggering. Can I
answer him in three thousand words or less? Doesn't he know he's in the heart
of what realtors call "the most dynamic and innovative retail shopping area
in the United States?" Is he unaware that he has entered—da-da da-da da-
da—the Gluttony Zone?

Before I lead him down the gustatory garden path I attempt to assess his
level of knowledge. He arrived in town yesterday from SUNY Binghamton
and has come to do graduate work in microbiology. No, he has never heard
of the gourmet ghetto. He has missed the articles about it in *The New York
Times, Newsweek,* and *The Nation.* He doesn't know that the East Coast
press loves to do a dance on how the Berkeley Left has become the food establishment, how "the counterculture has become the counter culture," how the
radicals now eat radicchio, how the barricades have been replaced by the
wheels of brie. No, he is just a new kid in town asking what appears to be a
perfectly simple question. For him, and for all the other new recruits, the

young men and women who are even now arriving from the provinces, I'd like to offer this modest guide to Berkeley.

If you dare to wander beyond the campus, beyond the dorms, beyond your "pig runs" and "animal houses" you will find a place that gets curiouser and curiouser. The first rule is that Berkeley, like Tina Turner, never does anything nice and easy. If you keep this in mind you won't be surprised when what would seem to be the simplest of civic acts—from tree trimming to garbage disposal—become issues of heated debate, protest, emotion, and political intrigue.

But let's start with that innocent question: where to get food around here. I answer the young man by pointing out that we have just passed Poulet, the gourmet chicken deli, the Virginia Bakery, Borrelli's, an Italian deli, the Griffon, a new Scandinavian restaurant, and Warszawa, a place that proves that Polish cuisine is more than a Spam upsidedown cake.

Across the intersection is Smokey Joe's Cafe, a monument to the mellow hippie. Next to it, on the site of a former funeral home, there is a complex of shops including Sweet Temptations, a chocolate and yogurt heaven, a Japanese place where you can achieve yakitori, a place that actually serves hamburgers, and one of the innumerable croissant and cappuccino filling stations that have become the McDonalds of Berkeley. (Surely over ten billion served by now.) Never mind that this mortuary mall once inspired angry protests in the community. That and the ability to park nearby are now history.

On the next corner is the Co-op, the Shattuck branch of a chain of cooperative supermarkets. This particular store is one of the largest volume supermarkets in the country. It too has experienced constant political infighting: should it sell the cheapest food, the wholesomest food, or those products untainted by the human or labor rights violations of the companies who make them? Newcomers can join or they can shop here without joining. If the clerk asks for your number you can say "Farmworkers" or "Free Clinic" and nobody will know you're a stranger. You will also want to check out the upstairs bulletin board where you might find a room to rent, a sofa, or your own true love.

My newfound friend and I proceed up Shattuck past the world-famous Chez Panisse and turn the corner to see the natives gather for coffee at a place called Peet's, which sells the sinsemilla of coffee beans as well as a variety of beans ordinaire. I tell him how on mornings here he'll find what my friend Sharon calls "independently wealthy mothers." These are the ones with working husbands and one perfect babe in an Aprica stroller. We listen as the men nearby bitch about how they're "not gettin' much."

You can even stop in at the Juice Bar for something as mundane as a turkey sandwich, I tell him. Just be sure you have a styrofoam cup in your hands at all times. This is your passport. Anyone caught wandering around the area without a styrofoam cup is immediately suspect. We have little gestapo type officers who approach you and ask to see "ze cup, pleeze!"

You'll probably want to stop in at Vivoli's for an Italian ice cream. I keep hoping they'll add some truly local flavors like Walnut Square or Nuclear Freeze but so far it's just plain old amaretto and fresh strawberry and stuff like that. Vivoli's represents a success story from one of Berkeley's unique minorities, the lesbian community. Unlike San Francisco, where the gay male community is ghettoized in the Castro district, the lesbian community is mostly mainstreamed into Berkeley life. It is speculated that there is one feminist therapist for every fifty people in Berkeley. A good thing too because you can't live here for very long without needing one of your own.

Nearby is Cocolat (Parlez-vous Berklaise?), recently the scene of a labor strike that forced chocolate decadence lovers to temporarily satisfy themselves with sex. Next door is a pathetic Northern California attempt at a Jewish deli redeemed by its Yiddishkeit live performances including, believe it or not, terrible Jewish comedians. Further up the street is Lenny's, a butcher shop where they'll "sell no swine before its time," and—what else?— another Italian bakery and restaurant. Then there's the Produce Center (always a bridesmaid to the the formidable Monterey Market), where you can get five kinds of berries and four kinds of mushrooms and have a friendly conversation with the only normal person in Berkeley. You'll know her when you see her.

Completing the food mania is a sushi dealer, the Berkeley Fish Market, and Pig By the Tail, or as one neighborhood wag has dubbed it, Pig By the Balls. And last, but not least, we come to the Cheese Board.

Ah, blame it on the Cheese Board, they started it all. And is their face and politics red. This is one of the oldest and most successful food businesses in town. The collective that runs it seems quite uncomfortable with their new-found fame. Not only did they introduce us to the wonders of brie and their mock Boursin and a myriad of goat cheeses, but they perfected that ultimate symbol of the new Berkeley—the baguette. If you play your cards right and have a lot of time to kill, you may be able to score one. In a form of torture, they pollute the neighborhood with the smell of this delicacy baking.

I imagine someday the Cheese Board will organize a mass community therapy-in. The whole of Berkeley will be invited to engage in a huge swash-buckler scene. Some therapist-cum-facilitator will be perched on a lifeguard platform on the grassy road-divider strip and sound the *en garde*. Then we will all pull our baguettes out of their long white sheaths and begin non-violently battering one another. "Have a nice day. Pow! Take that, you knave!"

I have another theory on the Cheese Board and their diabolically de-licious baguettes. No, they don't just want to constipate us. I think the plan is to get the whole community hooked and then baguette tease us. First it'll be "Sorry, no baguettes tonight, honey, the collective has a headache." From there it'll progress to "Baguettes for activists only." Before long nobody will get a baguette unless she submits to working for world peace and against nuclear weapons research. They'll franchise out branches to strategic lo-cales: The Cheese Board, Livermore; The Cheese Board, Los Alamos; The Cheese Board, Port Chicago. Believe me, if J. Edgar Hoover were alive today we'd have a five-hundred-page report on this small band of ragtag slicers and bakers, and its potential to wreak havoc by baguette denial.

Now that I've told you all about my neighborhood I want you to get out, leave, scram. I saw it first, and it's mine. If you must move beyond Larry Blake's or La Val's, go to somebody else's neighborhood. Wend your way through the maze of traffic diverters to another one of those islands in the Berkeley archipelago. Go to the Elmwood or Westbrae or Shattuck and Woolsey or College and Alcatraz or West Berkeley. There is actually better food to be had in these places than the ghetto. Some neighborhoods you can actually park in.

"But," protests the young man from the provinces, "all I wanted was to buy some bread and milk. That's all. If you really want to explain something, explain why it's so hard to find a place to live around here." (Phew! Couldn't he have asked me something simple like, "How can Reagan be removed from office?")

As I contemplate an explanation of the great Berkeley housing shortage, I hear Gene Pitney singing, "No, it isn't very pretty what a town without pity can do."

I walk him over to Henry Street behind the Safeway store (in North Berkeley, even Safeways have gourmet counters; I hear McDonald's is contemplating the introduction of Quail McNuggets). I point out a three-story cellblock-like building which extends back a full block to Milvia Street and bears the name Luxor Apts. This, I explain, is a classic Berkeley ticky-tacky circa 1966. Now look at the place next door. Note the porch columns, the stained glass, the elegant entrance. If you really want to know the story of Berkeley, it's told in windows, eaves, and brown shingles. Berkeley is basically a museum of houses, few of them all *that* grand but each magnificent in its details.

The ticky-tackies threatened this character and charm. Speculation in rental housing made tearing down two old elegant houses and putting up a 26-unit Luxor on the same lots a wise investment. Not three blocks from here is a row of ticky-tackies, one of them built on the site of a cottage where Allen Ginsberg reportedly wrote *Howl*. Would the English tear down Shakespeare's house and put up units?

Two forces conspired to stop the ticky-tackification of Berkeley. One was the riots of the Vietnam and People's Park era. Much anger was focused then on the concept that property was more valued than life. People showed their contempt for property by stoning, bombing, and placing graffiti on it. This didn't look so good when the developers brought the investors through for a looksee. The other force was rent control—for years a threat and finally a reality. Some feel rent control was necessary for neighborhood preservation and to maintain low-cost housing. Others feel it represents an unfair limitation on the supply of housing caused by mealy-mouthed no-growthers and argue that it ultimately contributes to gentrification.

"But," the young man inevitably asks, "what about the new building over there with the greenhouse windows, the skylights, and the wood shingles?" Sorry, pal, you can't afford it. Those are for the YUPs, the young urban professionals. They've been lured to Berkeley, in part, by bargains in condos and single-family homes—bargains, that is, relative to Marin, San Francisco, and the Peninsula. BART, a public transportation system convenient to Montgomery Street and few other places, is also a plus. The influx of these commuters has encouraged a new phase of speculation in commercial real estate, as creative capitalists and tax shelter artists sense a rising demand among the disposable income types for sophisticated shops selling unique items.

I give him an example. For days I passed a sign in the window of La Cuisine that proclaimed: "SALE! INGRID PARTY BALLS, $19.95." Curious, I went inside and asked, "What are Ingrid Party Balls?" "I don't know," the clerk answered.

"But you've had them on special all week."

She went and called another clerk. "Are you the one asking about the Ingrid Party Balls?" this one asked.

"Yes."

"I'm sorry," she said, "they're all sold out."

I considered calling up later and saying: this is Ingrid. Any messages?

I ask the young man if he understands now why he can't find a place to live.

"Sort of. But say, do you think there are any vacancies at the Luxor?"

"Don't tell me you want to live there. There are no fireplaces, no built-in redwood buffets, no window seats, no French doors—in short, none of the necessities of life."

"I think I could learn to survive without French doors. You ever try riding your bike from Pinole?"

I am about to suggest Oakland—"just over the rent control border," as they say in the real estate ads—but I can see something else is on his mind. He has one more question: "Do you know where ... this is kind of hard to ask ..."

Let's see. He said he was 23. (Was I ovulating in 1960?) "Look, I'm old enough to be your mother, boy. Ask me anything."

"Do you have any ideas on where I could meet girls?"

"Hey! Call us women," I retort—although, as I think about it, "girl" has had a slightly different ring to it since I've turned 35. (What really enrages me is when 23-year-old guys call me "ma'am.")

I try to break it to him gently how hazardous looking for love in Berkeley can be. I suggest he might want to join a men's group just to get the old Yin and Yang into balance before he comes on too strong or too weak to one of these young, assertive, hot-tub-on-the-first-date types. Next I suggest he make the necessary $25 investment in a haircut—one of those no-sideburn, parted-on-the-side specials. The long hair, I tell him, has got to go. I quote my friend Nina, who recently observed, "In the '60s I saw a guy with long hair and thought: brother. Now I see one and I think: mass murderer."

To meet women, he could try the clubs—Ruthie's, the Berkeley Square, Ashkenaz, etc., but I warn him that most of Berkeley closes at 9:00 p.m. Only the nocturnal creatures venture out after that, so he'd better be wary on the streets. Another approach would be to try the bookstores. (You probably think that there are so many bookstores because this is a town of intellectuals, but guess again—Cody's, Moe's, and their ilk have other uses.) I suggest he might be able to impress the right woman with, "Excuse me. Do you know where I can find a copy of Barbara Ehrenreich's book about men and the flight from commitment?" A more aggressive try would be "Have you seen a copy of *(How to Satisfy Your Lover With) Extended Sexual Orgasm?* I've already read about ESO myself but I need a copy for a friend." This will surely impress the red stiletto heels type. But what if he wants to meet a "Humboldt honey," an unshaven, Birkenstocked, Botticellian beauty? Here he might try, "I'm looking for a copy of *Death Begins in the Colon.* Do you know the book?"

While this bookish approach may work for recent East Coast arrivals, Californians generally prefer to get physical. A visit to the jogging track at Martin Luther King school may allow for a clever opener, such as "I couldn't help noticing how you never pronate." Or perhaps on a visit to Strawberry Canyon pool he could manage a quick "You swim laps often?" between strokes. I tell him the odds are even more favorable (one male: twenty females) at an aerobics class. While his head is between his legs, he can look to his right and say, "Good workout, huh?" He could also try hiking in Tilden Park—if he can find it.

Finally, if all else fails, there is Berkeley's favorite sport: hanging out, eating, and waiting for something to happen. So I hand the young man a step-by-step plan: "BERKELEY ON 5,000 CALORIES A DAY."

8:00 a.m.—Cappuccino at Caffe Mediterraneum. Walk up to a What's Left type (you know, Old Left, New Left, What's Left) and ask for an explanation of the mural at Telegraph and Haste. Jog up Dwight to College. Note woman in wheelchair helping blind man cross street.

9:00 a.m.—Vanilla malt at Elmwood Soda Fountain. Discover soda jerk is local sage. Grab a bag of watermelon Jelly Bellies from Sweet Dreams and a cruller from Dream Fluff Donuts. Check out the Ivy Shoppe. (This place, I predict, will be torn down soon, then reconstructed in fifteen years at considerable expense.)

10:00 a.m.—Bear claw and coffee at the Buttercup (the IRS willing). Too bloated to jog or walk. Call Taxi Unlimited and go down to Shattuck. Wander around Hink's—"a great store at home." Look at Berkeley Public Library.

11:00 a.m.—Optional snack at Edy's or Trumpetvine Court.

Noon—Szechwan Hot Sauce Noodles at the Taiwan Restaurant. Revitalized. Run down Hearst Street past Ohlone Park (who the hell was Ohlone?), noting St. Procopius Church and the Church of the Good Shepherd. Stop at grocery store at 7th and Hearst for homemade tortillas.

1:00 p.m.—Aerobics class at Goldies.

2:00 p.m.—Piece of pie at Bette's Diner. Meet beautiful woman with Mercedes who takes you to see her villa on San Luis Road.

4:00 p.m.—Stagger down to Fatapple's for a blueberry muffin and four cups of coffee with real cream and real sugar.

5:00 p.m.—Pick up ribs at Flint's Bar-B-Q.

6:00 p.m.—Pick up ribs at K C Bar-B-Q.

7:00 p.m.—Irish coffee at Brennan's. Get in argument over best barbecue place in Berkeley.

7:30 p.m.—Phone Herrick and Alta Bates Hospitals. Comparison shop for stomach pumping. Ask when Alta Bates cafeteria is open.

8:00 p.m.—Attend Berkeley City Council meeting. See our two political parties, the BCA and the ABC, in a ten-round exhibition match. (Tuesdays only.)

9:00 p.m.—Stroll Solano Avenue for Mu Shu Pork. Get a marble fudge cone at McCallums.

10:00 p.m.—Tune into KPFA for "Fat Is No Longer A Feminist Issue: A Look At Manorexics."

11:00 p.m.—Fries and Merlot at the Santa Fe Bar and Grill.

Midnight—*Rocky Horror Picture Show* at the UC Theatre (Saturdays only). See the children of Berkeley disguised as perverts.

As I hand him the list, I add a personal note. I came to Berkeley in the era of Dustin Hoffman's *The Graduate.* We wanted to get out of the rat race, out of the plastic, out of boredom and mediocrity just as Benjamin did. Now the movie is dated. Things have come full circle as a new generation desperately wants a crack at a good job, a home, some status. We, the class of '65, could reject those things when they seemed so readily available.

"*The Graduate* ..." he ponders. "I saw that on the late show. Isn't that the one where Dustin Hoffman has an affair with an older woman?"

"Yeah."

"Well, do you think maybe I could buy you a drink, ma'am?"

"What? Pollute my body with alcohol and other toxic chemicals? You've got to be kidding, Babycakes. Now beat it. And welcome to Berkeley."

Maxine Hong Kingston

✺ *from* Tripmaster Monkey

"WHY DID YOU ASK ME OUT?" ASKED NANCI.

Because you're beautiful, he thought, and maybe I love you; I need to get it on with a Chinese-American chick. He said, "I wanted to find out if the most beautiful girl of all my school days would come to me." There. Said. Would come to me. Intimate. He let her know that he used to be—and still was—in her thrall. "I'm calling you up," he had said on the phone, "to celebrate the first anniversary of our graduation. Come tell me, have you found out, 'Is there life after Berkeley?'" "I told you—we're having a reunion, a party for me."

"Shouldn't we be at Homecoming, then, with everyone else?"

What? Buy her a lion-head chrysanthemum, pin it on her tweed lapel? Do the two of us have to walk again past the fraternities on College Avenue, and admire their jungle-bunny house decorations? The Jew Guais too with Greek letters—Sammies—and Yom Kippur banners. Yeah, there were a Chinese fraternity and sorority, but if you were bone-proud, you didn't have anything to do with SOP sisters and the Pineapple Pies. Nor the Christian house, which let anybody in. The crowd let the city and county sawhorses route them, governments too co-operating with football. He was always walking alone in the opposite direction but ending up at Strawberry Canyon—the smell of eucalyptus in the cold air breaks your heart—among the group looking down into the stadium for free. Only he was up here for the walk, awaiting a poem to land on him, to choose him, walking to pace the words to

---

the rhythm of his own stride. And there was all this football interference. The Cal Marching Band, the drum booming, and the pompon girls kneeling and rotating an arm with pompons in the air, and the teams running toward each other with the crowd going oo-oo-OO-OH! How do all those people know you're supposed to stand and yell that yell at kickoff? The reason he didn't like going to football games was the same reason he didn't like going to theater: he wanted to be playing. Does his inability at cheers have to do with being Chinese? He ought to be in Paris, where everything is dark and chic.

"The Big Game soon," she said.

"Weren't you an Oski Doll? You were an Oski Doll, weren't you?"

"Come on. It was an honor to be an Oski Doll. It's based on scholarship too, you know? It's a good reference. Some of us Oski Dolls helped integrate the rooting section from you boys."

"'Here we go, Bears, here we go.' 'We smell roses.' 'All hail Blue and Gold; thy colors unfold.' 'Block that kick, hey.' 'Hold that line, hey.' 'The Golden Bear is ever watching.'"

"See? You did participate."

"Well, yeah, I went to the Big Game once. Stanford won." But most of the time I was participating in the big dread. "Those songs and cheers will stick in the head forever, huh?"

"I know your motive for wanting to see me," she said. "You want to know how you were seen. What your reputation was. What people thought of you. You care what people think of you. You're interested in my telling you."

He looked at the bitten nails of the fingers that held her cigarette and of her other fingers, both hands; they put him at ease. "Yes, if you want to tell me, go ahead."

"Well, let me think back," she said, as if school had been long ago and not interesting anymore. "It seems to me you were a conservative."

No. No. He had been wild. Maybe she thought it flattered a Chinese man to be called temperate? Safe. What about his white girlfriends? What about his Black girlfriend? His play-in-progress? That he read aloud on afternoons on the Terrace and at the Mediterraneum (called The Piccolo by those hip to the earlier Avenue scene). There had been no other playwright. Of whatever color. He was the only one. She hadn't cared for his poem in *The Occident?*

"Conservative like F.O.B.? Like Fresh Off the Boat?" He insulted her with translation; she was so banana, she needed a translation. "Conservative like engineering major from Fresno with a slide rule on his belt? Like dental student from Stockton? Like pre-optometry majors from Gilroy and Vallejo and Lodi?" But I'm an artist, an artist of all the Far Out West. "Feh-see-no. Soo-dock-dun," he said, like an old Chinese guy bopping out a list poem. "Gi-loy. Wah-lay-ho. Lo-di." But hadn't he already done for her a catalog of places? Repeating himself already. One of his rules for maintaining sincerity used to be: Never tell the same story twice. He changed that to: Don't say the same thing in the same way to the same person twice. Better to be dead than boring.

"I mean quiet," she said and did not elaborate, poured more espresso out of her individual carafe, sipped it, smoked. She wasn't deigning to go on. No examples. He had talked for four years, building worlds, inventing selves, and she had not heard. The gold went out of the day. He came crashing down. He must have been feeling good only because the sun was out amid grey weeks. (In the plague year, according to Defoe, the people's moods were much affected by the weather.)

"Well?" she said, pushing away from the table, her shoulders up, like a forties movie girl being hugged. "I have an appointment at three-thirty." As if she had come to the City for that important appointment and incidentally might as well have met with him too, a former classmate, after all. But there was no guile on her face, which seemed always uplifted. Was she joyful, or was that curve the way her mouth naturally grew? The way some cats and dogs have smile markings. Yeah, it was not a smile but a smile marking.

"Hey, wait a minute," he said, and grabbed her hand, held hands with her, a sudden endearment achieved right smack through force fields. "Let's go for a walk. Come for a walk with me. I live near here. Yeah, I do. Let me show you where I live."

Since she, in truth, did not have an appointment, she agreed to go with him. Finding digs, having digs, arranging them interested each of them very much. *God's solitaries in their caves and bare retreats.*

"Let's walk," he said, stubbing out his cigarette. Let's amble the blue North Beach streets as the evening sun goes down into the far grey water.

Though they walked through the land of the wasted, no Malte sights popped out to hurt him, she dispelling them. By day, the neon was not coursing through its glass veins. The dancing girl in spangles and feathers had flown out of her cage, which hung empty over the street. Nobody barked and hustled at the doorways to acts and shows. The day-folks, wheeling babies, wheeling grandpas, holding children by the hand, were shopping for dinner at the grocery stores and the bakery, dropping by the shoe repair. Oh, the smell of the focaccia ovens—O Home. A florist with white moustachios jay-walked through traffic with armsful of leonine football chrysanthemums. Behind glass, at the all-day-all-night place on the pie-wedge corner, poets, one to a table, were eating breakfast. The Co-Existence Bagel Shop was gone. The old guys, *Seventh Seal* knights, had played chess with Death and lost. The Bagel Shop, Miss Smith's Tea Room, Blabbermouth Night at The Place—all of a gone time. Out from the open door of La Bodega, a folksy guitar sweetened the air. The guitar was being passed around, and each played the tune he knew. You should have been there the night Segovia dropped by and played flamenco. Wittman musefully sang as if to himself a Mose Allison riff.

> *A young ma-a-an*
> *ain't nothin' in this world today.*
> *Because the ol' men's*
> *got all the money.*

The air of the City is so filled with poems, you have to fight becoming imbued with the general romanza. Nanci's long black hair and long black skirt skirled with the afternoon breezes. The leather of her shoulder bag strapped a breast. Her arms and outstretching legs were also long and black; she wore a leotard and tights like an old-fashioned Beat chick but, honestly, a dancer, dance togs for a good reason. Here he was: Wittman Ah Sing profiling down the street with a beautiful almost-girlfriend, clipping along, alongside, keeping up with him, the two of them making the scene on the Beach, like cruising in the gone Kerouac time of yore.

He ducked into the bookstore. She followed right on in. She stood beside him, browsing the rack of quarterlies, quite a few brave Volume I Number Ones. There were homemade books too, mimeo jobs, stencils, and small-press poetry that fit neat in the hand. On the top rack—right inside the door at eye level for all to see coming in or going out—was: an artistic avant-garde far-out new magazine that had published—in print—a scene from his play-in-progress—the lead-off piece—with his byline—right inside the front cover. He could reach over and hand it to her, but it would be more perfect if she happened to pick it out herself, come upon his premiere on her own, and be impressed. (F. Scott Fitzgerald, trying to impress Sheilah Graham, had driven to every bookstore in L.A., but could not find a copy of any of his books.)

Wittman went downstairs to the cool basement, where among the bookshelves were chairs and tables with ashtrays. He had first come to this place when he was a high-school kid on one of his escapes from Sacramento, Second City to Big City. No *No Free Reading* sign. No *No Smoking*. You didn't have to buy a book; you could read for nothing. You had a hangout where you didn't have to spend money. Quiet. All the radios in Chinatown blaring out the ball game, but here, we don't care about the World Series. He hadn't known the City Lights Pocket Book Shop was famous until the *Howl* trial, which he had cut school to attend. "Shig" Shigeyoshi Murao was the one charged with selling an obscene book. The muster of famous poets had blown Wittman away—everybody friends with everybody else, a gang of poets. He, poor monkey, was yet looking for others of his kind.

There had been a Chinese-American guy who rode with Jack and Neal. His name was Victor Wong, and he was a painter and an actor. Wittman had maybe seen him, or someone Chinese with the asymmetrical face of a character actor; he wore a white t-shirt with paint streaks and "hand-tooled leather shoes." Victor Wong, who went to the cabin in Bixby Canyon with Jack Duluoz and Neal/Cody. All this written up in *Big Sur*, where Jack calls Victor Wong Arthur Ma ("Little Chinese buddy Arthur Ma." Shit.), and flips out of his gourd walking in the moonless night above the wild ocean that rants for his life. Jack hangs on to the side of the mountain and listens and shouts back and sings. "Mien Mo Big Sur killer mountain for singing madly in." It would have been better if Victor/Arthur had been a writing man like the rest of them, but anyway he talked a lot and was good at hallucinations. "Little Arthur Ma [yet again "little"!] who never goes anywhere without his drawing paper and his Yellowjacket felt tips of all colors, red, blue, yellow, green, black, he draws marvelous subconscious glurbs and can also do excellent objective scenes or anything he wants on to cartoons—." They stay up all night, and Arthur Ma keeps making it up; he's not one of those storytellers who has to rehearse in the bathroom. Wittman had not gone up to the man with the character actor's face—one eye big, one eye small—and grabbed him by the arm and introduced himself. The poets at Big Sur fall asleep but not Arthur, who stays awake with Jack, the two of them yelling till dawn. "... and Arthur Ma suddenly yells: 'Hold still you buncha bastards, I got a hole in my eye.'"

John Oliver Simon

✎ Fuchsia

for Clarence Breland

And the sunset still seems to be bleeding
in the red wax flukes of fuchsia
and the purple cones of stock,
the marigold's orange dollars
and coyote lily's outrageous flags,
flowers for Ernestine who passed from here
the first week of March—Clarence told me
she was a strong woman—had worked
everywhere he was stationed in World War II—
eight years older than him—one daughter—
a devout Jehovah's Witness—Clarence ain't
a devout anything—once,
when he was very drunk
and his 280 pounds had to be hoisted
all the way up the stairs by the Lopez kids and me
he sang, and he called her
my old stand-by—she cleaned rich
people's houses—did her work and saved
her wages, and Clarence carpentered and plumbered
hauled stuff in the old red truck

and Ernestine drove to work in a new Datsun.
All hunched up in a skinny jacket
she would wait, while she was dying
for her ride to the Kingdom Hall
like a woman who was once a slave.
And naturally I never hugged her,
but she's blown into air, into thin air
and now Jake down the block
and the guy across the corner—
Clarence says he's gonna move to Mississippi
soon as he sells so death won't
catch him here, and I tell
him the story of the appointment
in Samarkand and Clarence
slaps his knee and says that's a good one.

🦋 Flatlands Backyard Infrastructure

Flatlands backyard infrastructure. You can't go out and buy it; takes awhile
to live in, sow seeds, sink roots, become neighbors with folks who might not
be your same age or color. My neighbor Clarence Breland and I have been
talking over our fence about gardens, baseball, and politics for a quarter of
a century—the current fence and its predecessor. "Ain't nothin holdin up
that fence but what we growin on it, John," he said. Clarence tells me how he
left Mississippi (Sheriff at the front door, him out the back door, ran all night
barefoot, hopped a freight, didn't stop till he got to Chicago) and the beauty
of island volcanoes erupting at night in the South Pacific during World War
II. I've found chips of obsidian digging in my garden. This year I'm growing
corn, pumpkins, beans, tomatoes (Mesoamerican staples) plus two kinds of
basil, red chard, celery, lettuce, purple cauliflower, radicchio, mustard,

arugula, yellow and red onions, cilantro, oregano, artichokes, rhubarb, strawberries, raspberries and marigolds. There's no soil anywhere sweeter than East Bay flatlands dirt. My daughters grew up here and now they've each moved one block away in backyard cottages. My mother and daughter calico cats think this backyard wilderness Eden was created especially for them. I won't disillusion them.

Brenda Hillman

☙ Several Errands

The shoe repairman works behind the married shoes,
his whole hand inside the boot he's shining,
everything cozy in the glass displays, laces paired
on gravel he's spread out in the window, shoes
placed as though they're walking, and beside them
propped up, the wooden tongues of shoe horns, poised
to serve the inanimate world ... He comes out mildly
attentive, soft accent, possibly a Scottish
childhood, possibly sheep to tend ... Clear day,
first summer divorced in Berkeley, a time of seamless,
indescribable grief; he waits kindly in his blue apron,
fingering the well-worn inner sole, and I am grateful
for those who serve us knowing nothing of our lives ...

*

The cleaner waits behind the silver bell;
he's from Cambodia and has free Christian literature
on the counter. He greets me with pleasant chatter,
searches through the coats, some left for years,
he says; they make a soft blue whistle as they circulate
on the ovals like the ones under those automatic boats.
As the clothes pass, little checks and prints under

the whooshing of motion, I see my husband's coat—
how long will I call him my husband—like an old friend
passing by quickly not bothering to greet me. Odd now,
I don't have to pick it up, the serious plaid will go
around between the women's suits and stay all night ...

*

I watch the young butcher flipping over the young
chicken: he takes one wing and sort of spins it,
first on its back, flinging the trimmed, watery
lemon-colored fat into the trash, then before
he starts on the legs he puts his hand so deeply in
that the finger comes out the neck ... The other butcher
sets the slab of beef under the saw: the riveting
intricate swirl as the dead flesh pulls away;
he goes off, shouts short words from the deep freeze—
to me or to the carcass hanging by the shank?—
I can wait, but the spaces can't, there's a slight
ticking, then the carcass swings and swings ...
Somehow I thought we would know everything
through the flesh. Perhaps. But my days have become
spirit. The young butcher splits the chicken
down the back, seems to enjoy the crack of the knife
as it enters the bone, so I try to. Housewives lean
against the cool glass to convey holiday news and he
responds without really looking up; I love that.

*

    oh Berkeley summer mornings, aren't they—
what? past the French Hotel, the glint of tiny spoons
so briefly and soberly allowed to rest on white saucers,
the plums just about over, the agapanthus—"lilies of denial"—
in the center dividers, blooming, or just about to—
like me, hearty and hesitant, not wanting to write it,
not wanting the ruin the perfection of the poem
by writing it ... At the dentist, the little mirror,

the dinosaur prong is put into the mouth. Mouth:
the first darkness. Nearby: the mobile with straw
eyeless fishes. The dentist will go home to her family,
having briefly reached inside the visible mystery
and found nothing ... I imagine Wisdom in the text
is like this, creating the cosmos from the mind of God,
looking interested and competent; she touches
the physical place with her prong, and the pain shines ...

Janice Gould

🌾 A Berkeley Life

1.
Most of my life I looked out
over the bay, over the blue
water and bridge
to the white city that gleamed
in the morning sun.
Beyond the white city was the ocean
curving into an infinity of birds
and waves. Somewhere
at the far end of the imagination
lay Japan, from whose fishing fleet
drifted the glass floats
we sometimes found
among dry strands of seaweed
on excursions to the beach.

The hills were a place of mud and rain,
of pungent chaparral, of oak,
laurel, and thistle. Past the narrow
asphalt streets and the gray-leaved eucalyptus,
we took our dogs into the hills
on foggy mornings, or cloudless
winter evenings, when my father

returned tired from work
and his long commute.
We watched as Berkeley changed—
the university expanded, the city
widened streets or blocked off others,
the traffic became busier.

And on those evenings, one year
or another as I got older,
a girl and I would sometimes
walk out to the steep green hills
above the labs and think tanks,
above the groves, the stadium,
the student housing.

Lit from underneath, the fog
glared over the city.
The sound of traffic rose to our ears,
a continuous throb. Then,
not looking at her face,
I would put my arm
around her shoulder.
If she did not move away—
if she leaned her head toward me—
we would stand thus, together
in a world that did not see us.

2.
Flowering trees, wind,
the south slope of sun,
a Mediterranean pine,
blossoming yucca.
The night smell
of star jasmine.
This was my neighborhood:
streets clean, almost

suburban.
Inside people's houses
I imagined bookcases,
a piano, the sideboard
with its carafe of rich liquor,
matching glasses.
Warm light. Adults
in conversation, children asleep
in cartoon-patterned pajamas.

The men are lawyers,
accountants, university professors.
They live
a good life:
opera, theater,
foreign films,
art openings, things
I cannot imagine.
They drive Volvos,
Peugeots, the occasional
Mercedes. And their wives
dress in linen
or chic satin
evening clothes.
I babysit their children
in homes that are always clean.
(The cleaning lady
comes on Friday.)

I look out the large windows
of their new houses.
The wooden frames smell fresh,
the glass is unbuckled.
Outside, the sky is very dark,
so dark you can see stars
though the lights below twinkle.

Shoes still on,
I fall asleep
on their cream-colored sofa.
They come home quietly,
their voices low, clothes
rustling. They pay cash.
The husband drives me home,
while the wife who is
so beautiful, so pale,
removes her clothes,
her makeup. She
waits for him
to return.

He drops me off at
the curb of my house
with its tangled
vegetation, old trees,
steep stairs.
I enter the hall
with its dog smell,
musty dampness,
the smell of disorder
and family secrets.

3.
"Dennis, goddamit,
come back here!"
That was my older sister
hollering from the porch
at her boyfriend
whom my mother,
in a fit of compassion,
had invited to live with us.
The motor of the '49 Ford
Mom gave him

roars as Dennis
peels away.
My sister cries,
slams doors,
tells our mother to
shut up!
Dennis will call later that evening,
drunk, but sobered from fear:
he has slammed the car into a telephone pole
by the canyon bar, a bar for misfit
cowboys in the Oakland hills.

He will come home reeking of liquor
and stumble into the room
where my younger sister and I sleep.
Trying to kiss her,
slobbering,
he stinks of beer,
cigarettes, shaving lotion.
He paws her with his rough
strong hands.
"Get away," shrieks my younger sister.
"Quit bothering me!"

Dennis will be crying, unsteady,
stupid. In the morning
Mother will be mad at him.
But as if he's her son,
or the man in the family,
she will pick up
his jeans and shorts,
cook his breakfast,
do his laundry—
laundry I fold, iron,
and place on the bed
in his room.

He flatters my mother
with his dog-like appreciation.
She believes in his innocence,
and berates my older sister.
"You're no better than a whore,
you chippy. You'll never
amount to anything!"
My dad, meanwhile, says nothing.
He gets up each morning
and drives away.

Our older sister is bad-tempered,
angry.
She hates us.
We keep away from her.
Every day
she screams,
slams doors.
She can never say
what happened.

Every day
the structure of our Berkeley life
promises to give way.

Julia Vinograd

For Moe Who Died

I keep thinking it's an April fool's trick
and Moe'll come back growling contemptuously
over his cigar,
"You people'll believe anything,
whadda you mean, dead?"
I've still got a Moe's trade slip, Moe money
with his picture and the slogan
"in God and Moe we trust."
I'll feel funny about using it now.
I never minded George Washington being dead
but some people just aren't supposed to die.
I remember Moe's voice loudly unharmonizing
with whatever blues the ceiling was playing.
"She done him wrong" would drift upstairs
and splash over the book I was browsing,
hunched on a stool or poring thru the rickety carts.
I remember the continual cheerful grumble
that came out of Moe like cigar smoke
and of course the cigars.
Freud said "sometimes a cigar is just a cigar"
but not now.
I want all cigars to have Moe's face on the gilt band.
I want Berkeley's no-smoking ordinance to go up in cigar smoke

at Moe's memorial, they can re-instate the silly thing
afterwards, if they have to.
I want to plant cigars on Moe's grave instead of flowers
and see what grows, something will.
I want exploding cigars.
I want to watch the endangered whales
blow waterspouts out of Moe's bald spot.
I want every book in all 4 floors of Moe's bookstore
to be about Moe because I don't know much about him
and I never needed to before,
he'd obviously always be there.
I want Moe back.
I recognized Moe's photo in the shop window,
it's from the employees' bathroom
and it's one of a pair of photos in the same frame.
The other photo shows Moe with his back to the camera,
facing the john.
And I want that other photo to be in the shop window.
I want to see Moe pissing all over that April fool Death,
that fools everyone.

Biographical Information

C. L. Babcock lived in Berkeley in the 1970s. She submitted "The Bancroft Way" for publication in *City of Buds and Flowers* (1977), an anthology published by John Oliver Simon at the *Aldebaran Review*. No further information about her work or life is available, but she is one of many writers who, without fanfare, have written about Berkeley life and quietly enriched its literary tradition.

Simone de Beauvoir (1908–1986) was a socialist, a feminist, and a leader of the existentialist movement. She lived in Paris most of her life. At the Sorbonne, she earned a degree in literature and philosophy, later receiving a professional teaching qualification from the École Normale Superiéure. She was named president of the French League of Women's Rights in 1974. Her books include *The Blood of Others* (1946), *The Second Sex* (1949), *America Day by Day* (1953), *The Mandarins* (1954), and her autobiography, *The Prime of Life* (1960). She and her lifetime companion, Jean-Paul Sartre, viewed literature as a terrain of imaginative freedom and used it to fight against institutional sexism, bourgeois hypocrisy, and organized religion.

Bishop George Berkeley (1685–1753) was born in Kilkenney, Ireland. He was a student and later a professor at Trinity College in Dublin before taking his Holy Orders at the Church of Ireland. Best known for his book *The Principles of Human Knowledge* (1710), he wrote beautiful prose that attempted to stem the rise of atheism in England and Ireland. Berkeley did missionary work in America and hoped to establish a college in the Bermudas. While he never saw this dream realized, he did contribute land and resources to Harvard and Yale Universities. A century after Berkeley wrote "Verses on the Prospect of Planting Arts and Learning in America," Frederick Billings stood in a field overlooking the Golden Gate and proposed to name the university *Berkeley*—after the man who coined the phrase "westward the course of empire takes its way."

Anthony Boucher (1911–1968) was the pseudonym of William A. P. White, a prominent book critic, editor, music scholar, and mystery writer. He was a graduate student at U.C. Berkeley in the early 1930s and lived at the International House, the

Sequoia Apartments on Haste Street, and at 2643 Dana Street. Writing as Anthony Boucher, he published seven novels and two collections of short stories. He was a three-time winner of the prestigious Edgar Award for best mystery criticism.

John F. Boyd (1843–1912) wrote "The Berkeley Heroine" while he was an undergraduate at U.C. Berkeley. It was published in *The Berkeley Heroine & Other Stories* (1900) and in *Under the Berkeley Oaks* (1901), a collection of works by U.C. Berkeley students. The "Bold Baggage Buster of Beautiful Berkeley," as he was called, went on to become the proprietor of Oakwood Park Stock Farm in Danville, California, where racehorses were stabled and bred.

Cornelius Beach Bradley (1843–1936) was born in Bangkok. He received a B.A. from Oberlin College in 1868 and a B.D. from Yale University in 1871. Following his studies, he spent three years as a missionary in what is now known as Thailand. He later attended U.C. Berkeley, where one of his professors was Lincoln Steffens. After earning an M.A., he stayed on and became a professor of rhetoric. He was fond of gardening and was a charter member of the Sierra Club. Bradley was a prolific writer whose works include *Suggestions to Teachers of English in Secondary Schools* (1894), *Four Great Humanists* (1907), *Stevenson and California* (1909), and *A Half Century Among the Siamese and the Lao* (1912).

Dorothy Bryant (1930–) is a native San Franciscan. She received a B.A. in music and an M.A. in creative writing from San Francisco State University. Bryant has published twelve books since she began writing in 1960, including *The Kin of Ata Are Waiting for You* (1976) and *Confessions of Madame Psyche* (1986), which won the American Book Award. The first of her three plays, *Dear Master*, was judged best script by the Bay Area Critics Circle. She lives in Berkeley with her husband.

Laura Chester (1949–) was born in Cambridge, Massachusetts, and grew up in Milwaukee. She received her B.S. from the University of New Mexico in 1972. She is an accomplished editor, poet, and prose writer. Her works of fiction include *Bitches Ride Alone* (1992) and *The Story of the Lake* (1995). Chester has also edited several anthologies, including *Deep Down* (1988), *Cradle and All* (1989), and *The Unmade Bed* (1992).

Philip K. Dick (1928–1982) was a cult figure in the world of science fiction. His novel *Do Androids Dream of Electric Sheep?* was made into the popular movie *Blade Runner*. *The Transmigration of Timothy Archer* (1982) is the third book in a trilogy that includes *VALIS* (1981) and *The Divine Invasion* (1981).

Robert Duncan (1919–1988) studied at U.C. Berkeley in the 1930s. The National Poetry Award was created in 1985 to honor *Ground Work: Before the War*, a collection that encompasses nearly twenty years of Duncan's poetry. He had a significant influence on his peers, many of whom would go on to become celebrated writers of the Beat Generation. He was a close friend of Jack Spicer and a mentor to Thomas Gunn.

Larry Eigner (1927–1996) was born in Swampscott, Massachusetts. Cerebral palsy confined him to a bed or wheelchair throughout his life. He was educated at home and took correspondence courses from the University of Chicago. He moved to Berkeley in 1978 and lived there for the rest of his life. His books of poetry include *From the Sustaining Air* (1953), *On My Eyes* (1960), and *Windows/Walls/Yard/Ways* (1994). His life was the subject of *Getting It Together*, a 1973 documentary.

John Kenneth Galbraith (1908–) was born in Iona Station, a small town in Ontario. After earning a degree in agricultural economics at Ontario Agricultural College, he came to U.C. Berkeley in 1931 for graduate study in economics. Upon finishing his thesis, he accepted an instructorship at Harvard University. World traveler, ambassador, and social philosopher, he is a pioneer of modern economic theory and has written more than twenty books, most of which deal with market failure and the problems of "private affluence and public squalor." His works include *The Affluent Society* (1958), *Economics and the Public Purpose* (1973), *The Age of Uncertainty* (1977), and *Annals of an Abiding Liberal* (1979).

Allen Ginsberg (1926–1997), the gay, Buddhist, Jewish poet, was dubbed the father of the 1950s San Francisco Renaissance and was one of the most prominent members of the Beat Generation. In 1943, he won a scholarship to Columbia University, where he majored in English and prepared to become a labor lawyer. There he met his lifelong friends Gregory Corso, Lucien Carr, and Jack Kerouac. In 1948, he moved to California. After a six-week stint as a graduate student at U.C. Berkeley, he went on to become a prominent poet and political activist. His 1956 poem "Howl" involved him in a famous obscenity trial. "A Supermarket in California" was inspired, in part, by a visit to a small Berkeley market.

Janice Gould (1949–) is a mixed-blood Native Californian whose tribal affiliation is Koyangk'auwi Maidu. She grew up in Berkeley and earned degrees in linguistics and English at U.C. Berkeley. She has published two collections of poetry—*Beneath My Heart* (1990) and *Earthquake Weather* (1996)—and teaches creative writing and Native American literature at the University of Northern Colorado.

Susan Griffin (1943–) is a poet, playwright, and feminist philosopher. Her work has been influential in shaping both feminist and ecological thought. Her books include *Women and Nature* (1978), *Pornography and Silence* (1981), *Made from This Earth* (1982), and *The Eros of Everyday Life* (1995). Her most recent collection of poetry, *Unremembered Country* (1987), won the Commonwealth Prize for poetry, and *A Chorus of Stones: The Private Life of War* (1992) won the Bay Area Book Reviewers Association Award. She was the recipient of a MacArthur Grant for Peace and International Cooperation, and she was awarded an Emmy for her play *Voices*. She lectures throughout the United States and Europe and lives in Berkeley.

Robert Hass (1941–) was born in San Francisco. He received a B.A. from St. Mary's College in 1963 and went on to earn an M.A. and a Ph.D. from Stanford. Hass won the Yale Series of Younger Poets Award in 1972 and the William Carlos Williams Award in 1979. He was a Guggenheim Fellow in 1980, and, in 1995, he was named Poet Laureate of the United States. His volumes of poetry include *Field Guide* (1973), *Praise* (1979), *Human Wishes* (1989), and *Sun under Wood* (1996). He teaches English at U.C. Berkeley.

Brenda Hillman (1951–) received a B.A. from Pomona College in 1973 and an M.F.A. from the University of Iowa in 1976. Hillman's collection of poems *White Dress* (1985) was honored with the Poetry Society of America's Norma Farber First Book Award. Her other works include *Fortress* (1989), *Death Tractates* (1992), and *Bright Existence* (1993).

James Hopper attended U.C. Berkeley around the turn of the century. "The Proud Dig and the Lazy Student" was published in *Under the Berkeley Oaks* (1901).

Alice Kahn (1943–) was born in Chicago. She taught high school English in San Lorenzo, California, and is now a nurse practitioner in Berkeley. Her trenchant and humorous essays have appeared in the *Express, West,* and the *San Francisco Chronicle.* Her books include *Multiple Sarcasm* (1985), *My Life as a Gal* (1987), and *Luncheon at the Cafe Ridiculous* (1990).

Jack Kerouac (1922–1969) was born in Lowell, Massachusetts. He studied briefly at Columbia University, dropping out to work as a cotton-picker, gas station attendant, and sportswriter for the *Lowell Sun.* In the late 1950s, he became the unofficial leader of the California artists and free spirits known as the Beat Generation (a term he coined). Kerouac became a legend after the publication of his 1957 autobiographical novel *On the Road,* which he claimed was written in just three weeks.

Maxine Hong Kingston (1940–) was born and raised in Stockton, California. She received a B.A. from U.C. Berkeley in 1962. Kingston's novels include *The Woman Warrior* (1977), winner of the National Book Critics Circle Award for nonfiction, *China Men* (1980), and *Tripmaster Monkey: His Fake Book* (1989). She lives in Berkeley and spends summers with her husband, Earl Kingston, at the Grand Canyon. She is a member of the English department at U.C. Berkeley.

Suzanne Lipsett (1943–1996) was born in New York City and attended U.C. Berkeley. Her books include *Coming Back Up* (1985), *Out of Danger* (1987), *Remember Me* (1991), and *Surviving a Writer's Life* (1994).

David Lodge (1935–), literary critic and prize-winning novelist, has published ten novels, including *Nice Work* (1989) and *Paradise News* (1991), ten volumes of literary criticism, and three plays. He is an honorary professor of modern English literature at the University of Birmingham in England, where he taught from 1960 to 1987. In 1969, he was a visiting associate professor at U.C. Berkeley. He lives in Birmingham with his wife.

Jack London (1876–1916) was born in San Francisco. By turns, London was an oyster pirate, seaman, Yukon prospector, tramp, U.C. Berkeley student, and world traveler. His first published story, "An Odyssey of the North," appeared in the *Atlantic Monthly* in 1899. In 1905, he unsuccessfully ran for mayor of Oakland on the Socialist ticket. He was extremely popular in his lifetime, authoring such favorites as *The Call of the Wild* (1903), *White Fang* (1906), and *Martin Eden* (1909). Sadly, he drank himself out of his fortunes, eventually dying of kidney failure.

Henry F. May (1915–) is a professional historian. He was raised in Berkeley and attended U.C. Berkeley as an undergraduate. He went to Harvard for graduate school and later returned to Berkeley as a professor of history. A passage from his memoir *Coming to Terms: A Study in Memory and History* (1987) is excerpted in this anthology.

Josephine Miles (1911–1985) was born in Chicago and moved to Berkeley when she was a year old. She received a Ph.D. from U.C. Berkeley in 1938, where she taught English for three decades. In 1972, she was the first woman to be appointed Professor of English at U.C. Berkeley. She wrote numerous volumes of poetry that included *Lines at Intersection* (1939) and *Collected Poems* (1983). She won many literary prizes, most notably the MLA James Russell Lowell Prize. She patterned her poetry after real life: "I like the idea of speech—not images, not ideals, not music, but people talking—as the material from which poetry is made."

Czeslaw Milosz (1911–) was born in Lithuania and raised in Poland. An essayist, poet, and novelist, he led the avant-garde Polish Poetry Movement in the 1930s and was part of the Polish resistance in World War II. He came to the United States in 1960 and has been a professor emeritus of Slavic languages and literature at U.C. Berkeley since 1978. One of the most celebrated figures in twentieth century literature, he received the Nobel Prize in 1980. Milosz has published over forty books, many of which Robert Hass helped to translate. His most recent work is *A Book of Luminous Things* (1996), an anthology of international poetry. Milosz has said that writing "…is a constant struggle, an attempt to translate as many elements of reality as possible into form."

Valerie Miner (1947–) is a novelist, journalist, critic, and political activist who advocates a strong, international women's movement. She grew up in Washington, New York, and California. Miner has taught fiction and media in the Field Studies Program at U.C. Berkeley, and her articles have appeared in *The Economist*, the *New York Times*, and *Ms*. Miner's novels include *Murder in the English Department* (1982), a mystery set on the Berkeley campus, as well as *Movement* (1982), *Winter's Edge* (1985), and *All Good Women* (1987).

Glenn Myles (1933–) was born in Carthage, Texas, and grew up in Phoenix. He is an artist, actor, and poet. His poems and drawings have been published in *The New Black Poetry*, *Yardbird Reader*, *Dices*, and *Black Bones*. He won third prize from the National Library of Poetry for his poem "Writing Down the Bison." He has published one volume of his illustrations and poetry, *Down and Country: The Art and Poetry* *of Glenn Myles* (1974). Myles is working on a new book, and he also works as a free-lance graphic designer and illustrator.

Frank Norris (1870–1902) was born in Chicago and grew up in San Francisco. After two years in Paris, he enrolled in U.C. Berkeley's English department. There he enjoyed fraternity life, wrote for the San Francisco literary journal *The Wave*, and finished the first draft of his 1899 novel *McTeague*. He later wrote *The Octopus* (1901), a novel chronicling the construction of railroads in the West.

Thomas Parkinson (1920–1992) was one of the first writers to take up the cause of the Beat Generation. A Yeats scholar, he taught at Wesleyan and in Germany before becoming a professor of English at U.C. Berkeley. His play *What the Blindman Saw: Twenty-five Years of Endless War* was produced by the Berkeley Department of Dramatic Art in 1971. His books of poetry include *Men, Women, Vines* (1959), *Homage to Jack Spicer & Other Poems* (1970), and *Collected Poems* (1980).

Dale Pendell (1947–) is a poet, software engineer, and longtime student of ethnobotany. His poetry has appeared in many journals, and he was the founding editor of *KUKSU: Journal of Backcountry Writing*. He is the author of *Pharmako/Poeia: Plants, Powers, Poisons, and Herbcrafts* (1995). A companion volume, *Pharmako/Gnosis*, will be published by Mercury House in 1998.

Thomas Pynchon (1937–) was born in Long Island, New York, and graduated from Cornell University in 1958. He is the author of four famously labyrinthine novels: *V.* (1963), *The Crying of Lot 49* (1966), *Gravity's Rainbow* (1973), and *Vineland* (1990). His most recent book is *Mason & Dixon* (1997). Pynchon won the National Book Award for *V.* and, in 1989, the MacArthur "genius" award. A recluse who refuses to divulge his life story, release a personal photograph, or reveal his whereabouts, Pynchon was also awarded (but never claimed) a William Faulkner First Novel Award.

Ishmael Reed (1938–) has written numerous essays, nine novels, and four volumes of poetry, and has edited several anthologies, including *Yardbird Lives!* (1978). Songwriter, publisher, playwright, and a senior lecturer at U.C. Berkeley, Reed perpetually challenges the status quo with his anti-Eurocentric point of view. Reed—along with writers such as Rudolfo Anaya—co-founded the Before Columbus Foundation to promote and disseminate contemporary American, multicultural literature.

Raquel Scherr is a noted feminist, author, and editor. Her work includes *A Voice Against Silence: Feminist Poetics in the Early Work of Rosario Castellanos* (1979). She is the co-author of *Face Value: The Politics of Beauty* (1984) and a co-editor of *West of the West: Imagining California* (1989).

Bobby Seale (1936–) was born in Dallas, Texas, and grew up in Oakland. As a young adult, Seale became interested in education as a way to empower the residents of his black neighborhood. A vehement, passionate political activist, Seale helped found the Black Panther Party in 1966 and was one of the famous Chicago Eight. During the trial, Seale had to be bound and gagged to stop his courtroom disruptions. He has written two autobiographies: *Seize the Time* (1970) and *A Lonely Rage* (1978).

John Oliver Simon (1942–) is a fifth-generation Californian. His great-great-grandfather was mayor of San Francisco in the 1860s, and his great-grandfather owned the largest bordello on the Barbary Coast in 1899. Simon arrived in Berkeley in 1964, just in time to sit beside the stranded police car in Sproul Plaza during the Free Speech Protest. He has lived in the same flatlands cottage since 1968. Simon has worked with the California Poets in the Schools Program and is now writing a book about his travels in Latin America.

Louis Simpson (1923–) was born in the West Indies and emigrated to the United States at age seventeen. He studied at Columbia University and at the University of Paris. He is the author of eleven volumes of poetry, including *In the Room We Share* (1990), *There You Are: Poems* (1995), an autobiography, a novel, and five works of literary criticism. He won a Pulitzer Prize for his book *At the End of the Open Road* (1960) and became a Prix de Rome Fellow at the American Academy of Arts and Letters in 1957. He has taught at U.C. Berkeley and SUNY Stonybrook.

Shelley Singer (1939–), a novelist, journalist, editor, and screenwriter, lives in Berkeley. She is the author of a series of mystery novels set in Northern California that includes *Samson's Deal* (1983) and *Full House* (1986). She credits the Berkeley Police Department as an important source of information for her books.

Jack Spicer (1925–1965), who has been called the foremost surrealist of the Beat Generation, was remembered by Thomas Parkinson as the student who "disrupted" a poetry writing workshop that he, Leonard Wolf, and Josephine Miles once taught at U.C. Berkeley. Parkinson made him a teaching assistant, channeling Spicer's rebellious energy into the writing of vivid, surreal poetry that filled five books during his short lifetime. His work was gathered together in *The Collected Books of Jack Spicer* (1975).

Lincoln Steffens (1866–1936) was born in Sacramento and moved to Berkeley in 1884. He became fascinated by history when he discovered that "... history was not a science, but a field of research." An investigative reporter and incorrigible moralist, Steffens was one of the first muckrakers in American journalism. In his book *The Shame of the Cities* (1904), an investigation into governmental corruption, he invented what became a popular idiom for the interdependence of American institutions—"the system." *The Autobiography of Lincoln Steffens* (1931) has become a classic of American literature.

George R. Stewart (1895–1980) taught English—mainly at U.C. Berkeley—from the 1920s until the 1960s. He published more than twenty-five books between

1930 and 1970, including several volumes of historical and biographical works and seven novels. His bestselling fiction includes *Storm* (1941), *Fire* (1948), and *Earth Abides* (1949).

Yoshiko Uchida (1921–1992) was born in Alameda, California, and grew up in Berkeley. Uchida began writing stories at the age of ten. She finished high school in two and a half years and entered U.C. Berkeley at age sixteen. She majored in English, philosophy, and history. She could not cross the stage to receive her diploma, however, as she and her family were at that time incarcerated in a World War II internment camp for Japanese-Americans in Topaz, Utah. After the war, Uchida earned a master's degree in education from Smith College. She wrote thirty-three books for children and four adult works—all addressing the tensions of multiracial life in America. In 1952, Uchida traveled to Japan on a Ford Foundation Fellowship, collecting folktales that she later published as *The Magic Listening Cap* (1955).

Julia Vinograd (1943–), the "Street Samurai," is a poet who lives on—and loves—the streets of Berkeley. She was born and raised in Berkeley and received a B.A. from U.C. Berkeley and an M.F.A. in creative writing from the University of Iowa. Vinograd has published more than twenty-seven books of poetry, including *Street Scenes* (1987).

Benjamin Ide Wheeler (1854–1927) was educated at Brown and received his Ph.D. from Heidelberg University. After teaching philology at Harvard and Cornell, he came to U.C. Berkeley in 1899, where he became one of the most important presidents of the University. His twenty years of strong leadership helped transform a provincial school into the world-renowned campus of today. He attracted prestigious scholars to the faculty and helped implement the many building projects and educational programs of U.C. benefactor Phoebe Hearst.

Gale Wilhelm (1908–) was born in Eugene, Oregon, and moved to San Francisco in 1925. Wilhelm has lived in Berkeley since 1985. She had some early sonnets published in *The Overland*, and her novels include *We Too Are Drifting* (1935), *Torchlight to Valhalla* (1938), *Bring Home the Bride* (1940), *The Time Between* (1942), and *Never Let Me Go* (1945).

Al Young (1939–) has written five books of poetry, including *Geography of the Near Past* (1976), and four novels. He taught creative writing at U.C. Santa Cruz and now teaches at Stanford. Young has received numerous awards, ranging from the Guggenheim to the Joseph Henry Jackson. He collaborated with Ishmael Reed on works such as *Yardbird Lives!* (1978) and *Calafia: The California Poetry* (1979).